Locus Amoenus

Renaissance Studies Special Issue Book Series

This series of special issue books is published in association with the journal *Renaissance Studies*. Both the journal and book series are multi-disciplinary and publish articles and editions of documents on all aspects of Renaissance history and culture. The articles range over the history, art, architecture, religion, literature, and languages of Europe during the period.

Also available:

Locus Amoenus: Gardens and Horticulture in the Renaissance
Edited by Alexander Samson

Re-thinking Renaissance Objects: Design, Function and Meaning
Edited by Peta Motture and Michelle O'Malley

The Renaissance Conscience
Edited by Harald E. Braun and Edward Vallance

Spaces, Objects and Identities in Early Modern Italian Medicine
Edited by Sandra Cavallo and David Gentilcore

Approaching the Italian Renaissance Interior: Sources, Methodologies, Debates
Edited by Marta Ajmar-Wollheim, Flora Dennis and Ann Matchette

Beyond the Palio: Urbanism and Ritual in Renaissance Siena
Edited by Philippa Jackson and Fabrizio Nevola

The Biography of the Object in Late Medieval and Renaissance Italy
Edited by Roberta J. M. Olson, Patricia L. Reilly and Rupert Shepherd

The Renaissance and the Celtic Countries
Edited by Ceri Davies and John E. Law

Asian Travel in the Renaissance
Edited by Daniel Carey

Locus Amoenus

Gardens and Horticulture in the Renaissance

Edited by Alexander Samson

A John Wiley & Sons, Ltd., Publication

This edition first published 2012
Originally published as Volume 25, Issue 1 of *Renaissance Studies*
Chapters © 2012 The Authors
Editorial organization © 2012 The Society for Renaissance Studies and Blackwell Publishing Ltd

Blackwell Publishing was acquired by John Wiley & Sons in February 2007. Blackwell's publishing program has been merged with Wiley's global Scientific, Technical, and Medical business to form Wiley-Blackwell.

Registered Office
John Wiley & Sons Ltd, The Atrium, Southern Gate, Chichester, West Sussex, PO19 8SQ,
United Kingdom

Editorial Offices
350 Main Street, Malden, MA 02148-5020, USA
9600 Garsington Road, Oxford, OX4 2DQ, UK
The Atrium, Southern Gate, Chichester, West Sussex, PO19 8SQ, UK

For details of our global editorial offices, for customer services, and for information about how
to apply for permission to reuse the copyright material in this book please see our website at
www.wiley.com/wiley-blackwell.

The right of Alexander Samson to be identified as the authors of the editorial material in this work has been asserted
in accordance with the UK Copyright, Designs and Patents Act 1988.

Library of Congress Cataloging-in-Publication data is available for this book.

Locus amoenus : gardens and horticulture in the Renaissance / edited by Alexander Samson.
p.   cm.
"Originally published as volume 25, issue 1 of Renaissance studies"–T.p. verso.
Includes bibliographical references and index.
ISBN 978-1-4443-6151-3 (paper) – ISBN 978-1-4443-9675-1 (ePDF) – ISBN 978-1-4443-9677-5
(Wiley Online Library) – ISBN 978-1-4443-9676-8 (ePub)
1. Gardens–Europe, Western–History–16th century.   2. Gardens–Social aspects–Europe, Western–History–
16th century.   3. Gardening–Europe, Western–History–16th century.   4. Horticulture–Europe, Western–History–
16th century.   5. Gardens, Renaissance–History.   6. Gardens in literature.   7. European literature–Renaissance,
1450-1600–History and criticism.   8. Renaissance.   9. Europe, Western–Social life and customs–16th
century.   10. Europe, Western–Intellectual life–16th century.   I. Samson, Alexander.   II. Renaissance studies.
SB466.E92L63 2012
635.09′031–dc23
2011042245

A catalogue record for this book is available from the British Library.

Set in 10/12 pt New Baskerville by Toppan Best-set Premedia Limited

1 2012

English School, detail of *Portrait, probably Sir George Delves*, 1577, oil on panel, 218 × 133.8 cm (© Walker Art Gallery, National Museums Liverpool)

Front Cover: English School, *Portrait, probably Sir George Delves*, 1577, oil on panel, 218 × 133.8 cm (© Walker Art Gallery, National Museums Liverpool)

Contents

Notes on contributors

Brian Dix is an archaeologist specializing in historic gardens and their landscapes. He has worked extensively throughout mainland Europe in addition to investigating major British sites. He is a former Course Tutor at the Architectural Association, London and co-author of *Peopling Past Landscapes* among other publications.

Brent Elliott is the Historian of the Royal Horticultural Society, having previously been its Librarian and Archivist for twenty-five years. He is the author of *Victorian Gardens* (1986), *Flora* (2001), and *The Royal Horticultural Society: a History 1804–2004* (2004) among other works. Formerly the editor of *Garden History*, he is currently the editor of *Occasional Papers from the RHS Lindley Library*. Most recently, he has been editing for publication part of The Paper Museum of Cassiano dal Pozzo, due to appear in 2012 as series B Volume VII of that catalogue raisonnée under the title *Flora: the Paris Manuscripts*.

Paula Henderson is an independent architectural and garden historian. Her many publications include articles in *Architectural History*, *Garden History* and *The British Art Journal*, as well as essays in *Albion's Classicism: The Visual Arts in Britain, 1550–1660* and *Patronage, Culture and Power: The Early Cecils, 1558– 1612*. Her first book, *The Tudor House and Garden: Architecture and Landscape in the 16th and Early 17th Centuries*, won the Berger Prize for British Art History. She is currently completing a book on gardens in Tudor and Stuart London.

Claudia Lazzaro is Professor of History of Art at Cornell University. She is the author of *The Italian Renaissance Garden* and many articles on villas and gardens, as well as co-editor of *Donatello among the Blackshirts: History and Modernity in the Visual Culture of Fascist Italy*. She is currently working on images of cultural identity in sixteenth-century Florence.

Jennifer Munroe is Associate Professor of English at the University of North Carolina at Charlotte, where she teaches courses on early modern literature and culture, Shakespeare, film, and literary theory. She is author of *Gender and the Garden in Early Modern English Literature* and editor of *Making Gardens of Their Own: Gardening Manuals For Women 1550–1750*. She is also co-editor of *Ecofeminist Approaches to Early Modernity*. Her current book project looks at the relationship between women and the natural world as it bears on the development of early modern science.

Alexander Samson lectures in Golden Age Literature in the Spanish and Latin American Studies department at University College London. He has published widely in the fields of Anglo-Spanish intercultural relations, Mary Tudor and her marriage to Philip II, translation, early modern travel writing and the *comedia.*

Susan C. Staub is Professor of English at Appalachian State University, where she teaches Early Modern literature. She is author of *Nature's Cruel Stepdames: Murderous Women in the Street Literature of Seventeenth Century England* and various essays on Spenser, Shakespeare, and Gascoigne and is editor of *The Literary Mother: Essays on Representations of Maternity and Childcare* and *Mother's Advice Books*, Volume 3 in *The Early Modern Englishwoman: A Facsimile Library of Essential Works*, series II. Her book-in-progress is on Shakespeare's gardens.

Introduction
Locus amoenus: *gardens and horticulture in the Renaissance*

ALEXANDER SAMSON

Annihilating all that's made
To a green thought in a green shade.

Andrew Marvell, 'The Garden'.[1]

Gardens, horticulture and their literary representation intersected with many of the critical, defining social transformations of the early modern period; from shifting patterns of land use to evolving political discourses of magnificence and power, new scientific ideas about the natural world, botany and medicinal writing, religious changes and aesthetics. The natural world was invoked to justify and make sense of unprecedented social, cultural and political change. However, gardens also reflected new forms of self-fashioning, leisure and pleasure. Garden history has not been revolutionized by the emergence of environmental criticism, instead gardens have become intertwined in other disciplinary areas from archaeology to gender studies, art history to literary studies. This volume seeks to demonstrate the ubiquity of the garden in Renaissance culture, whether as metaphor, symbol or real space, as a site for contemplation, agricultural production or cultural inscription, and at the same time reflect the diversity and range of academic writing on the subject. Woodcut illustrations in herbals (medicinal treatises about plants) were pirated and reused to the point of being unrecognizable and of no practical use in the identification and classification of plants. This points to the persistent tension between experience and authority in the way the natural world was understood. The emergence of horticulture and botany as

---

[1] John Dixon Hunt (ed.), *The Oxford Book of Garden Verse* (Oxford: Oxford University Press, 1993), 56. One of the most important writers on gardens, landscape architecture and the natural world in literature of his generation, John was due to contribute to this volume but was sadly unable to. We would like to dedicate it to him. Founder of the *Journal of Garden History, Word & Image,* and series editor of Penn Studies in Landscape Architecture, whose recent publications include Raffaella Fabiani Giannetto's *Medici Gardens: From Making to Design* (Philadelphia: University of Philadelphia Press, 2008), he is the author of classics like *Garden and Grove: the Italian Renaissance Garden in the England Imagination, 1600–1750* (London: J. M. Dent & Sons Ltd., 1986) and *The Figure in the Landscape: Poetry, Painting and Gardening during the 18th Century* (Baltimore: Johns Hopkins University Press, 1976).

empirical sciences paralleled a broader dignification of gardening as a liberal rather than mechanical art. Attempts to read historic gardens aesthetically point to the inadequacy of art historical categories like 'Renaissance' or 'Baroque' and the differences not simply between national but also regional traditions. Changing fashions in flowers reflected a democratization of the garden and its appropriation for aesthetic, non-utilitarian ends, as a space for new forms of leisure, contemplation and moral improvement. The changing role gardens played in mediating between people and the natural world were reflected and appropriated in literature and art. The complex interplay between poetics and gardening saw art understood through metaphors drawn from the garden and the garden recast as a living form of art.

WRITING GARDENS IN EARLY MODERN EUROPE: BOTANY, HORTICULTURE AND LITERATURE

The explosion of writing on gardens and horticulture in the early modern period, beginning with translations and printings of classical authors, reflected the different ways in which the return to nature was used to ground and make sense of the shifting relationship between people and the natural environment. In the case of England, Xenophon's treatise on household management and agriculture, the *Oeconomicus*, for example, was published in a Latin translation as early as 1508 and then reprinted in five further editions by 1526, before being Englished in 1532. Virgil's *Eclogues/Bucolics* and *Georgics* appeared in English in 1575 and 1589 in translations by Abraham Fleming. An underlying factor in the growing popularity of writings on agriculture and gardening was economic: low rents and labour costs alongside rising food prices as a result of the growing population persuaded landowners to end demesne and enter into commercial farming, taking closer economic control of how their estates were managed. This return to farming by magnates after generations without direct experience of agriculture was accompanied by a practical interest in classical writing on husbandry.[2] Barnabe Googe, a kinsman of William Cecil, and major conduit for the dissemination of Spanish literary culture in England, translated in 1577 the German humanist and servant of the Duke of Cleves, Konrad Heresbach's *Four Books of Husbandry*, first published in Latin 1570.[3] At precisely this time, Cecil was expanding and

[2] Joan Thirsk, 'Making a Fresh Start: Sixteenth-Century Agriculture and the Classical Tradition', in Michael Leslie and Timothy Raylor (eds.), *Culture and Cultivation in Early Modern England: Writing and the Land* (London: Leicester University Press, 1992), 15–34, esp. 15–16 and 19.

[3] *Ibid.*, 25. Googe translated Jorge de Montemayor's *Diana*, the most widely read pastoral novel in early modern Spain and was the first person to translate verse by Garcilaso de la Vega, whose *Églogas*, an *imitatio* Castilianising Viriglian landscape resonated in the Spanish literary imagination throughout the rest of the century.

developing 'the most influential Elizabethan garden' at Theobalds, which was overseen by the herbalist John Gerard, who dedicated his *Herball* to Burghley in 1597.[4]

Alongside a revived aristocratic interest in agriculture, a democratizing impulse is apparent throughout Europe in much writing on gardens. The first gardening handbook to appear in England, Thomas Hill's *A Most Briefe and Pleasaunt Treatyse howe to dress, sowe and set a Garden* of *circa* 1558 aimed 'to please the common sort, for whose onelye sake, I have taken these paines and have published this Booke'.[5] A similar popularizing aim had impelled William Turner, father of English botany, whose works were condemned in 1546 under Henry VIII and in 1555 under Mary, to publish *Libellus de Re herbaria* (1538) and then translate it as *The Names of Herbes* (1548). He complained that his plant list was needed because herbalists were not communicating their knowledge to their fellow Englishmen.[6] Eleven herbals and eight horticultural treatises appeared in England across the sixteenth century.[7] The first book in English dedicated exclusively to vegetable growing was Richard Gardiner's *Profitable Instructions for the Manuring, Sowing and Planting of Kichin Gardens* of 1603, while the first book to focus on flowers was John Parkinson's *Paradisi in sole paradisus terrestris or A Garden of all sorts of pleasant Flowers* of 1629.[8] Perhaps the biggest selling book of poetry from the Elizabethan period with eighteen editions before the end of the century, was Thomas Tusser's agricultural treatise *A hundredth good pointes of husbandrie* of 1557, expanded in a second edition of 1562 to consider more fully 'huswifery'; — eventually becoming the *Fiue hundredth points of good husbandry* in 1573.[9] Tusser took it for granted that the garden was the special province of the housewife, listing the plants she should grow. Ironically, this horticultural theorist was less than successful as a farmer; unsuccessfully attempting to farm at Cattiwade in Suffolk, then West Dereham, Norfolk and finally Fairsted in Essex. Tusser's text is also of interest for its defence of enclosure.

Underlying changes in land usage in this period played out against this background of an increasingly informed and textually mediated understanding of cultivation. Rising food prices, then as now, did not just add impetus to commercial farming, but also made it more attractive for private individuals to grow their own. Tusser was dismissed by Gabriel Harvey as a poet 'for common

[4] Roy Strong, *The Renaissance Garden in England* (London: Thames and Hudson, 2nd ed., 1998), 52 and 54.

[5] The only extant copy of the first edition is in the University of Glasgow library and is undated: Thomas Hill, *A Most Briefe and Pleasaunt Treatyse howe to dress, sowe and set a Garden* (London: Thomas Marsh, 2nd ed. 1563), cited in Martin Hoyles, *Gardeners Delight: Gardening Books from 1560 to 1960* (London: Pluto Press, 1994), 7.

[6] *Ibid.,* 9.

[7] *Ibid.*

[8] Richard Gardiner, *Profitable Instructions for the Manuring, Sowing and Planting of Kichin Gardens* by Richard Gardiner (London: Edward Allde for Edward White, 1603) and John Parkinson, *Paradisi in sole paradisus terrestris or A Garden of all sorts of pleasant Flowers which our English ayre will permit to be noursed up* (London: Thomas Cotes for Richard Royston, 1629). See Eleanour Sinclair Rohde, *The Old English Gardening Books* (London: Martin Hopkinson, 1924), 27 and her essential bibliography.

[9] Thomas Tusser, *A hundredth good pointes of husbandrie* (London: Richard Tottel, 1557).

life, and vulgar discourse'.[10] While in Spain, Andrés Laguna, the translator of
Dioscorides, the foremost classical source for botanical knowledge and
herbals, suggested that his treatise would help grandees and noblemen plan-
ning great agricultural estates and gardens to avoid the pitfall of supposed
'experience'.[11] Gregorio de los Rios argued similarly that his 1592 treatise
Agricultura de jardines 'será luz y provecho para los jardineros, pero también
para los dueños de los jardines en todo estados de gentes' [will illuminate and
profit gardeners, but also the owners of gardens from all estates of society].
On the other hand, he underlined that 'no metiéndome en las medicinales,
sino en aquellas que tienen buena flor y vista . . . podré decir con razón ser yo
el primero que escribe esta materia' [I do not deal with medicinal plants but
rather pretty ones with flowers . . . I can rightly say that I am the first person to
do so] and 'Debiéndoseme dar crédito en lo que *por experiencia* he descubier-
to . . . no se puede probar con autoridades de otros' [I should be trusted for
what I have discovered through *experience* . . . it can not be proved according to
the authority of others].[12] Not only were the precise status of gardening and
horticulture as branches of knowledge being negotiated in this period, but
also who the space of the garden belonged to, whether professional or
amateur, male or female, landlord or commoner. The very function of
gardens themselves was also the subject of debate, whether utility or pleasure,
contemplation or commerce, science or art.

POLITICAL LANDSCAPES

Until the fifteenth century, gardens had depended on empirical experience
and were not seen as works of art, lacking an underlying conceptual process.
By the mid-sixteenth century, however, gardens had begun to reflect the ideas
of architects like Francesco di Giorgio and Sebastiano Serlio, involving conceptual thinking, models and drawing. With the concept of the garden as a
work of art came iconography, gardens that told a story through their inter-
twining of motifs, themes, and complex mythological schema. Giovanni Battista Ferrari's 1633 *De florum cultura* provided the first complete theory of
garden design akin to those formulated for architecture. Botany, aquatic
engineering and the medicinal uses of plants, as well as their association with
cookery, tipped the balance of gardening and gardens towards being considered liberal rather than merely mechanical arts.[13] Leon Battista Alberti was

[10] *Oxford Dictionary of National Biography*, http://www.oxforddnb.com/view/article/27898 (accessed November 2010).
[11] On botanical gardens, see John Prest, *The Garden of Eden: The Botanic Garden and the Re-creation of Paradise*
(New Haven: Yale University Press, 1981).
[12] Gregorio de los Rios, *Agricultura de Jardines (Madrid: P. Madrigal, 1592)*, ed. Agustín de Amezúa (Madrid:
Sociedad de Bibliofilos, 1951), 19 and 21. My italics.
[13] See Alain Renaux, *Louis XIV's Botanical Engravings* (Aldershot: Ashgate, 2008).

perhaps one of the first thinkers to define them as liberal arts.[14] Luis Cabrera de Córdoba, biographer of Philip II, was the son of the superintendant of the grounds and gardens at El Escorial. He wrote a twenty-nine canto, 23,000 line-plus poem, *Laurentina* (*c.* 1580–90) for Philip II. Only a fragment (seven cantos) survives in a manuscript presentation copy at the Biblioteca de El Escorial with the dedication, first canto and those parts of the poem relating to San Lorenzo (cantos 24–28).[15] The poem's protagonist is the river Tagus, who describes the woods of Aranjuez (canto 1, octaves 32–97) and the estate around the monastery at El Escorial (canto 24, octaves 36 – 97), and the gardens annexed to it (canto 26, octaves, 17 – 9).[16] An even more striking example of this process of dignification was the French gardener and land-scape architect André Le Nôtre, who when offered a coat of arms by Louis XIV suggested that they should figure three snails, a cabbage and a spade.[17]

Large formal gardens were expressions of power and courtly magnificence. When Richmond Palace was rebuilt by Henry VII following a fire that destroyed the old palace in 1497, it became the first in England to possess extensive formal gardens.[18] His son's first essay into gardens at Hampton Court Palace in the 1530s with alterations first to the Privy Orchard and then the Privy Garden were captured in Anthonis van Wyngaerde's famous pan-orama of Hampton Court from the Thames, *circa* 1558.[19] Gardens reflected the magnificence of their creator's mind 'magnificenza dell'animo suo': 'exotic planting and expensive ornamentation of ephemeral materials con-veyed the magnificence of a garden's owner, so too did the ordered squares and rows of trees, manifested above all in a view of that garden.'[20] Visual depictions of gardens, painted or engraved views, followed conventions and sought to replicate the modes of viewing gardens that their layout and design encoded, with raised walkways (as at Hampton court or Valladolid in 1605) or parterres creating specific ways of seeing and reading the spaces. Knot gardens, formal terraces and walkways symbolized through geometry, the ability to shape and control nature. Branching out from the medicinal monastic gardens dissolved during the Reformation and royal palace gardens

---

[14] His treatise is discussed by a number of the contributors, see especially Carrigan and Lazzaro.

[15] Biblioteca Real de San Lorenzo, El Escorial, MS e.IV.6.

[16] Discussed by Felipe Pedraza Jiménez, 'De Garcilaso a Lope: jardines poéticos en tiempos de Felipe II', in Carmen Añón Feliú, dir., *Felipe II: El Rey Íntimo. Jardín y Naturaleza en el siglo XVI* (Madrid: Sociedad Estatal para la Conmemoración de los Centenarios de Felipe II y Carlos V, 1998), 307–30, here 320.

[17] Ian Thompson, *The Sun King's Garden: Louis XIV, André Le Nôtre and the Creation of the Gardens of Versailles* (London: Bloomsbury, 2007), 11.

[18] David Loades, *The Tudor Court* (Oxford: Davenant Press, 2003), 6, 7 and 10.

[19] See Simon Thurley (ed.), *The King's Privy Garden at Hampton Court Palace, 1689–1995* (London: Apollo, 1995) and Mavis Batey and Jan Woudstra, *The Story of the Privy Garden at Hampton Court* (London: Barn Elms, 1995). Anthonis van Wyngaerde's famous panorama of Hampton Court from the Thames, *c.* 1558, showing the gardens is in the Ashmolean, Oxford, see Henderson in the present volume, Fig. 3.

[20] Claudia Lazzaro, *The Italian Renaissance Garden: From the Conventions of Planting, Design, and Ornament to the Grand Gardens of Sixteenth-Century Central Italy* (London: Yale University Press, 1990), 71, note 2 (297) and from Bartolomeo Taegio, *La villa* (Milan, 1559), 101.

reflecting magnificence and providing a backdrop for chivalric, heraldic and dynastic propaganda, numerous distinctions between different kinds of garden developed during the course of the sixteenth century: kitchen gardens with vegetables and herbs; leisure gardens, dominated by flowers, statuary, fountains and architectural structures; and the philosophical garden, private, leisurely retreats for conversation and contemplation.[21]

The dignification of horticulture as a liberal art was connected to the increasing politicization of gardening and gardens. Gardens were frequently invoked in political discourse as a metaphor for the ideal republic; their harmonious unity of sense and smell, animal and plant life, contemplative and spiritual qualities, evoked nostalgia for a prelapsarian Eden, a golden age when every need was supplied by nature's spontaneous, natural abundance free from conflicts brought about by private property. By the second half of the seventeenth century in England, cultivation, in this case of trees, was seen as political in this way. The first major publication of John Evelyn, now generally known as a diarist, the first 'Publique Fruit of your Royal Society' as he wrote in the dedication to Charles II, was about 'Woods, [which] contribute to your Power, as to our greatest Wealth and Safety . . . For, as no Jewel in your Majesties resplendent Crown can render you so much Lustre and Glory as your regards to Navigation.'[22] Forest, chase and warren had been traditionally exempt from common law and forbidden to any but the king 'privileged for wild beasts and foules', 'for his princely delight and pleasure, which Territorie of ground, so privileged, is meered and bounded with unremovable, markes, meeres, and boundaries'.[23] The laws governing forests had fallen into disuse by the Restoration and the resultant change of land use had led to the cutting down and decimation of plantations that Evelyn objected to.

He underlined the fact that Pliny and Cicero had 'disdain'd not to exercise themselves in these Rusticities'.[24] The virtuous republican ideal and citizen in contrast to the decadence and corruption of imperial Rome was often symbolized by the figure of Lucius Quinctius Cincinnatus, the Roman called away from his plough to save the republic. In the accompanying almanac, Evelyn's patriotism extended to a concern for his fellow countrymen's spiritual well-being:

> As Paradise (though of Gods own Planting) had not been Paradise longer then the Man was put into it, to Dress it and to keep it . . . there is not a more laborious life then is that of a good Gard'ners; but a labour full of tranquility,

---

[21] See the discussion of the philosophical garden in Justus Lipsius, *De constantia/ On Constancy (1605)*, trans. Sir John Stradling (Exeter: Bristol Phoenix Press, 2006), Book 2, Chapters 1–3, 75–81. I would like to thank my colleague Angus Gowland for drawing this to my attention.

[22] John Evelyn, *Sylva or a Discourse of Forest-Trees, and the Propagation of Timber . . . To which is annexed Pomona . . . Also Kalendarium Hortense* (London: John Martyn and John Allestry, 1664), sig. A3r and v.

[23] Quoted in Sylvia Bowerbank, *Speaking for Nature: Women and Ecologies of Early Modern England* (London: Johns Hopkins University Press, 2004), 15.

[24] Evelyn, *Sylva*, sig. B1v.

and satisfaction; Natural and Instructive, and such as (if any) contributes to Piety and Contemplation, Experience, Health and Longevity. In sum, a condition it is, furnish'd with the most innocent, laudable and purest of earthly felicities, and such as does certainly make the neerest approaches to that Blessed state, where only they enjoy all things without pains[25]

The cottage garden came to be seen as a site for self-improvement, a symbol of fruitful labour and the morally salutary effects of gardens. The word paradise derived from Old Persian meaning an enclosure, park or orchard.[26] While the etymology of 'hortus' the Latin word for garden also meant 'enclosure' and conjured up the notion of retirement, self-reliance and content away from the public world of politics. With boundaries, however, also came the possibilities of transformation, exclusion and transgression.[27] In the classical world priapus was the guardian deity of gardens and tension between the sensual and spiritual is a constant theme of gardens and their description. Justus Lipsius in his *De constantia* exclaims to his friend 'You have heaven here, Langius, and no garden', to which Langius replies with a diatribe against the collectors of 'strange herbs and flowers'.[28] The commonplace of gardens as another Eden, alerts us to the way in which the study of gardens crosses over into more general considerations of evolving conceptions of nature.[29] Antonio de Torquemada's philosophical and theological treatise *Jardín de flores curiosas* [*Garden of curious flowers*] (1570) invoked Aquinas' definition of nature as the representation of the 'voluntad y mente de Dios' [mind and will of God].[30] Evelyn's particular formulation here of the relationship between God and nature, sets improving labour at the centre of man's purpose within the divine plan.

John Parkinson's *Paradisi in Sole* (1629), alluded to above, exemplified the notion of the garden as a lost paradise. In his dedication to the queen, he prayed 'that your Highnesse may enioy the heauenly Paradise, after the many yeares fruition of this earthly'.[31] Gregorio de los Rios argued that his treatise, despite the fact that, like Parkinson's, it dealt with flowers, was suitable even for monks and nuns:

para religiosos es honesto y loable, cuando, después de cumplir con sus obligaciones, ocupan la vista en aquella hermosura y variedad de flores y verduras; con

---

[25] *Kalendarium Hortense: Or, the Gardners Almanac* (Printed by John Macock for John Martyn and John Allestry, 1664), sig. H2r.

[26] On the *locus amoenus* in literary tradition from Dante to Tasso see Angelo Bartlett Giamatti, *The Earthly Paradise and the Renaissance Epic* (Princeton, NJ: Princeton University Press, 1966), 11.

[27] Victoria Emma Pagán, *Rome and the Literature of Gardens* (London: Duckworth, 2006), 10–11 and 23.

[28] Justus Lipsius, *De constantia*, 75 and 78.

[29] On this see Keith Thomas, *Man and the Natural World: Changing Attitudes in England 1500 – 1800* (London: Allen Lane, 1983), 236.

[30] Antonio de Torquemada, *Jardín de flores curiosas*, ed. Giovanni Allegra (Madrid: Clásicos Castalia, 1982), 105.

[31] Parkinson, *Paradisi in sole*, sig. **2r.

lo cual y con la suavidad de sus olores levantan el espíritu en gloria y alabanza de su Criador, [este] regalo . . . aparta de murmuraciones, juegos y otros vicios.[32]

[it is honest and praiseworthy for those of a religious calling, when after they have fulfilled their obligations, they occupy their sight with that beauty and variety of flowers and greenery; with which and with the gentle smells their spirits are raised up in glory and praise of their Creator, [this] pleasure . . . keeps them away from slander and gossip, gambling and other vices.]

Nostalgia for an 'idealized collective-agrarian' feudal communitarian past was frequently expressed in 'fantasies of liberating regression to garden and wilderness'.[33] Notions of the good Christian steward achieving equilibrium between the human and natural orders, civility governed by natural law, a reason or rationality founded in the revelation of God's will in the inner workings of the natural world, were central to the popularizing writings on horticulture. An ordered and fruitful nature shaped by human ingenuity and art reflected early modern discourses of mastery and stewardship.

LITERARY ARCADIAS

Trends towards seeing landscapes instrumentally, for maximizing profit by better exploitation of the land through enclosure, drainage and disafforestation, were countered by literary trends that sought to re-enchant the natural world through romance or mythify the economic structure at the centre of the countryside, the country house.[34] As nature was being transformed by the New Science into a 'governable utilitarian object', writers like Mary Wroth strove at 're-enchanting, or better, reinventing nature according to vitalist principles'.[35] At the same time that new ways of exploiting the land were being employed, changes to the countryside, concerns about rural depopulation, the absence of sturdy yeoman to people armies for defence, or trees for ships, as Evelyn argued, underlined that sustainability was already an issue even in the seventeenth century. However, claims of scarcity as objective facts about the natural environment, whether of grain or timber, need to be treated cautiously as strategies to create value and manufacture control.[36] For Watson, nostalgia for unmediated contact with the world of nature, efforts to identify with flora and fauna, an objective of seeing things in themselves, without recourse to prosopopeia, anthropomorphism or personification, was a response to 'epistemological anxieties brought on by mediation', a crisis of representation

[32] Gregorio de los Rios, *Argicultura de Jardines*, 19.
[33] Robert Waston, *Back to Nature: The Green and the Real in the Late Renaissance* (Philadelphia: University of Pennsylvania Press, 2006), 6.
[34] These themes were explored at a conference *Land, Lanscape and Environment, 1500–1700*, Early Modern Research Centre, University of Reading 2008, convened by Adam Smyth.
[35] Sylvia Bowerbank, *Speaking for Nature*, 18.
[36] Robert Waston, *Back to Nature*, 4.

and the 'internal referentiality and historical instability of any verbal system'.[37] Chorographies and the country house poem invested place with the mythic solidity of the age-old, ancient and unchanging, obscuring the true conditions behind nature's bountiful production of plenty.

As Raymond Williams wrote more than three decades ago with characteristic lucidity of Ben Jonson's country house poem for the Sidneys, 'To Penshurst', their plenty was raised 'unlike others, "with no man's ruine, no mans grone"; with none, "that dwell about them" wishing them "downe" . . . [rather through] the gentle exercise of a power that was elsewhere, on their own evidence, mean and brutal'.[38] The Edenic vision of natural plenty and order, linking Christian and classical myth, deliberately set out to exorcise the curse of the fall, guilt at consumption without labour. There is 'more than a hint . . . of that easy, insatiable exploitation of the land and its creatures – a prolonged delight in an organized and corporative production and consumption – which is the basis of many early phases of intensive agriculture . . . this natural order is simply and decisively on its way to table'.[39] This vision of providence is decisively linked by Jonson to human sharing and charity. The Arcadian ideal in sixteenth- and seventeenth-century England was inexorably linked, whether as palimpsest or not, to changes in the early modern rural economy and impact of copyhold land tenure.[40] There is an important difference between this leisured Arcadianism mediated through Virgil's *Eclogues* and the poetry of husbandry and agriculture inspired by Virgil's *Georgics*, Xenophon's *Oeconomicus* and Thomas Tusser. Agriculture was also, of course, at the centre of colonial enterprise, the plantation being at the centre of the civilizing processes of colonization.

Gardens were always part of a 'wider cultural experience', more than simple reflections, they were 'cultural landscapes', 'sites where human beings discover and realize whole patterns of belief, authority, and social structure'.[41] This is particularly true of the refraction of Italiante models in English gardens, tracing an ambivalent cultural relationship of emulation and rejection. The generally accepted picture is one of a change away from the architectural settings of the Carolingian masque with avenues of trees, water features, topiary, arbours and grottoes, a rejection of formal parterres, staged effects, fountains and mythological Baroque statuary, towards variety and wilderness, blurring the boundaries between the formal garden and the woodland and agricultural land that surrounded it. This more 'natural' style of landscaping, however, became political in highly sophisticated and subtle

---

[37] *Ibid.*, 13 and 15.

[38] Raymond Williams, *The Country and the City* (London: The Hogarth Press, 1985), 29.

[39] *Ibid.*, 30.

[40] See Adam Nicholson, *Earls of Paradise: England and the Dream of Perfection* (London: Harper Press, 2008).

[41] John Dixon Hunt, *Garden and Grove: The Italian Renaissance Garden in the English Imagination 1600–1750* (Philadelphia: University of Pennsylvania Press, 1996), xiii.

ways.[42] Despite this, the English landscape garden 'owed much to a continuing emulation of Italian Renaissance models'.[43] The simultaneous presence and absence of the Italianate garden is crucial to the aesthetic, moral and political understanding of English gardens from this period onwards. English visitors tended to elide historical differences and regional variations in Italian gardens, even the gardens of the Medici villas in Tuscany differed markedly from each other.

Italianate gardens possessed important religious and political associations in the early modern English literary imagination. At the same time that the Earl of Leicester was creating the first Italianate, Renaisssance garden in 1575 at Kenilworth, Spencer's Guyon was destroying the 'Bower of Bliss': an extensive garden populated by sweet-smelling flowers, scented herbs, the burbling of running water and fountain, erotic pictures 'of naked boyes', the melodious trilling of songbirds and a series of perspectives that required the spectator to read and interpret the scene and apply the moral.[44] The rejection as opposed to sophisticated, knowing enjoyment of the 'Bower of Bliss' and by extension Italianate gardens by Spenser's Guyon, stems from their mythological, heathen schema and religious distaste with what they connoted. The classical, Ovidian gardens and landscapes alluded to in eulogizing the beauties of the 'bower' all signify death.[45] The rejection of lascivious statuary, mythological themes and structures, topiary, lettering and heraldic symbolism, the falsity of image, sexual temptation and seduction through the senses and sensuality is part of a broader Protestant rejection of Roman Catholic aesthetics. It is not just that gardens of this type were Italianate but more specifically Roman and Florentine, with all the associations of immorality that came with it of sodomy, murder and corruption.

The antitype of the 'Bower of Bliss', the 'Garden of Adonis', opposed Roman luxuriousness, decadence and immorality, nature as feigning simulacrum, to the Venetian Republican's utilitarian virtue, exemplified by Trissino, according to which nature is productive, pleasure and utility combined, garden, villa and farm interrelated, nature cultivated and improved rather than traduced with automata or suggestive erotic imagery.[46] Venice was generally anti-papal, something that endeared it to Protestant observers, who were most likely to visit the Veneto, England's most significant trading area in Italy.[47] Roman tyranny and oppression, its Baroque aesthetic of visual trickery and allusive, complex allegorical/mythological symbolism were anathema to

---

[42] Tim Richardson, *The Arcadian Friends: Inventing the English Landscape* (Bantam Press, 2007), 3–14.

[43] Dixon Hunt, *Garden and Grove*, xvii.

[44] This whole paragraph relies heavily on the brilliantly illuminating article by Michael Leslie, 'Spenser, Sidney, and the Renaissance Garden', *English Literary Renaissance* 22 (1992), 3–36. Section on the 'Bower' is at Edmund Spenser, *The Faerie Queene*, II, xii, 42–87.

[45] Edmund Spenser, *The Faerie Queene*, II, xii, 52. A chapter in Dixon Hunt is devoted to how Ovidian mythological themes featured in England, see *Garden and Grove*, Chapter 4 – Ovid in the Garden, 42–58.

[46] Edmund Spenser, *The Faerie Queene*, III, vi, 30 – 54.

[47] Leslie, 'Spenser, Sidney, and the Renaissance Garden', 27.

both Eastern European and English Protestants – in Philip Sidney's *The Countess of Pembroke's Arcadia* this style is embodied by Basilius' star-shaped lodge, modelled on the country house known as the Jagdsschlosses outside Prague designed by the Archduke Ferdinand of Tyrol, a zealous Catholic who re-established papal authority in Prague and introduced the Jesuits. Sidney had visited Prague in 1575 and then 1577 shortly after the accession of the ecumenical Rudolf II. Another house, Kalander's, as in Spenser provides a foil in Sidney's poem, with its 'well-arrayed ground', 'neither field, garden, nor orchard – or rather it was both field, garden and orchard . . . set with trees of the most taste-pleasing fruits . . . new beds of flowers, which being under the trees, the trees were to them a pavilion, and they to the trees, a mosaical floor'.[48] It is curious that biblical imagery is almost totally absent from Renaissance gardens, despite the potentially rich theme of Christ as Gardener and providential understandings of nature.[49]

The Italian painter Federico Zuccaro had been invited to England by Leicester in the same year as the Kenilworth entertainment, having worked on frescoes in the Villa Farnese at Caprarola and Sala Regia in the Vatican, underlining that his garden was a self-conscious emulation of Italian models.[50] The mercer and his servant Robert Langham described how the garden was 'beautified with many delectable, fresh and umbragioous Boowerz, aberz, seatz, and walks, that with great art, cost, and diligens wear very pleazauntly appointed'.[51] At the centre of the garden was a fountain where there

> wear things ye see, moought enflame ony mynde too long after looking: but whoo so was foound so hot in desyre, with the wreast of a Cok waz sure of a coolar: water spurting upward with such vehemency, az they shoold by and by be moystned from top too to.[52]

This amusing jape alerts us to the theatricality of gardens, the ways they employed humour and jokes as part of how they were to be experienced, controlling perspectives and their own interpretation, like the terraces constructed to give particular prospects over the garden and surrounding parkland and also link house and garden. Water jokes were common in Italian gardens such as the Villa Medici in Castello and Villa Lante at Bagnaia, and known as 'burladores' or tricksters in Spanish.[53] Elizabeth I commissioned a fountain for Hampton Court, finished in 1590, that included a *giochi d'acqua* sometimes catching bystanders unawares with water spurting out of marble

[48] Philip Sidney, *The Countess of Pembroke's Arcadia (The New Arcadia)*, ed. Victor Skretkowicz (Oxford: Clarendon Press, 1987), 14 and see *ibid.*, 33.

[49] See Lazzaro, *The Italian Renaissance Garden*, 131.

[50] Leslie, 'Spenser, Sidney, and the Renaissance Garden', 8.

[51] Robert Langham, *A Letter*, ed. Roger J. P. Kuin (Leiden: Brill, 1983), 37. Garden is described, 69–73.

[52] *Ibid.*, 72.

[53] Lazzaro, *The Italian Renaissance Garden*, 65–8.

columns.[54] The ability of the garden to erotically excite and at the same time sooth and tranquilize against passion deliberately exploited the tension between the sensual and spiritual we have already noted.

FASHION FOR FLOWERS

Concerns with profit and pleasure, art and nature, authority and authorship link gardens, garden writing and poesie with changing concepts of land and landscape. Evolving notions of private property and ownership read estates as not solely available for economic exploitation and personal pleasure. Their improvement, as for Evelyn, was a patriotic imperative, improving and strengthening the kingdom and its natural resources while being simultaneously morally beneficial to those involved in such a project. Labour and its moral benefits accrued not just to the great retired soldiers and statesmen of the age as they celebrated their achievements, but for everyone down to the humble huswife. Gardens were not just other Edens, their cultivation was a way back to the prelapsarian world for those who cultivated them. Pruning to control nature's wanton excess and reign in the sprouting of wild vegetation symbolized the constant need to police sexual desire.[55] As horticultural treatises proliferated, cuttings, splicing, transplanting and grafting became loaded with metaphorical resonances of the relationship between art and nature, art's ability to improve on nature, metaphors further extended to explore the nature of poetic ornament and rhetorical artifice. Sexual reproduction and the life of plants became intertwined in a shared language by which new hybrids, bastard scions or offshoots, new growths grafted onto old rootstock and dynasty or familial hierarchies were envisaged through hortulan language. One metaphor eliding the boundaries between body, landscape and natural world figured mining as an abortion. Family trees and genealogies proliferated at the same time as chorographies invented a new language with which to celebrate landscape and the sites of historical memory. The distinctions between gardens and landscapes specifically shaped for leisure, landscape architects as opposed to mere gardeners, emerged or were blurred while the purpose and understanding of gardens, for utility or pleasure, art or science evolved. There is no doubt that gardens were 'ideologically charged spaces' that conveyed 'social meaning', particularly as sites where gender power relations and those between men and women and the natural world were shaped, negotiated and formulated.[56] Changing fashions in flowers reflected the way in which gardening encoded ongoing reaffirmations of social difference; as gillyflowers and carnations proliferated and became

---

[54] See Paula Henderson's chapter, note 40.

[55] Rebecca Bushnell, *Green Desire: Imagining Early Modern English Gardens* (London: Cornell University Press, 2003), 96.

[56] See Jennifer Munroe, *Gender and the Garden in Early Modern English Literature* (Aldershot: Ashgate, 2008).

accessible to people lower down the social scale, tulips and auriculas became fashionable among the upper classes. A 'preoccupation with novelty, rarity and hybridization',[57] led to the importation of exotic, tropical delicates kept alive in heated greenhouses.

The first tulip had of course been brought back by the Habsburg embassy to Suleiman the Magnificent's court in Constantinople in 1555, allegedly by the Flemish ambassador Busbecq. They were seen in Augsburg gardens by the naturalist Conrad Gesner, including that of the Fuggers a few years later.[58] Lope de Vega in the dedicatory letter to his play *Lucinda perseguida* [*Lucinda pursued*] addressed to the Flemish Emmanuel Sueyro, thanked his friend for some tulips he had sent for the poet's garden of 'varios colores, hermosa y peregrina vista' [various colours, beautiful and rarely seen].[59] Frustrated social ambition cast a shadow over Lope's brilliant career. In Justus Lipsius' neo-Stoic dialogue, aspirational fashions in flowers were denounced: 'that sect . . . who . . . hunt after strange herbs and flowers, which having got, they pre-serve and cherish more carefully than any mother does her child; these are men whose letters fly abroad into Thracia, Greece, and India only for a little root or seed', whereas gardens 'were ordained for modest recreation, not for vanity; for solace and not for sloth', the 'true end and use of gardens, to wit, quietness, withdrawing from the world, meditation, reading, writing'.[60] Francis Bacon in his essay 'Of Gardens' dismissed medieval 'knots . . . under the windows of the house on that side which the garden stands, they be but toys: you may see as good sights many times in tarts', along with topiary ('I, for my part, do not like images cut out in juniper or other garden stuff; they be for children') and statuary – 'great princes' 'sometimes add statua's, and such things, for state and magnificence, but nothing to the true pleasure of a garden.'[61] The more formal and splendid gardens concerned with display and magnificence were tainted and tarnished by their hollowing out of nature.

While there may have been a desire to see things in themselves, related to the empirical and scientific interest of gardens, the personification of nature, anthropomorphism and prosopopeia ran riot in the early modern garden, compensating for nature's disenchantment. Comparisons of teaching to gar-dening were commonplace in humanist educational treatises, as were meta-phors likening books to gardens.[62] Gardens were a symbol of self-fashioning and the ability of art to improve on nature. Baltasar Gracián wrote that art:

---

[57] See Susan Staub's chapter in this book, note 56.

[58] Anne Goldgar, *Tulipmania: Money, Honor and Knowledge in the Dutch Golden Age* (Chicago: Chicago University Press, 2007), 32.

[59] Cited by Agustín de Amezúa y Mayo, *Opúsculos Histórico-Literarios*, 3 tomos (Madrid: Consejo Superior de Investigaciones Científicas, 1951 – 3), Tomo 3, 376–412, 'Felipe II y las Flores', 381.

[60] Justus Lipsius, *De Constantia*, 78–9 and 80.

[61] Francis Bacon, *Essays or Counsels, Civil and Moral*, ed. Brian Vickers (London: The Folio Society, 2002), 166 – 7 and 170.

[62] Rebecca Bushnell, *Green Desire: Imagining Early Modern English Gardens* (London: Cornell University Press, 2003), 1.

'complemento de la naturaleza y un otro segundo ser que por extremo la hermosea . . . Suple de ordinario los descuidos de la naturaleza, perfeccionándola en todo; que sin este socorro del artificio quedara inculta y grosera' [a complement of nature and a second being that greatly beautifies it . . . It makes up for nature's defects, perfecting in every way; without this aid from artifice it would be coarse and uncultivated].[63] Iago's extended conceit to Rodrigo in *Othello* rejects the idea that it is not in his power to bend his will away from temptation:

> our bodies are gardens, to the which our wills are gardeners, so that if we will plant nettles, or sow lettuce, set hyssop, and weed up thyme; supply it with one gender of herbs, or distract it with industry, why, the power, and corrigible authority of this, lies in our wills.[64]

From the Muses' garden or Apollo's garden, the garden came to symbolize art, creative power, the shaping and improvement of nature, a metaphor for humanity's divine nature and ability to impose spirit and reason on matter, disorder and chaos. Numerous similes compared gardening to poetry. George Puttenham for example argued that when the poet 'speaks figuratively . . . he doth as the cunning gardiner that vsing nature as coadiutator, furders her conclusions & many times makes her effectes more absolute and straunge.'[65] Poetic ornament like gardening worked with nature, to embellish and improve on her through art. Collections of *romances*, the indigenous Castilian metre dating back to the medieval period, were frequently titled with the names of plant-life: from Juan de Timoneda's *Rosas* [Roses] (1573) to various 'silvas de romances' [forests of romances] (Barcelona 1561, Zaragoza 1588) and of course Pedro de Mexía famous prose miscellany *Silva de varia lección*, 'ramillete' [posy] and simply 'flores' [flowers].[66] As Susan Staub points out in this book the term anthology derives from the Greek for flower collection, like its Latin synonym 'florilegium' which means flower culling. There was a fundamental ambiguity in relation to the garden as a space of intimate retirement, female leisure and pleasure and as an extension of the public space of the household. The pleasure or walled garden was specifically created as a female space. Fertility and the well-ordered household were reflected by it. Although it also had a negative opposite, a dark other as a sexual space, of

---

[63] Baltasar Gracián, *Obras Completas*, ed. Manuel Arroyo Stephens, 2 vols (Madrid: Turner, 1993), 'El Criticón', Part I, Crisis VIII, Vol. 1, 106.

[64] William Shakespeare, *Othello*, ed. Maurice R. Ridley, Arden Shakespeare (London: Routledge, 1994) I. iii. 320–26, p. 40. The note suggests his horticultural examples simply emphasize contrasting humours, the nettle hot and dry, the lettuce cold and moist, likewise hyssop and thyme. The passage is discussed by Stephen Greenblatt, *Renaissance Self-Fashioning: From More to Shakespeare* (London: University of Chicago Press, 1980), 235 in relation to Iago's shaping power as a role-player.

[65] George Puttenham, *The Arte of English Poesie*, ed. Gladys Doige and Alice Walker (Cambridge: Cambridge University Press, 1936), 307. See Christine Coch, 'An arbor of one's own? Aemilia Lanyer and the early modern garden', *Renaissance and Reformation* 28 (2004), 97–118, here 102.

[66] Pedraza Jiménez, 'De Garcilaso a Lope', 309.

secret assignations and a means of access through secret hidden doors. Gardens, women and poetry had long been associated in the early modern period, the poetic bower being the clichéd place of choice for literary and perhaps real amorous encounters.

The first literary garden of early modern Spain is Melibea's 'huerto' or 'huerta', garden or orchard, the walled space created for her pleasure into which Calisto trespasses and first speaks to her, where their relationship will be graphically consummated and from whose walls her lover will fall symbolically to his death before she commits suicide throwing herself from a tower into the same place.[67] While the country could be read providentially in terms of morally improving labour, in contrast to the city's moral confusions, it could equally be seen as a space of sexual freedom, a liberation from stifling bureaucratic norms of the emergent modern state. Lope de Vega's play *El villano en su rincón* [*The Peasant in his Niche*] based on an apocryphal story of Francis I becoming lost while out hunting and spending the night in a woodcutter's hut, explores the confrontation between king and unrepentant old peasant, who wishes to avoid at any cost meeting the royal gaze that bound the subject through awe to a semi-divine majesty and brought the individual into being in a political sense, providing a model for emulation, and a mirror where a morally exemplary human being is reflected. While, for the king it is a philosophical awakening to the truth of his own condition, through confronting his own self, divested of the trappings of majesty and royal business, a *desengaño* and self-awareness crucial in his development as king, for the peasant the plot's denouement with his installation as chamberlain at court, is a deeply ambivalent 'elevation'.[68]

AMERICAN IMPORTS

Perhaps the final, important stimuli behind horticultural and garden writing in the early modern period were the challenges of the Americas.[69] New introductions quickly spread across western Europe. Floral treasures introduced through Spain included the African marigold, the Marvel of Peru, and

---

[67] Fernando de Rojas, *La Celestina: Tragicomedia de Cailsto y Melibea*, ed. Francisco Lobera *et al.* (Barcelona: Crítica, 2000), pp. 25–7.

[68] See the magisterial analysis of the play in relation to contemporary political discourse in Alban K. Forcione, *Majesty and Humanity: Kings and Their Doubles in the Political Drama of the Spanish Golden Age* (New Haven: Yale University Press, 2009), esp. 24–100.

[69] The most important sources are found in the *Cuadernos Valencianos de Historia de la Medicina y de la Ciencia*, Serie A (Monografías), Tomos XL, LI, and LIII (see note 70): XL – José Pardo Tomás and María Luz López Terrada, *Las primeras noticias sobre plantas americanas en las Relaciones de viajes y Crónicas de Indias (149 –1553)* (Valencia: Universidad de Valencia, Instituto de Estudios Documentales e Histróricos Sobre la Ciencia, 1993); LI – José María López Piñero and José Pardo Tomás, *La influencia de Francisco Hernández (1515–1587) en la constitución de la botánica y la materia médica modernas* (Valencia: Universidad de Valencia, Instituto de Estudios Documentales e Histróricos Sobre la Ciencia, 1996).

Morning Glory.[70] By 1571, the prickly pear was being cultivated by the London apothecary Hugh Morgan.[71] These new, exotic plants posed a problem for the classificatory schemes of descriptive botany inherited from the classical world and encouraged a concept of geographical distribution in the understanding of plant life absent from an exclusively Mediterranean science. By the end of the sixteenth century, it was clear that American nature had overrun the descriptive possibilities of traditional interpretative schemes and detailed descriptive studies were required, a need fulfilled by José de Acosta's *Historia natural y moral de las Indias* (1590) [*Natural and Moral History of the Indies*].[72] Despite its date and wealth of information, the *Suma de geographia* (1519) [*Geographical Summary*] of Martín Fernández de Enciso remained on the margins of the introduction of botanical knowledge, despite a translation of the section on America into English in 1578, which probably circulated mostly amongst cosmographers and 'pilotos'.[73] The most important early texts were *De la natural historia de las Indias* (1526) [*Natural History of the Indies*] and *Historia general y natural de las Indias* (1535) [*General and Natural History of the Indies*] by Gonzalo Fernández de Oviedo. It is notable that it is American nature that is central to the historic importance of these early accounts. Later, Francisco López de Gómara brought together material from Angleria and Oviedo in *Historia de las Indias* (1552) [*History of the Indies*]. This account was translated into English by Thomas Nicholas (1578 and 1596), who also rendered the *Historia del descubrimiento y conquista del Peru* (1555) [*History of the Discovery and Conquest of Peru*] by Agustín de Zárate into the vernacular in 1581. The same translator also published *Nuevas . . . del gran Reino de China* [*News . . . from the Great Kingdom of China*] in 1577.[74]

Perhaps the most important text in the dissemination of knowledge about American plants was Nicolás Monardes' *Historia medicinal de las cosas que se traen de nuestras Indias Occidentales* (three parts apperaed between 1565–74) [*Medicinal History of Things Brought Back from our West Indies*]. Monardes was translated by Frampton in 1577, reissued in the same year and then in augmented editions in 1580 and 1596.[75] Hariot's *A briefe and true report* refers the reader back to this translation, *The ioyfull newes from the West Indies*. Gerard's *The Herball* (1597) derived much of its information on American plants from Dodoens, who in turn was heavily influenced by Monardes.[76] In the story of

---

[70] John H. Harvey, 'Spanish Gardens and Their Historical Background', *Garden History* 3 (1974), 7–14, here 12.

[71] See Brent Elliot, 38–39.

[72] José María López Piñero and María Luz López Terrada, *La influencia española en la introducción en Europa de la plantas americanas (1493–1623)*, Tomo LIII (Valencia: Universidad de Valencia, Instituto de Estudios Documentales e Histróricos Sobre la Ciencia, 1997), 126.

[73] Piñero and Terrada, *La influencia española*, 20–1.

[74] *Ibid.*, 29–30.

[75] See Donald Beecher, 'The Legacy of John Frampton: Elizabethan Trader and Translator', *Renaissance Studies* 20 (2006), 320–39, here 324–5 and note 13.

[76] Piñero and Terrada, *La influencia española*, 121.

descriptive botany, Clusius one of the three inheritors of Fuchs is a pivotal figure in relation to the Americas and Spain.[77] He maintained a close friendship with Arias Montano in Antwerp 1568–75 working on the *Biblia sacra* for Philip II, and was published like him by the Plantin Press. He visited Spain as the preceptor of Jacob Fugger, whose family were early cultivators of the tulip, arriving in Vitoria in mid-1564 and staying in Seville around January 1565 before returning to Madrid in April. He maintained correspondence with the Seville-based naturalist Simón de Tovar who died in the city in 1596. Clusius of course produced an annotated translation of Monardes in 1574 printed by Plantin, getting hold of copies in London in 1571, only a few months after they were published in Seville, as well as producing his own account of Iberian flora, *Rariorum aliquot stirpium per Hispanias observatarum historia* (1576).[78] In these texts, a metaphorical language was born around plants to think about the relationship between the Old World and the New, through notions of geographical distribution, of a natural sympathy between climate and type, exoticism, transplanting and hybridity.[79] These ideas associated particular plants with national types and the natural philosophy that linked climate and character.

LOCUS AMOENUS AND GARDEN HISTORY

The academic study of gardens is a relatively recent phenomenon. According to Roy Strong,[80] garden history took off 'as a serious academic industry' in 1979 following the exhibition at the Victoria and Albert museum entitled *The Garden.*[81] Paula Henderson discussed the sources on gardens in England in her book on *The Tudor House and Garden* – from the great surveys of Willian Camden and John Norden, to foreign visitors' accounts, as well as, of course, books on gardening and husbandry and estate maps. Many of these accounts make frustrating assumptions about the visual evidence in front of them, the way that Renaissance gardens actually looked are difficult to reconstruct, caught between plans, general structural descriptions and the more detailed scientific attention to specific plants. Surviving verbal accounts by travellers or participants in outdoor festivities, in addition to visual evidence in engravings, paintings, gardening manuals and so on, supplemented by archaeological evidence for the structure, architecture and layout of groundworks allow us to go some way towards reconstructing them. However, gardens never remain

---

[77] See Brent Elliot's chapter in this book.

[78] Piñero and Terrada, *La influencia española*, 67 and 89–90.

[79] See Londa Schiebinger and Claudia Swan (eds.), *Colonial Botany: Science, Commerce and Politics in the Early Modern World* (Philadelphia: University of Pennsylvania Press, 2006), esp. Daniela Bleichmar, 'Books, Bodies and Fields: Sixteenth-Century Transatlantic Encounters with New World Materia Medica', 83–99.

[80] Roy Strong, *The Renaissance Garden in England* (London: Thames and Hudson, 1998), 6.

[81] A book was produced to accompany the exhibition, John Harris (ed.), *The Garden: A Celebration of One Thousand Years of British Gardening* (London: New Perspectives, 1979).

constant, changing with the seasons, the tending and maintenance lavished
on them, subject to the tastes, fashions and needs of a given time. The most
difficult thing to recover are planting schemes, although looking at the plants
imported for big, lavish princely gardens may give us some idea of when
flowers, herbs or trees took root in particular countries' gardens. Any investigation of these green spaces runs into the problem that gardens are constantly in flux and change, alive and never the same, sprouting beyond and
breaching the limits of wall, fence, bed and frame that separate them from
nature and attempt to contain them apart from the landscape that surrounds
them. Roy Strong noted in the preface to his 1997 reissue of *The Renaissance
Garden in England*[82] that the one avenue through which massive advances have
been made in our understanding of this subject has been garden archaeology.

The essays in this volume seek to contribute to and expand on debates
about gardens and environmental thought in the early modern period in
areas from botany and art history to gender studies, literature and archaeology. Brent Elliott's essay confronts and draws our attention to the ways in
which the technology of the book itself affected the spread of botanical
knowledge, with pirated illustrations slowly more worn eventually become all
but unrecognizable; the dependence of the herbal on tradition and authority
and the ways this dependence influenced the development of new classificatory schemes and the prestige of particular examples of this early modern
genre. The first systematic attempt to respond to the attack on the medieval
herbal (treatises on medicinal plants) that had begun in 1492 with a text
pointing out the confusions, discrepancies and misidentifications within classical sources (in particular Pliny and Dioscorides) was the *Herbarum vivae
eicones* (1531) by Otto Brunfels, a Basel-based physician. Plants introduced
from the Americas gave impetus to the concept of geographical distribution
and certain environments being suitable for particular flora. Leonhart Fuchs's
De historia stirpium (1542) described American introductions like maize and
was possibly the first herbal based on observation rather than imitation. Maize
had of course been brought back from the Carribean by Columbus on his
third voyage, the first illustration of it appearing in Fernández de Oviedo.

Paula Henderson author of the seminal *The Tudor House and Garden*[83]
considers here the issue of whether the English garden had a 'Renaissance' at
all, looking at the patchy evidence from estate maps for the survival of medieval features from galleries to banqueting houses, earthworks and snail
mounts to moats well into the sixteenth century; in the same way that earlier
gothic and chivalric forms continued to haunt the architecture, visual art and
literary imagination of the Tudor and Stuart period. William Lawson's *A New
Orchard and Garden* of 1618 demonstrates the availability of Italian Renaissance

---

[82] Strong, *The Renaissance Garden in England*, 6.

[83] Paula Henderson, *The Tudor House and Garden: Architecture and Landscape in the Sixteenth and Early Seventeenth Centuries* (London: Yale University Press, 2005). Any consideration of gardens in early modern England will necessarily use this source as a point of departure.

ideas, with its promotion of statuary, symmetry and geometry, classical or mythological-inspired fountains and schemes governed by ordered and harmonious design. Nevertheless, the water garden continued to be popular, chiming with the popularity of the ornamental canal in the Low Countries, often also a functional feature providing drainage on the flat flood plains and the French enclosure of pleasure gardens and houses within moats and canals. Understanding the mutually influencing factors producing English gardens in this period, the movement between past and present, indigenous and foreign, as an evolution reinforces the prejudices of later architectural historians and obscures the eclectic and heterogeneous confluence of culture, politics, geography and religion producing the landscapes and topography of Tudor England. A shift in emphasis from heraldic to classical motifs on the indigenous table fountains of John Harington and Lord Lumley is one of the fragmentary pieces of evidence to betray the influence of Italian Renaissance imagery. The English Heritage reconstruction of the fountain at Kenilworth is also discussed. Pyramids and obelisks, free-standing statuary all cropped up with greater frequency towards the end of the sixteenth century. Nevertheless, in Jacobean England it seems that fantastic or romantic medievalism made a return that foreshadowed the political revival of the gothic in the eighteenth century, both resurrections were intertwined with patriotic fervour. Garden history is complicated by its non-linear phases and evolution, the difficulties of tracing influence even when enough evidence survives for us to gain a rough approximation of what a garden actually looked like.

Some of the best surviving evidence of the complexity of mapping gardens onto broader art historical categories are the Giusto Utens lunettes of Medici villas from around 1599–1602 (Fig. 1). The Cafaggiolo garden from the mid-fifteenth century (panel d) typifies an ideal of rural retreat, a productive, enclosed, agricultural style that persists into the seventeenth century and was mirrored at Collesalvetti (panel a). By contrast the Tuscan Villa La Petraia of 1575 (panel c) is more self-consciously architectural, with house and garden drawn together on one scale, also found in the mannerist dell'Ambrogiana depicted as it was at the end of the sixteenth century (panel b) still probably in the process of being rebuilt.

Claudia Lazzaro explores the political and cultural uses of colossal statues of ancient river gods unearthed in Rome in the early sixteenth century, which soon found their way into papal and then, through imitations, later Medici gardens. Their settings, mounted on trays with rippling or trickling water against natural backdrops, blurred distinctions between art and nature, and eventually led to their use in fountains with water incorporated into the figure's design. These anthropomorphic figures were also used in entries and gardens as assertions of territorial lordship, symbolizing the relationship between the fertility of a given state and its rulers. The age of a river could be symbolized by the figure's youth; its having changed course through the crossing of its legs; and a male-gendered natural abundance through water spurting from its penis.

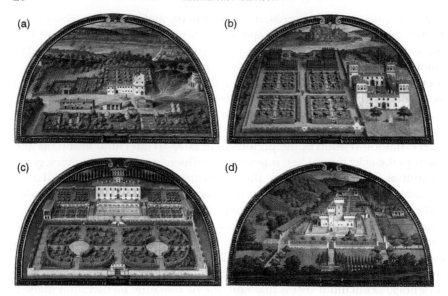

Figs. 1a–d   Giusto Utens, *Villa Collesalvetti, Villa dell'Ambrogiana, Villa La Petraia, Villa Cafaggiolo,* from a series of lunettes depicting views of the Medici villas, *c.* 1599–1602, tempera on panel, Florence, Museo di Firenze com'era

Some were given new identities like that transformed into the Arno, complete with Medici symbolism carved around the rim of the vase it was holding. Stylistically it echoed the work of Michelangelo and came to adorn the sculpture garden of the Florentine Medici Pope Leo X. If nature was holy, a mask for the creator, then the personification of river gods reflected the evolving ways in which this sacredness was imagined in political, artistic, gendered and cultural terms. From ideas about natural science to good lorship in flood defences and acqueducts, the river god was a gauge of evolving relationships between the natural world, its artistic representations, its stewards and their territories, mankind's place in the changing geographies of their environment. This was a landscape shaped above all by Medici patronage, the artistic genius of Michelangelo and the centrality of the city of Florence.

Susan Staub's subject in this volume, George Gascoigne, had been involved by Leicester in composing the Kenilworth entertainments and commemorated them in his *The Princelye Pleasures at the Courte at Kenelworth* (1576). He had appeared as a savage man dressed in ivy. As well as his *The Noble Arte of Venerie or Hunting,* a translation of 1575 of works on hunting by Jacques du Fouilloux and Gaston de Foix, he had also unsuccessfully tried his hand at farming, leasing the manor at Willington in Bedfordshire in 1562. There is a reconfiguration of authorship between the first and second editions of Gascoigne's poetry, from that in *A Hundreth Sundrie Flowres* of an anonymous editor of a coterie volume circulated in manuscript, bringing together a bunch of disparate blooms, to that in *The Posies of George Gascoigne* where a controlling and directing authorial voice already announced on the title page categorizes the plants in order to direct his readers' interpretation and understanding of them. Poetic collections and gardening manuals betray similar social aspirations. This essay explores the meaning of gardens in the sixteenth and seventeenth centuries, through the conversation between garden rhetoric, a burgeoning discourse of horticulture, in gardening manuals and herbals, and other forms of writing. Gascoigne's purpose, like that of garden writers, was to uncover for readers a privileged and cultivated private world, and appeal to their 'green desire'[84] to become involved with the making of England as hallowed, fertile and profitable ground, the result of morally improving labour.

The issue as to whether gardens were more properly the domain of men or women in this period is explored in this volume in Jennifer Munroe's consideration of Mary Somerset (1630–1715), Duchess of Beaufort, whose 'innocent diversions' on her estate at Badminton, centred on collecting, categorizing and analysing plants. These 'innocent diversions' blurred the line between gardening, horticulture and botany. Far from displaying deference to the male scientific establishment, she was part of an inner circle of natural scientists working on plant classification, cataloguing and description. Her extensive correspondence with Sir Hans Sloane, botanist and long-time president of the Royal Society underlines the scientific value of her investigations and classifications of plants, which were compiled in a twelve-volume manuscript, the *Herbarium*. She was sent copies by Sloane of his printed works and those of another botanist, John Ray, who was lent Sloane's copy of her manuscript and made copious annotations on it. Without the monumentalization of a print edition, however, Mary Somerset's labours were as ephemeral as the garden she dedicated her life to. Despite the fact that her contemporaries clearly took her seriously, her reputation has wilted and been forgotten.

My contribution to the volume departs from a consideration of the Spanish lexis for outdoor spaces, arguing that climatic conditions played a crucial role in shaping the invocation and imagination of gardens in early modern Spain. The climate affected the boundaries between public and private spaces in the baking plains of Castile, with shade and water – which were dominant features of literary evocations of the natural world – found most frequently on riverbanks. The word 'jardín' did not enter common usage until the eighteenth century, rather *huerto/a*, an outdoor space for leisure or recreation defined by trees for shade and running water, a stream or river to cool and freshen the air. The permeable borders of the *huerto/a* reflected the ambivalent meanings

---

[84] Phrase taken from the title of Rebecca Bushnell's *Green Desire: Imagining Early Modern English Gardens* (London: Cornell University Press, 2003).

of gardens by the end of the seventeenth century as spaces of danger and temptation as well as spiritual contemplation, places of moral and mortal effects.

The newest critical tool for understanding gardens in the past is represented in this volume by Brian Dix, whose chapter looks at the uses of garden archaeology and how much what lies beneath the contours of great gardens can tell us about what was originally there and serve as a critical tool in carrying out sensitive reconstructions, such as those in recent years at Kenilworth and Vaux-le Vicomte.[85] He points to the inherent limitations of relying on any single source of evidence and that this tool is at its most powerful where archaeology can be combined with several other generically different ones. There is a certain irony about what the archaeological evidence tells us about Kenilworth. The reconstruction is a monument to a kind of solidity and permanence that the original garden clearly did not possess, its impermanence and ephemerality suggesting it was erected just for the duration of the queen's stay. Only thirty years later, little remained, the obelisks mentioned in Langham's description of the entertainments, probably wood painted to look like stone, unmentioned. The planting at the manor of Sir Thomas Tresham at Lyveden may have paid tribute to his Catholicism with willows around the moat canals and roses and raspberries, associated with Christ's passion apparent in the circular beds emanating out from the central Edenic orchard.

The profusion of recent writing on nature is finally beginning to reflect its own wild abundance, sprouting up everywhere, endlessly fertile and only with difficulty controlled by pruning, weeding and digging over.[86] The material in this volume is inevitably selective encompassing only certain aspects of the early modern garden, but nevertheless we have been lucky enough to attract writing from scholars of garden history, botany, archaeology, art history, gender and early modern natures. The arrival of ecocriticism, championed by among others Jonathan Bate, might have been expected to have given new impetus to the consideration of landscape, horticulture and figurations of the natural world in this period.[87] Ecocriticism – nature not just as a projection of human values, an irreducible nature beyond anthropomorphism, prosopopeia, and personification – and a recovery of early modern 'nature' is underway.[88] Recent critics have demonstrated that early modern writers were

[85] English Heritage have attempted to reconstruct at Kenilworth the paradise garden built by Leicester for the festivities with which Elizabeth I's visit in 1575 was feted; described by Robert Laneham, a mercer in Robert Dudley's court, see Robert Langham, *A Letter*, ed. Roger J. P. Kuin (Leiden: Brill, 1983) and on the reconstruction John Watkins' forthcoming edited book.

[86] An 'Early Modern Gardens in Context Research Network' has been set up at Trinity College Dublin co-ordinated by Anatole Tchikine, based in their Centre for Medieval and Renaissance Studies.

[87] A good recent survey of these approaches is Thomas Hallock, Ivo Kamps and Karen Raber (eds.), *Early Modern Ecostudies: From the Florentine Codex to Shakespeare* (New York: Palgrave Macmillan, 2008). See also Jonathan Bate, *The Song of the Earth* (London: Picador, 2000).

[88] See Laurence Coupe (ed.), *The Green Studies Reader: From Romanticism to Ecocriticism* (London: Rouledge, 2000) and Greg Garrard, *Ecocriticism*, The New Critical Idiom (London: Rouledge, 2004).

aware of the complexity and fragility of ecosystems, that nature was not eternal and unchanging, how monsters and cats cut across distinctions between the natural and unnatural, domestic and wild, and of the shifting relations between human beings and their unstable environments. However, it is clear that '[e]nvironmental criticism in literature and the arts clearly does not yet have the standing within the academy of such other issue-driven discourses as those of race, gender, sexuality, class and globalization.'[89] Ecocriticism initially sought to bring literary studies closer to life sciences in a way that underlined the disjunction between the natural and human. A turn away from this critique of discourses of nature and the natural and the employment of organicist models saw the questioning of distinctions between natural and human environments. From controversies about the historical reconstruction of early modern gardens and their fake fruit, to the political and aesthetic implications of plants, gardens, statuary and landscape, it is clear that the *locus amoenus* is still very much central to the study of the Renaissance.

---

[89] Lawrence Buell, *The Future of Environmental Criticism: Environmental Crisis and Literary Imagination* (Oxford: Blackwell, 2005), 129.

1

The world of the Renaissance herbal

Brent Elliott

A herbal is a treatise on medicinal plants, traditionally intended for an audience of doctors and apothecaries; the purpose was to enable them to know which plants to use for medical purposes, and how to identify them in the field. As a genre, the herbal extends back into classical times, though there is only one title that has survived in complete form from that period: the *Materia medica* of Dioscorides, dating from the first century AD.[1] There was a mediaeval tradition, passed initially through Arab hands, which was in large part based on Dioscorides, but added to over the centuries by local herb lore and legend; the first printed herbals of the late fifteenth century fell into this tradition.[2]

What we may define as the Renaissance herbal arose in reaction against this tradition. During a period of a little over a century, between 1530 and the 1640s, the Renaissance herbal developed and reached its prime. This paper is far too short to give a very detailed account of its subject, but I will attempt to convey the most salient points about a genre that has received too little attention from scholars of Renaissance literature, however much attention it has received from botanists.[3]

HERBALS AND THE DEVELOPMENT OF BOTANY

What we may term the Renaissance herbal arose specifically from the demand that the traditions of plant lore be re-examined, and that the works of Pliny and Dioscorides be separated from the accumulated encrustation of centuries of myth and folklore.

---

[1] For a recent consideration of Dioscorides, see John M. Riddle, *Dioscorides on Pharmacy and Medicine* (Austin, TX: University of Texas Press, 1985).

[2] The mediaeval herbal tradition has been inadequately studied, primarily because most writers on the history of herbals have been botanists, who like to tune into the story in 1530. The best treatment so far is Minta Collins, *Medieval Herbals: the Illustrative Traditions* (London/ Toronto and Buffalo: British Library/ University of Toronto Press, 2000), but see also Wilfrid Blunt and Sandra Raphael, *The Illustrated Herbal* (London: Frances Lincoln, 1979), 10–119, and Frank J. Anderson, *An Illustrated History of the Herbals* (New York: Columbia University Press, 1977), 30–120.

[3] The standard history of herbals is Agnes Arber, *Herbals: Their Origin and Evolution: a Chapter in the History of Botany, 1470–1670*, first published in 1912; see the 3rd edn., edited with an excellent bibliography by William T. Stearn (Cambridge: Cambridge University Press, 1986). Other general surveys of importance are: Eleanour Sinclair Rohde, *The Old English Herbals* (London: Longmans, Green & Co., 1922); Claus Nissen, *Kräuterbücher aus fünf Jahrhunderten: medizinhistorischer und bibliographischer Beitrag* (Munich: Robert Wölfle Antiquariat, 1956); Blanche Henrey, *British Botanical and Horticultural Literature before 1800* (London: Oxford University Press, 1975), Vol. 1, 5–54, 79–92; and Frank J. Anderson, *Illustrated History*.

Locus Amoenus, First Edition. Edited by Alexander Samson. © 2012 The Authors.
Journal compilation © 2012 The Society for Renaissance Studies and Blackwell Publishing Ltd.

The attack on the mediaeval herbal began with Niccolo Leoniceno, whose tract *De Plinii aliorumque erroribus in medicina* [On the errors of Pliny and others in medicine] was published in 1492. His arguments that Pliny had misidentified plants because of confusions over etymology were immediately and fiercely debated,[4] but left a growing uncertainty in the academic world about the validity of traditional identifications. The first systematic attempt to resolve the uncertainty came in 1530, when Otto Brunfels, a physician of Basel, published *Herbarum vivae eicones*, a work which has long had the reputation of being a mediocre compilation, notable for its illustrations but not for its text.[5] But this is to judge Brunfels by the standards of a later generation; his purpose was not to publish new descriptions of plants but to collate the information about them provided by Dioscorides, Pliny, and other sources, drawing attention to disparities. In 1531 Brunfels supplemented his work with *Novi herbarii tomus II*, 216 pages of which (Appendix, 'De vera herbarum cognitione') consisted of an anthology of extracts from Leoniceno and other writers about the identification of plants in classical sources. So, regardless of the quality of plant identifications and descriptions in Brunfels's own text, he helped to stimulate further the interest in re-examining the accepted traditions, and thus prepared the way for Fuchs (one of whose earliest publications was a contribution to Brunfels's appendix).[6]

Despite the attack on Pliny, the major effort of the early Renaissance herbal was not so much an attempt to break free from the classical authors, as to recover the authentic texts of the classical authors and free them from subsequent interpolations. The first printed texts of Dioscorides were published simultaneously in Basel and Cologne in 1529; the 1598 edition, published by Andreas Wechel in Frankfurt, remained the standard edition until the nineteenth century. In the meantime, Pietro Andrea Mattioli's commentary on Dioscorides, first published in 1544, had passed through at least thirty-six editions in different languages.[7] Mattioli attempted to identify conclusively the plants described by Dioscorides, but he would not be the last to do so.[8] There

---

[4] For Leoniceno, and the interpretation of his criticism of Pliny in terms of the local politics of Poliziano's circle, see Peter Godman, *From Poliziano to Machiavelli: Florentine Humanism in the High Renaissance* (Princeton: Princeton University Press, 1998), 96–106; Brian W. Ogilvie, *The Science of Describing: Natural History in Renaissance Europe* (Chicago, IL: University of Chicago Press, 2006), 126–33.

[5] Thomas Archibald Sprague, 'The Herbal of Otto Brunfels', *Journal of the Linnean Society: Botany*, Vol. 48 (1928), 79–124; Arber, *Herbals*, 52–5; Anderson, *Illustrated History*, 121–9.

[6] Further editions of *Tomus II* appeared in 1536, 1537, and 1539; by the 1536 edition the entire work had been retitled *Herbarium*, and had grown to three volumes. The 'Appendix de vera herbarum cognitione' appears in the 1536 edition on pp. 97–313, Leoniceno's extract being on 180–205, and Fuchs's 'Annotationes aliquot herbarum & simplicium' on 245–271.

[7] See Sara Ferri (ed.), *Pietro Andrea Mattioli, Siena 1501 – Trento 1578: la vita, le opere con l'identificazione delle piante* (Perugia: Quattroemme, 1997), 391–6, for a list of editions in the Biblioteca Comunale di Siena, but this does not include foreign translations, the 1586 *Epitome* and its successors, etc.

[8] While Mattioli was supremely confident in his identifications of Dioscorides' plants, not all were equally impressed, and two centuries later John Sibthorp would make an expedition to Greece, resulting in his famous *Flora Graeca* (1806–1830), for exactly the same purpose.

had been no significant concept of geographical distribution in the early sixteenth century, until previously unknown plants began to be introduced from the Americas. Brunfels, in 1530, showed no real awareness that the flora of Germany might differ from that of Greece and the Near East. His coeval Euricius Cordus, whose *Botanologicon* was published in 1534, deliberately omitted what we would now regard as significant details from plant descriptions on the grounds that they exhibited regional variations; he at least recognized that some plants had been discovered since the time of Dioscorides.

Leonhart Fuchs was the first herbalist to describe American introductions like maize; his *De historia stirpium* (1542) has traditionally been regarded as the first botanical work in which both the text and the illustrations were based on personal observation rather than copying. It was given an abridged translation into German the following year, as the *New Kreüterbuch*, and several octavo editions followed.[9]

Fuchs set the initial standards for plant description which most subsequent herbalists attempted to meet or surpass. From the point of view of the development of descriptive botany, his most important successors were a trio of Flemish authors all published by the firm of Christopher Plantin of Antwerp: Rembert Dodoens, Mathieu de L'Obel (more usually called Lobel or Lobelius), and Charles de l'Ecluse (more usually called Clusius). These authors between them, in addition to writing herbals as traditionally understood, laid the foundations of the modern regional flora. The *Stirpium adversaria nova* of Lobel and his colleague Pierre Pena (1571) described the plants of the Montpellier area (while including a miscellany of rare and recently introduced plants); Clusius' *Rariorum aliquot stirpium per Hispanias observatarum historia* (1576) described the plants observed in a tour of Spain and Portugal. In his *Exoticorum* (1605), he reproduced a number of texts describing plants of the Americas.[10]

From Brunfels to Clusius, the standards of descriptive botany improved steadily: clearer and more detailed descriptions, an increasing consistency of vocabulary used to describe plant anatomy, an awareness of the need to record locations. (No herbal, in this respect, surpassed John Gerard's *Herball* of 1597; Gerard relied on a network of correspondents around England to send him

[9] Arber, *Herbals*, 64–70; Anderson, *Illustrated History*, 137–147. A facsimile and translation of the *De historia stirpium*, unfortunately in monochrome, has been published under the title *The Great Herbal of Leonhart Fuchs*, edited by Frederick G. Meyer *et al.* (Stanford, CA: Stanford University Press, 1999).

[10] Arber, *Herbals*, 82–91; Anderson, *Illustrated History*, 173–180. For Lobel, see Armand Louis, *Mathieu de l'Obel 1538–1616: épisode de l'histoire de la botanique* (Ghent-Louvain: Story-Scientia, 1980). For Clusius, see Friedrich Wilhelm Tobias Hunger, *Charles de l'Escluse (Carolus Clusius): Nederlandsch kruidkundige 1526–1609* ('S-Gravenhage: Martinus Nijhoff, 1927); Florike Egmond *et al.* (eds.), *Carolus Clusius: Towards a Cultural History of a Renaissance Naturalist* (Amsterdam: Koninklijke Nederlandse Akademie van Wetenschappen, 2007); and see the chapter 'Americana in the *Exoticorum libri decem* of Charles de l'Ecluse' in Peter Mason, *Before Disenchantment* (London: Reaktion Books, 2009), 124–48.

notices of localities where plants had been found.)[11] In other matters there was, from the modern point of view, little progress. There were no recognized standards for nomenclature. So long as there were few species to distinguish, everyone was happy with a two-word name, but the more related plants there were to distinguish, the longer and more descriptive the names became; and there was no accepted rule for the order in which the terms appeared in the name. As early as 1620, Caspar Bauhin felt it necessary to publish a dictionary of synonyms for plant names (*Pinax theatri botanici*). But there could be no generally acceptable resolution of the problem of naming when there was no agreement on how plants were to be classified. There were no distinct concepts of genus, species, or variety, let alone higher-order classifications like family. From Lobel onwards, a variety of classification schemes was tried, but until the mid-seventeenth century most herbalists were content to group plants by a mixture of criteria; medical, morphological, utilitarian, and sometimes etymological.[12] (There is no space here to enter into the debate about Renaissance encyclopaedism and its criteria for inclusion and organization of information, beyond saying that a more detailed consideration of herbals would prove a useful test case.)[13]

BOTANICAL ART IN THE HERBALS

The earliest printed herbals were the heirs to a long mediaeval tradition of plant illustration, one that has attracted an insufficient degree of scholarly attention in modern times, but for perfectly understandable reasons. For the botanist, plant illustration before the 1530s is a matter of antiquarian interest only, as manuscript and early printed illustrations alike are virtually useless for botanical purposes. We know from Pliny that classical botanists attempted to produce illustrated works on plants, but abandoned the attempt; when hand-copying was the only means of reproducing images, it did not take many generations of copying before the resulting images had ceased to resemble the originals exactly enough to be useful for purposes of identification. Botanists therefore relied on written descriptions, and anyone who has attempted

[11] For Gerard's regional network, see Robert H. Jeffers, *The Friends of John Gerard* (Falls Village, CT: Herb Grower Press, 1967–1969).

[12] The most detailed analysis of descriptive standards and taxonomic ideas in the herbals is to be found in Edward Lee Greene's *Landmarks of Botanical History*, the first part of which was published in 1909, and the remainder not until Frank Egerton's edition (Stanford, CA: Stanford University Press, 1983). Despite Greene's cantankerous and pugnacious approach, it remains unfailingly interesting, instructive, and as yet unsurpassed. For the most recent discussion of the species concept as it existed in the Renaissance, see John S. Wilkins, *Species: a History of the Idea* (Berkeley, CA: University of California Press, 2009), 84–7.

[13] For some contributions to the debate about the nature of Renaissance encyclopaedism which specifically deal with the question of herbals, see Giuseppe Olmi, *L'inventario del mondo: catalogazione della natura e luoghi del sapere nella prima età moderna* (Bologna: Società Editrice il Mulino, 1992); Brian W. Ogilvie, 'The Many Books of Nature: How Renaissance Naturalists Created and Responded to Information Overload', *Journal of the History of Ideas*, Vol. 64 (2003), 29–40; Ogilvie, *Science of Describing*, esp. 139–208.

to identify a plant from a description alone will understand why descriptive botany made few strides until the invention of printing.[14]

Manuscript and early printed herbals suffered from the recycling of a limited number of stylized images, which could be usefully employed only by those who already knew the plants in question, and did not need to use the images as field guides. Take the illustrations in *The Grete Herball* (printed by Peter Treveris, 1526): they are all printed from blocks of a standard size, with no indications of scale; they offer outlines only; flower and leaf shapes are highly schematized; and in some cases, mythological or emblematic consider-ations take precedence over description (mandrakes have human bodies, iris flowers are reduced to fleur-de-lis shapes). The anonymous artist need never have seen the plants he was depicting: they are based on the illustrations seen in earlier publications (Figs. 1 and 2).

In 1530, the first printed plant illustrations drawn from actual plants were published in Strasbourg by Johann Schott, in the first volume of Brunfels's *Herbarum vivae eicones*, whose title means 'Images of living plants' (Fig. 3). The artist was Hans Weiditz, some of whose original drawings survive in the Felix Platter Herbarium in Geneva.[15] While Brunfels's text was meagre as a work of descriptive botany, its polemical message about the importance of subjecting the inherited body of writing on plants to modern criticism served as a justification for the use of actual plants rather than existing illustrations as models. Weiditz's illustrations were carved at life size, and depict actual specimens rather than idealized versions. Little more than a decade later came Fuchs's *De historia stirpium*, where for the first time illus-trations drawn from actual plants were accompanied by descriptions based on personal observation (Fig. 4). The work contained portraits both of Fuchs and of his artists: Heinrich Füllmaurer, who drew the plants on paper; Albrecht Meyer, who copied the drawings onto woodblocks, and Veit Rudolph Speckle, who carved the blocks (Fig. 5). (Two centuries would pass before the next time an artist had his portrait in a botanical work – G. D. Ehret, in C. J. Trew's *Plantae selectae* (1750–73).) The Füllmaurer illustrations are, like those of Weiditz, largely drawn and printed at life size (though this advantage was lost when they were recarved for octavo editions). As in the work of their immediate predecessors, the woodcuts are largely simple outlines, but for reasons acknowledged in the preface: an awareness

---

[14] Pliny's account will be found in Book 25, Chap. 4 of his *Historia naturalis*. For a sprightly consideration of the implications of Pliny's account, see William M. Ivins Jr., *Prints and Visual Communication* (London: Routledge & Kegan Paul), 1–20. There are now many histories of botanical art which include discussions of the illustrations in Renaissance herbals, but still the standard work is Wilfrid Blunt and William T. Stearn, *The Art of Botanical Illustration*, 3rd edn. (Woodbridge: Antique Collectors' Club, 1994), 61–87. See also Brent Elliott, 'The Birth of Botanical Illustration', *The Garden*, Vol. 120 (1995), 81–3.

[15] The Weiditz watercolours were discovered by Walther Rytz; see his works, *Das Herbarium Felix Platters: ein Beitrag zur Geschichte der Botanik des XVI. Jahrhunderts* (Basel: Buchdruckerei Emil Birkhäuser & Cie, 1933.), and *Pflanzen Aquarelle des Hans Weiditz aus dem Jahre 1529: die Originale zu den Holzschnitten im Brunfels'schen Kräuterbuch* (Berne: Verlag Paul Haupt, 1936.) See also Blunt and Stearn, *Botanical Illustration*, 61–3.

Fig. 1 Woodcut, allegedly of a black hellebore but actually of an iris, from the fifth Venice edition of the Herbarius Latinus, printed by Alessandro de Bindoni in 1520. Even if the picture had been properly identified, how useful would it have been as a guide to identification? (Royal Horticultural Society, Lindley Library)

that purchasers of the book would probably want to have the pictures coloured, so there was little point in cluttering the images with lines and shading that would be effaced.[16]

The history of the illustration of printed herbals is not a story of simple progress toward the goal of exact representation. As many herbals were published in octavo or small quarto formats, illustration at life size was not always possible; in some herbals a compromise was reached, which remained influential well into the eighteenth century: if the plant was too large to be accurately rendered on the page, some important detail would be rendered at life size, in addition to the reduced depiction of its general habit. The best and most detailed plant illustrations printed from woodblocks are to be found in the editions of Mattioli's commentary on Dioscorides, beginning with the 1565 Venice edition published by Valgrisi, in which large woodcuts by Giorgio Liberale and Wolfgang Meyerpack were first printed. It would be difficult to

[16] Blunt and Stearn, *Botanical Illustration*, 64–71.

Fig. 2 Figures of male and female mandrake, from *The Grete Herball* (1526) (Royal Horticultural Society, Lindley Library)

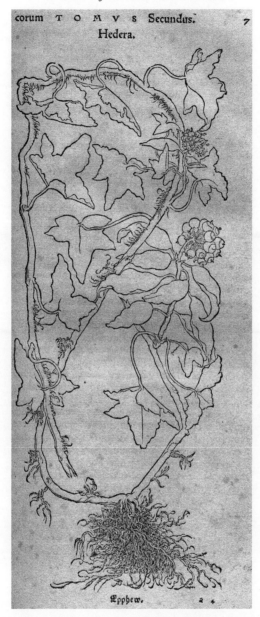

Fig. 3   Ivy, from Otto Brunfels, *Herbarium*, tom. II (1536) (Royal Horticultural Society, Lindley Library)

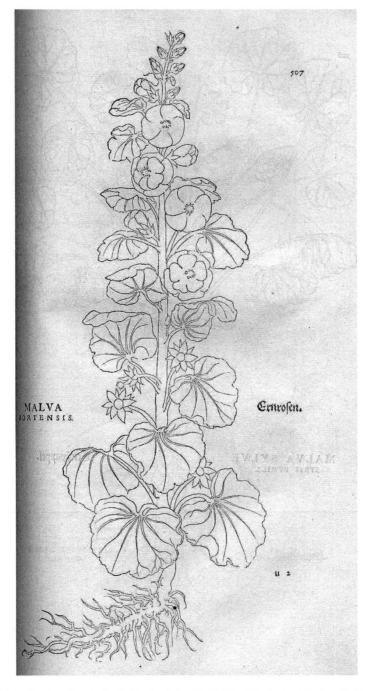

Fig. 4   Malva, from Leonhart Fuchs, *De historia stirpium* (1542) (Royal Horticultural Society, Lindley Library)

Fig. 5 The artists of Fuchs's *De historia stirpium*: top right, Albrecht Meyer, who drew the plants; top left, Heinrich Füllmaurer, who copied the drawings onto the woodblocks; below, Veit Rudolph Speckle, who carved the blocks (Royal Horticultural Society, Lindley Library)

produce finer definition of lines by whittling a woodblock, and indeed German editions of Mattioli tended to copy the smaller illustrations used in Valgrisi's 1554 edition.[17]

---

[17] Arber, *Herbals*, 92–7; Anderson, *Illustrated History*, 163–72; Blunt and Stearn, *Botanical Illustration*, 73–6; Ferri, *Pietro Andrea Mattioli, Siena 1501 – Trento 1578*; William Patrick Watson *et al.*, *The Mattioli Woodblocks* (London: Hazlitt, Gooden & Fox, 1989).

PUBLISHING HISTORY OF THE HERBALS

Herbals became a genre with a strong market, and all the publishing traditions of plagiarism and competition can be traced during the course of the
sixteenth and seventeenth centuries. What is often regarded as the first court
case brought over infringement of copyright involved a herbal. In 1532
Johannes Schott of Basel, Brunfels' publisher, issued a German translation of
his *Herbarum vivae eicones* under the title of *Contrafayt Kreüterbuch* (the title was
varied in later editions).[18] In 1533 he brought a suit in the Imperial Chamber
Court against Christian Egenolph, a printer in Frankfurt, for violating the
terms of the Imperial privilege accorded to him by reprinting his translation
without authorization. The Reichskammergerichtsakten do not record a
verdict in the case of Schott v. Egenolph, but it has been generally assumed
that judgment was made for the plaintiff.[19] Egenolph was a notorious pirate,
helping himself freely to other publishers' work, and recycling the same
illustrations under various titles; as early as 1542 Fuchs criticized him for his
continual republication of flagrant errors.[20] His firm's greatest success was the
herbal compiled by his son-in-law Adam Lonitzer, a work for which the phrase
'scissors and paste' could have been invented, but which stayed in print longer
than any other herbal, being reissued more or less continuously until 1783.[21]
Lonitzer was commemorated by Linnaeus by giving the honeysuckles the
Latin name *Lonicera*, but this honour must be attributed to affection for a work
remembered from his youth rather than recognition of superior qualities.

The copying of illustrations was a standard publishing practice in the sixteenth century; original, standard-setting achievements in depiction were
regularly cribbed, especially by provincial publishers, and the results easily
identified by the right-to-left reversal of the image. So we find that the first
important English herbal, William Turner's *Herbal*, the first botanically important English herbal (published in three parts in 1551 and 1568, the first in
London and the remainder in Cologne), copied illustrations from Fuchs
(Figs. 6 and 7).[22]

The two editions of John Gerard's *Herball* present a much more complicated problem. The *Herball* was very much a publisher-led book. The printer,

[18] The Lindley Library's edition of this work is a 1546 reissue by Hermann Gulfferich of Frankfurt under the
title *Kreuterbuch contrafeyt*.

[19] Friedemann Kawohl (2008) 'Commentary on Schott v. Egenolph (1533)', in *Primary Sources on Copyright
(1450–1900)*, ed. Lionel Bently & Martin Kretschmer, http://www.copyrighthistory.org/cgi-bin/kleioc/0010/
exec/ausgabeCom/%22d_1533%22 (accessed November 2010).

[20] Carsten Jäcker (ed.), *Christian Egenolff* (Limburg: Glaukos, 2002).

[21] It first appeared in 1557 as the *Kreütterbuch*, though in fact it was merely a revision of Theodoric Dorsten's
Botanicon (1540), itself a revision of Eucharius Rösslin's *Kreutterbüch* (1533), itself a cobbling-together of two
previous works, Peter Schoeffer's *Gart der Gesundheit* (first edition 1485) and Hieronymus Brunschwig's *Buch zu
Distillieren* (first edition 1500). For some discussion, see Anderson, *Illustrated History*, 156–62; see also Arber,
Herbals, 70–72.

[22] For Turner, see Henrey, *British Botanical and Horticultural Literature*, Vol. 1, 21–6; Anderson, *Illustrated
History*, 148–57. Turner's *Herbal* has been republished in facsimile by Cambridge University Press (1995).

John Norton, wanted to publish a good English-language herbal, and planned to commission a new translation of Dodoens's herbal (already translated in 1578), and accompany it with the best of recent plant portraiture. Having seen the *Eicones plantarum* of Tabernaemontanus (1590) at the Frankfurt Book Fair, he arranged to rent the woodblocks from Nicolaus Bassaeus, the publisher, and a comparison between Gerard and Tabernaemontanus reveals that the illustrations were printed from the same blocks: not only is there no right-to-left reversal, but when photocopied onto transparent acetate and overlaid, the two images correspond exactly. The first author that Norton engaged left the work unfinished on his death, so Gerard was hired instead, with Lobel correcting the text, and it was Lobel himself who first launched accusations of plagiarism against Gerard. The fact that the text was fitted to a series of illustrations made on the continent helps to explain why Gerard included some plants he acknowledged were not to be found in England.

In the early 1630s, a new edition of Gerard's *Herball* was commissioned – again a publisher-led enterprise, conceived in order to cut out a competitor. John Parkinson – whose *Paradisus terrestris* (1629), the first English book purely on garden flowers rather than medicinal plants, had been a great success – was reported to be working on a new herbal to replace Gerard's. Norton's widow and her colleagues commissioned the apothecary Thomas Johnson to revise the text; his enlarged and improved edition was published in 1633, with a further reissue in 1636. (Parkinson's herbal, *Theatrum botanicum*, eventually appeared in 1640.) This time the illustrations were taken, not from Tabernaemontanus, but from Christopher Plantin; Johnson claimed in his Preface to have 'made use of those wherewith the Workes of Dodonaeus, Lobel, and Clusius were formerly printed', and at the end of the volume – apologizing for some out-of-sequence addenda – 'This worke was begun to be printed before such time as we received all the figures from beyond the Seas'.[23] However, a comparison of superimposed acetate copies reveals that the illustrations were not printed from the same blocks as in Plantin's publications, but were copied, in most cases without right-to-left reversal. I suspect that the Plantin woodcuts were copied onto paper that was then treated with turpentine or an equivalent in order to make it transparent, so that the paper could be turned over for re-copying onto the blocks.

HERBALS AND THE GARDEN

Herbals can have an additional relevance for the history of gardening, for they can provide information about the introduction of new plants into the garden. From Fuchs, for example (cap. lxix), we can tell that *Momordica balsamina* was being grown in Germany by 1540, decades before the generally

---

[23] Arber, *Herbals*, 129–35; Henrey, *British Botanical and Horticultural Literature*, Vol. 1, 36–54; Anderson, *Illustrated History*, 218–26; Louis, *Mathieu de l'Obel*, 269–74.

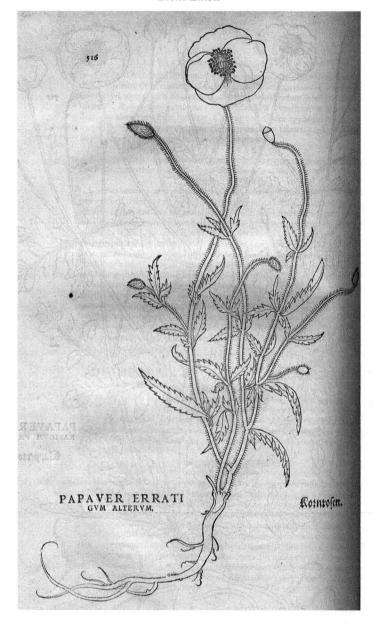

Fig. 6   Poppy, from Leonhart Fuchs, *De historia stirpium* (1542) (Royal Horticultural Society, Lindley Library)

Fig. 7 Poppy, from William Turner, *Herbal* (1568), copied from Fuchs with right-to-left reversal (Royal Horticultural Society, Lindley Library)

accepted date, and the first reference to potatoes being grown in England is found in Gerard's *Herball* (Fig. 8). It should not be assumed that the herbalists are necessarily sources of accurate information about new introductions; the ambiguity of the term 'Indies' alone resulted in a massive circulation of misinformation, and Gerard's statement that potatoes were introduced from

Fig. 8   The first printed illustration of the potato, from John Gerard, *Herball* (1597) (Royal Horticultural Society, Lindley Library)

'Virginia' misled scholars for centuries. But the herbals frequently contain the best information the period can provide on the subject, and the spread of maize and potatoes throughout Europe has been documented in large part from these publications.[24] Nor is it only medicinal plants that are thus documented: Pena and Lobel, in their *Stirpium adversaria nova* (1571), reported

[24] John J. Finan, *Maize in the Great Herbals* (Waltham, MA, 1950: Chronica Botanica); Redcliffe N. Salaman, *The History and Social Influence of the Potato* (Cambridge University Press, 1949).

that the London apothecary Hugh Morgan had a collection of West Indian cacti in his garden, from which they produced the first published illustration of a prickly pear.[25]

I have already remarked on the lack of generally accepted concepts of species and variety in the sixteenth century. Gerard's *Herball* went beyond its brief and included detailed accounts of cultivated varieties of plants like auriculas, daffodils, crocuses, irises, anemones, ranunculus – to such an extent that it is considered a gardening book as well as a herbal (Fig. 9). And while Parkinson's *Paradisus terrestris* (1629) provided a precedent for books dealing specifically with garden plants, some writers of herbals followed Gerard's example, most notably William Salmon in his *Botanologia. The English herbal* (1718). This massive work, dismissed ever since its publication for its belated adherence to Galenic principles of medicine, is only now being recognized as a source of useful information for the student of plant fashions.[26]

THE DECLINE OF THE HERBAL

The Renaissance herbal effectively came to an end in the mid-seventeenth century. The hiatus in publication resulting from the Thirty Years' War meant that the return to 'normal' publishing coincided with the foundation of scientific societies in various countries, a shift of emphasis in botanical writing, and altered standards in publishing. The Civil War in England did not result in such a devastating break, but even so, botanical publication largely lapsed until the Restoration; John Parkinson did publish a 'second edition' of his *Paradisus terrestris* in 1656, but in fact it consisted entirely of unsold sheets of the 1629 printing, with the title-page date altered.

The first factor affecting the production of herbals was the increasing preference given to engravings rather than woodblocks as illustrations. Engraving had been introduced into horticultural publication in the early seventeenth century with a new genre that came to be known as the florilegium: works dedicated to depicting the plants of a particular garden, and focussing largely on ornamental plants rather than medicinal.[27] Engraving was expensive, and difficult to incorporate within the same page as text; while different strategies were employed to resolve the effective break between the description and the illustration, the role of the herbal as a handy guide to plant identification in the field became difficult to sustain.

In the second half of the seventeenth century, botanical encyclopaedias superseded herbals as a genre. Where upmarket herbals survived, they tended

---

[25] Pierre Pena and Mathias Lobel, *Stirpium adversaria nova* (London: Thomas Purfoot, 1571), 41–73. For the history of the documentation of cacti in herbals, see Gordon Rowley, *A History of Succulent Plants* (Mill Valley CA: Strawberry Press, 1997), 41–73.

[26] On Salmon, see Henrey, *British Botanical and Horticultural Literature*, Vol. 2, 5–7; Brent Elliott, 'The Forgotten Herbal', *The Garden*, Vol. 134 (2009), 42–3.

[27] Brent Elliott, 'The Florilegium', *The Garden*, Vol. 120 (1995), 204–07.

600   THE SECOND BOOKE OF THE

Fig. 9   Marigold cultivars, from John Gerard, *Herball* (1597) (Royal Horticultural Society, Lindley Library)

to have strong institutional affiliations: Robert Lovell's *Pambotanologia . . . or, a complete herball* (1659; 2nd ed. 1665) was based closely on the collections of the Oxford Botanic Garden, and Elizabeth Blackwell's *Curious herball* (1739) on those of the Chelsea Physic Garden. John Pechey's *Compleat herball* (1694) was the first to divide the text between British natives and exotic plants. The word 'herbal' survived, but publications like James Newton's *Compleat herbal* (1752) and John Edwards' *Edwards' herbal* (1770) are in fact largely collections of engraved illustrations, the former case a pocket encyclopaedia and the latter effectively a florilegium.

There had long been an inconsistency in the sources of medical advice: on the one hand, a long academic tradition of Galenic medicine, and on the other, folk advice based to some degree on practical observation, handed down orally until it entered the literature in the sixteenth century. It is only recently that attempts have been made to distinguish these two sources.[28] The repudiation of Galen in the late seventeenth century, reflected in the dismissal of Salmon's *Botanologia*, meant that doctors and apothecaries in the eighteenth century wished to distance themselves from the herbal tradition. Progressively the word 'herbal' disappeared from the titles of works intended for university use or for the medical profession, to be replaced by the words 'medical botany'.

But the herbal did not disappear; it merely sank below the horizon of the learned, into the crepuscular world associated with almanacs, astrological treatises, and mass-market how-to books. The eighteenth century saw a progressive migration of herbals into the occultist fringe: Michael Bernhard Valentini's *Viridarium reformatum* (1718) was heavily alchemical, while Nicholas Culpeper's *English physitian*, first published in 1652, introduced astrology into the genre. Editions of Culpeper continued to appear regularly into the early nineteenth century, gradually turning into the *English physician and complete herbal*, and finally into *Culpeper's herbal*, while becoming progressively associated with both astrology and Freemasonry.[29] As the association between 'herbals' and quackery became fixed in the educated mind, so the very concept of the herbal fell into desuetude. In 1843, in response to a reader's enquiry, the magisterial *Gardeners' Chronicle* could say, 'We do not know what you mean by a Herbal. The term is disused.'[30]

What happened after that is a story of twentieth-century revivalism.

Lindley Library, Royal Horticultural Society

---

[28] This is primarily the accomplishment of Gabrielle Hatfield: see her *Memory, Wisdom and Healing: the History of Domestic Plant Medicine* (Stroud: Sutton Publishing, 1999), and David Elliston Allen and Gabrielle Hatfield, *Medicinal Plants in Folk Tradition: an Ethnobotany of Britain & Ireland* (Portland, OR: Timber Press, 2004).

[29] Henrey, *British Botanical and Horticultural Literature*, Vol. 1, 82–8. For a recent defence of Culpeper (alternative medicine v. the Establishment), see Benjamin Woolley, *The Herbalist: Nicholas Culpeper and the Fight for Medical Freedom* (London: HarperCollins, 2004). There has not yet been an historical bibliography of Culpeper; should anyone be inclined to tackle this project, the best collection of editions is at the Wellcome Institute.

[30] *Gardeners' Chronicle* 1843, 400.

2

Clinging to the past: medievalism in the English 'Renaissance' garden

PAULA HENDERSON

Historians of Tudor and early Stuart architecture used to emphasize the idea that art was inexorably 'progressive', evolving into purer, classical forms.[1] As a result, a building like Longleat (Wiltshire, begun in the 1560s), with its emphatic symmetry, superimposed orders and relative restraint, epitomized a 'momentary High Renaissance'[2] and the period up to 1585 represented a 'false dawn of an English Renaissance . . .'.[3] To many architectural historians, the promise of the Renaissance was only really fulfilled in the buildings of Inigo Jones, who himself had been 'reborn' once he experienced the architecture of Italy itself. To many of these same historians classical art was (and still is) deemed superior, so why would patrons in the sixteenth century, particularly those who were schooled in the Classics (anyone who really mattered), not wish to emulate an Italianate, classical style? The assumption was that once classical ideas were introduced into England, patrons would embrace them and art forms would become more classical, more continental. The problem is that the evidence suggests that, while patrons were happy to experiment with classical forms, at times they rejected classicism or simply adapted the vocabulary to complement earlier, 'medieval' forms, which they quite frequently preferred.[4]

This happened in most of the arts, including literature, where Edmund Spenser's *Faerie Queene* and Philip Sidney's *Arcadia* combined new classical forms with the romance of medieval chivalry to glorify the queen and nation. The cult of chivalry and the romance of medieval virtues were emphasized, too, in Accession Day tournaments and in many other entertainments given in

---

[1] For a discussion on the way in which the Tudors and early Stuarts read and adapted classicism, see the essays in Lucy Gent (ed.), *Albion's Classicism*, Studies in British Art 2 (New Haven and London: Yale University Press for The Paul Mellon Centre for Studies in British Art, 1995).

[2] John Summerson, *Architecture in Britain, 1530–1830* (9th ed., New Haven and London: Yale University Press, 1993), 62.

[3] Mark Girouard, *Robert Smythson & the Elizabethan Country House* (New Haven and London: Yale University Press, 1983), 30, (updated edition of *Robert Smythson & the Architecture of the Elizabethan Era*, (1967).

[4] On the appeal of medieval chivalry, see Girouard, *Robert Smythson*, 34–6 and, more recently, *Elizabethan Architecture: Its Rise and Fall, 1540–1640* (New Haven and London: Yale University Press, 2009), Ch. 8, 419–54.

Locus Amoenus, First Edition. Edited by Alexander Samson. © 2012 The Authors.
Journal compilation © 2012 The Society for Renaissance Studies and Blackwell Publishing Ltd.

honour of the queen. The virtues of chivalry and associations with the Arthurian legend formed the basis of a nascent nationalism that would echo down the centuries.

In painting, very sophisticated classical models were introduced in the reign of Henry VII (1485–1509). Henry's Book of Hours (*c.* 1500, BL Add MS 35254) includes an 'Annunciation' of great sensitivity and sophistication with depth, modelling and perspective.[5] Although a private book, there seems to be no reason that it could not have served as a model for other artists working for the crown had the monarch so wished. More accessible was the sculpture of Pietro Torrigiano, including the naturalistic terracotta bust of Henry and the fine funerary effigies of Henry and Elizabeth of York, placed on the classical sarcophagus in the Lady Chapel at Westminster Abbey.[6] Henry had brought the Florentine sculptor to England specifically for the purpose and his work should have provided a powerful model to those wishing to create up-to-date Renaissance monuments.

Even more dramatically, in the reign of Henry VIII, Hans Holbein the Younger brought to England a highly developed, virtuoso northern-Renaissance painting style, epitomized by the stunning double-portrait of Jean de Dinteville and Georges de Selve, known as 'The Ambassadors' (1533, National Gallery, London) in which the powerful and lifelike figures stand in a setting of great complexity and depth.[7] Later in his career, when Holbein had become the official painter to the king, the figures in his portraits stand or sit isolated in contracted, blank space: his famous portrait of Henry VIII (Thyssen Museum, Madrid, 1536) shows a three-quarter view of the king in all his finery against a flat, blue background. Certainly this was the result of the demands and expectations of the patron, rather than a deterioration in artistic style.[8]

Later in the sixteenth century, other foreign artists continued to adapt their style to the Elizabethan preferences for rigid, iconic images. Although Elizabeth had been ex-communicated from the Roman Catholic church, portraits of her were as fixed and symbolic as medieval images of the Virgin Mary. It wasn't until the second decade of the seventeenth century that her successors – James I and Charles I – brought in the most sophisticated continental artists, including Peter Paul Rubens and Anthony Van Dyck, who finally established a robust, contemporary Baroque style.

The same thing happened in architecture. In the early Tudor period, Italian craftsmen were working for courtiers and the crown, adding such purely Renaissance details as the terracotta roundels with busts of the Caesars,

[5] Janet Backhouse, *The Illuminated Manuscript* (Oxford: Phaidon Press Ltd, 1979), 74.
[6] Carol Galvin and Phillip Lindley, 'Torrigiano's Portrait Bust of Henry VII', *Burlington Magazine*, Vol. 130 (1988), 892–902.
[7] Susan Foister, *Holbein and England* (New Haven and London: Yale University Press, 2004), Fig. 216, 214–22.
[8] Foister, *Holbein and England*, Fig. 189, 186–90. On later portraits, 226 ff.

Fig. 1   Wollaton Hall, Nottinghamshire (photo: author)

executed by the Italian Giovanni da Maiano at Hampton Court.[9] By the middle of the century, some houses – like Somerset House, London, and Longleat – demonstrated a more thorough adaptation of classical form with cohesive, symmetrically articulated facades. The great number of houses that were built in the latter half of the century, however, was far more eclectic, returning to archaic forms combined with new Mannerist influences from the continent. Many houses retained gatehouses with distinctly medieval profiles, for example, but embellished with subtle classical ornament. At Charlecote (Wiltshire), begun by Sir Charles Lucy in 1558, the passageway in the turreted gatehouse retains pendent fan vaulting, while fine, shell-headed niches flank the doorways into the porter's lodgings on each side.

Most spectacular is Wollaton Hall (Nottinghamshire), built by Robert Smythson in the 1580s for Sir Francis Willoughby, with its sophisticated Italianate plan and ornate, Dietterlinesque classical ornament (Figs. 1 and 2). The sprawling hulk of the building could hardly be mistaken for a continental building, particularly with the enormous prospect room perched on the top, reached via rounded tourelles. The traditional great hall was inserted into what would have been an open courtyard on the original continental plan with traceried clerestory windows providing the only light. The addition of a hammerbeam roof emphasizes the medieval prototypes of the hall itself. Taken as a whole, Wollaton is a splendid example of the highly individualistic manner in which patrons felicitously combined new and old elements.

When we look at gardens, we are far more limited in our evidence. The two most reliable visual sources for Tudor and early Stuart gardens are Anthonis

[9] On early Tudor classicism, see Maurice Howard, *The Early Tudor Country House, Architecture and Politics, 1490–1550* (London: George Philip, c. 1987).

Fig. 2 Wollaton Hall, Nottinghamshire: views of the middle roof with clerestory windows of hall (photo: author)

van den Wyngaerde's views of the royal palaces of *circa* 1560 (Ashmolean Museum, Oxford) and Isaac de Caus' drawing of the south front of Wilton House (*c.* 1630, Worcester College, Oxford) and his publication, Wilton Garden (*c.* 1640).[10]

At Hampton Court, the garden was divided into irregular, individual compartments with banqueting houses, ponds, a great spiral mount and numerous

---

[10] On Wilton garden, see Paula Henderson, *The Tudor House and Garden: Architecture and Landscape in the Sixteenth and Seventeenth Centuries* (New Haven and London: Yale University Press, 2005), 112–13.

heraldic beasts on posts (Fig. 3). The gardens were not symmetrical, nor were they aligned on an entrance to Henry's private apartments. There is no evidence of any classical references at all and one must assume that the gardens of Hampton Court had evolved naturally out of medieval forms, just as the palace itself did.

In contrast, the Earl of Pembroke's gardens at Wilton House (Wiltshire), created a hundred years later by Isaac de Caus, were aligned on the intended new south front of the house, although the building of the extended garden range was never completed (Fig. 4). That the gardens were created as planned is stunning evidence that they were part of an *a priori* programme of rebuilding. Like many continental gardens, the garden at Wilton was divided into three parts: a quadripartite *parterre de broderie* with figural fountains nearest the house; a wilderness; and an oval circus with a copy of the Borghese gladiator at the centre and a terrace and grotto at the end. Symmetry, axiality, complex hydraulics and classical sculpture clearly show that this was, in fact, a Renaissance garden.

These two seminal images provide a dramatic beginning and end of the Tudor/early Stuart garden: the first certainly linked to medieval traditions and the other to continental Renaissance gardens. How the one evolved into the other is not easy to determine, nor is the question of whether there was a tendency to retain or revive archaic forms in gardens, as there had been in the other arts. The only way to approach either of these questions is by looking at the evidence. But first, it is useful to consider what we know about English medieval gardens and, even more important, what the Tudors knew about them.

MEDIEVAL GARDENS

The dividing line between the 'medieval period' and the 'early modern period' was hardly as well defined then, as it appears to be now! John Leland, the first and only designated 'Royal Antiquary', travelled through England between 1540 and 1546, recording antiquities for Henry VIII.[11] Architecture was his primary focus and he rarely mentioned gardens, although he did describe parks, woodlands, rivers and streams. Gardens were certainly essential adjuncts to palaces, houses of the nobility, wealthy gentry and even modest homes would have had kitchen or physic gardens, orchards and perhaps even vineyards.[12] Greater houses would also have had pleasure gardens, sometimes called a 'pleasance' or 'herber', either adjacent to the living quarters or in a walled or moated enclosure in the larger landscape around it. These gardens generally had irregularly placed raised beds filled with native plants, flowers

---

[11] John Chandler (ed.), *John Leland's Itinerary: Travels in Tudor England* (Stroud, Gloucestershire: A. Sutton, 1993).

[12] On medieval English gardens, see John Harvey, *Medieval Gardens* (London: Batsford, 1981), Teresa McLean, *Medieval English Gardens* (London: Barrie & Jenkins, 1989), Sylvia Landsberg, *The Medieval Garden* (London: British Museum, 1995).

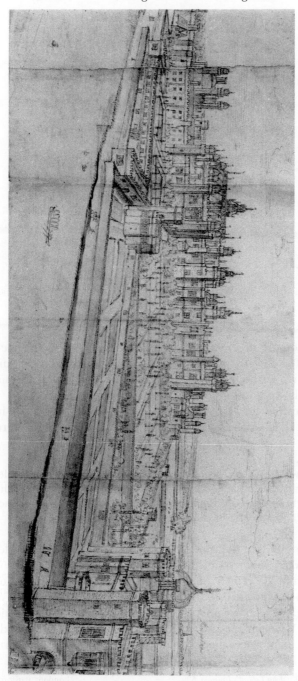

Fig. 3   Anthonis van den Wyngaerde, view of Hampton Court from the south (© Ashmolean Museum, Oxford)

Fig. 4   Isaac de Caus, drawing of Wilton House and garden, *c.* 1630 (© The Provost and Fellows Worcester College, Oxford)

and herbs; some had topiary and ornamental pots for delicate and exotic specimens. The finest gardens would have a fountain or conduit and some sort of shelter: an arbour or protected turf seat. Large pleasure gardens might have orchards, a mount, pool, aviary and a menagerie.

The few gardens (or garden features) that Leland wrote about included the snail mount at Wressle Castle, built by one of the younger Percys, earls of Worcester

> The castle wardrobe was exceptionally fine, as were the gardens inside the moat and the orchards outside. In the orchards were mounds with topiary hedges and a spiral flight of steps cut into them like the helix of a cockleshell, so that they could be climbed to the top without effort.[13]

Leland also described the more contemporary Thornbury Castle, left unfinished by Edward Stafford, third Duke of Buckingham after his execution for treason. Leland described the 'wooden gallery in the rear garden of the house, which was attached to the north side of the parish church'.[14] The stone walls of the gallery survive and are similar to a gallery at Richmond Palace (as recorded by Wyngaerde) and to others erected in the early Tudor period.[15] Leland also mentioned the gardens at Kenilworth Castle, particularly the

[13] Chandler (ed.), *John Leland's Itinerary*, 539.
[14] Chandler (ed.), *John Leland's Itinerary*, 186.
[15] Henderson, *Tudor House and Garden*, 153–5.

Pleasaunce, a double-moated island retreat on which Henry V had erected a banqueting house that, according to Leland, Henry VIII dismantled and re-erected in the outer courtyard of the castle.[16] Although the banqueting house disappeared long ago, the impressive earthworks of the Pleasaunce are clearly visible even today.

More specific information on medieval gardens is found in royal accounts.[17] For example, we know that Henry I built a menagerie in Woodstock Park, where he kept 'lyons, leopards, strange spotted beasts, porcupines, camells and such like animals', sent to him from 'diverse outlandish Lands'.[18] In 1256, Henry III built a cloister of marble columns (probably a gallery) in a garden at Guildford.[19] Richard II built a summer house with benches and trestle tables on an island in the Thames at Sheen with several rooms heated by fireplaces, a kitchen and a private chamber. He had new barges built to transport his guests from the palace to the island.[20]

'Rosamund's Bower' at Everswell (in the park at Woodstock), traditionally said to have been built by Henry II for clandestine meetings with his mistress Rosamund Clifford, was begun in 1166, when there were references to a 'well'.[21] Accounts also refer to pools of water, a 'great cloister' and a chapel, kitchen and wine cellar. Later kings made other alterations and what remained as late as the seventeenth century was recorded in an annotated sketch by John Aubrey.[22] A rectangular enclosure ('100 paces by 80 paces'), entered through a by then ruined gatehouse, contained what looks like a smaller enclosure with 'three baths in trayne', or three square pools of water linked by conduits supplied by a spring that still exists in the park at Blenheim. In Aubrey's time, the first pool retained its stone walls and there were traces of a wall seat and niches.

In spite of the limited evidence, it is clear that medieval gardens survived well into and beyond the sixteenth century. Furthermore, medieval gardens already contained many of the most important features associated with Tudor and early Stuart gardens: galleries, banqueting houses, and complex earthworks, including water gardens. Certainly the Tudors knew far more about medieval gardens than we do today.

TUDOR AND EARLY STUART GARDENS

Our knowledge of sixteenth- and early seventeenth-century gardens is also fragmentary, although we do have more written accounts and important visual

[16] Chandler (ed.), *John Leland's Itinerary*, 475.

[17] Howard Colvin, 'Royal Gardens in Medieval England', in Elisabeth B. MacDougall (ed.) *Medieval Gardens* (Washington DC: Meriden-Stinehour Press, 1986), 7–22. Howard Colvin (ed.), *The History of the King's Works* (London: H.M.S.O); Vol. I: *The Middle Ages, Part 1* (1963). Vol. II: *The Middle Ages, Part 2* (1963). Vol. III: *1485–1660, Part 1* (1975). Vol. IV: *1485–1660, Part 2* (1982).

[18] Colvin, 'Royal Gardens', 18 and n. 47.

[19] Colvin, 'Royal Gardens', 14–15.

[20] Colvin (ed.), *King's Works* II, 998.

[21] Colvin, 'Royal Gardens', 18.

[22] Bodleian Library MS Wood 276b, fol. 43v.

evidence, including drawings and estate maps. In addition, there are some
surviving garden features, including fountains, statuary, garden buildings and
earthworks. By putting this evidence in chronological order, it should be
possible to determine how gardens evolved and what elements were a con-
tinuation of indigenous, medieval forms and at what point continental ideas
intervened and dominated. Most important for this essay, is to try to determine whether archaic medieval features were re-introduced into gardens, as
they were in the other arts.

The relationship between the house and garden

The most informative visual sources that we have for gardens between the
1550s (Wyngaerde) and the 1640s (de Caus' Wilton) are estate maps.[23] These
maps suggest a growing emphasis on symmetry and alignment with the house,
both essential to the order and harmony of Renaissance gardens. In 1618,
William Lawson published *A New Orchard and Garden* in which he included a
pictorial plan of an ideal 'orchard' or garden (Fig. 5). At the top (to the
south) was the turreted house and, below it, a tripartite garden, flanked by
long, tree-lined walks. A river (or moat) ran across the top and bottom of the
garden with mounts in each of the four corners, each surmounted by a
building, shown with windows, finials and banners. The garden itself was
terraced with stairs providing access to each of the three levels. A central path
(on the axis of the house) divided the garden into six compartments, including (in the middle) an orchard planted in quincunxes and a knot garden. At
the lowest end were the kitchen gardens. The two compartments nearest the
house were shown with a large tree (perhaps a fine specimen tree) and figures
of a horse and swordsman, possibly suggesting either topiary or sculpted
ornament. At the centre of the garden was a conduit or fountain. Lawson's
book demonstrates that, by the second decade of the seventeenth century, the
principals of Renaissance design were being promoted to a wide audience.

Archaeological Evidence

There was a strong medieval tradition of moated houses and gardens and
many earthwork remains survive to this day.[24] In the sixteenth century, a
number of important builders incorporated medieval moats into their new
gardens. When Lord Burghley built his most important house at Theobalds
(Hertfordshire) in the 1570s, he used the old moat as a channel that ran

[23] Henderson, *Tudor House and Garden*, 5–7.
[24] Henderson, *Tudor House and Garden*, 2–3. See Christopher Taylor, *Parks and Gardens of Britain: a Landscape History from the Air* (Edinburgh: Edinburgh University Press, 1983) and Paul Everson and Tom Williamson (eds.), *The Archaeology of the Landscape: Studies Presented to Christopher Taylor* (Manchester and New York: Manchester University Press, 1998).

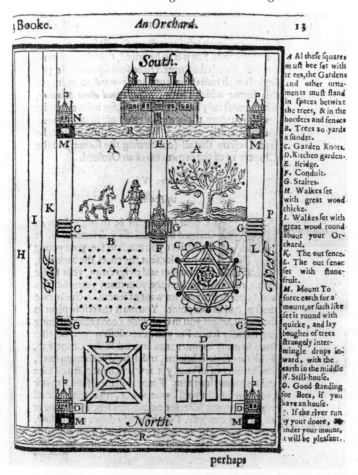

Fig. 5   William Lawson, an ideal garden from *A New Orchard and Garden*, 1618 (© The British Library Board, 966.b.28)

around his garden. The German traveller Paul Hentzner wrote, 'one goes into the garden, encompassed with a ditch full of water, large enough for one to have the pleasure of going in a boat, and rowing between the shrubs'.[25] The finest, surviving moated garden is at Lyveden New Bield (Northamptonshire), which Sir Thomas Tresham began at the end of the sixteenth century. He, too, extended an earlier moat into the much larger 'moated orchard' that he created there, which had pairs of mounts at each end (Fig. 6).[26] Like the mount at Wressle, two of these were 'snail mounts', with paths that spiralled

[25]   Paul Hentzner, *A Journey into England in the Year 1598*, Horace Walpole (ed.), (Strawberry Hill, 1757), 54.
[26]   On moated houses and water gardens, see Henderson, *Tudor House and Garden*, 128–37.

Fig. 6   Lyveden New Bield: one of the snail mounts and the garden lodge (photo: author)

upward toward the summit. The practice of excavating ponds and water gardens, often associated with the building of mounts and terraces, continued at the highest levels of society, with Viscount Howard of Bindon at Bindon Abbey (Dorset), Robert Cecil, first Earl of Salisbury at Hatfield (Hertfordshire), and Francis Bacon at Gorhambury (Hertfordshire), all creating (or intending to create) elaborate water gardens, often at a distance from the house (like the Pleasance at Kenilworth and Rosamund's Bower at Everswell). There were parallels in Dutch gardens, where ornamental canals were also helpful in draining the low, flat land, and in France, where houses and pleasure gardens were also often enclosed in moats. In Italy, the use of water in such large expanses was rarely possible.

Garden buildings

Pleasant retreats were found in most gardens, initially in the form of an arbour, but gradually built in more permanent materials. We have already noted the substantial buildings in the garden at Everswell and the marble cloister erected in the thirteenth century by Henry III at Guildford. Throughout the sixteenth century, 'cloisters' were added to many houses and gardens, presumably the equivalent of the classical loggias that were so important in continental gardens.[27] The continued use of the term 'cloister' throughout

---

[27] See Paula Henderson, 'The Loggia in Tudor and Early Stuart England: The Adaptation and Function of Classical Form', in Lucy Gent (ed.), *Albion's Classicism*, Studies in British Art 2 (New Haven and London: Yale University Press for The Paul Mellon Centre for Studies in British Art, 1995), 109–45.

the Tudor and early Stuart periods suggests that the associations were as medieval, as they were classical.

Leland's reference to the pretty 'banqueting house' that Henry VIII moved from the Pleasaunce at Kenilworth to the castle precinct may be one of the earliest uses of a term that would become almost generic for all Tudor and early Stuart garden buildings and also for the little turrets on rooftops of houses that served the same purpose.[28] In Henry VIII's garden at Hampton Court, there were narrow towers (or belvederes) built into the perimeter walls on the east side of the privy garden, more complex buildings with elaborately glazed upper rooms and stair turrets to the roofs and, most impressive of all, a three-storey 'great round arbour' on the mount, begun in 1533 (all visible in Wyngaerde's view).[29]

The joy in experimentation with these little buildings is evident in the wide variety of plans used over the century: octagonal, hexagonal, squares with projecting bows (Montacute), and lozenges (Hardwick). Classical ornament, initially added randomly to these little buildings, gradually gave way to buildings that sounded (at least in descriptions) more temple-like: at Theobalds, a very Plinian semi-circular banqueting house was adorned with statues of the emperors.[30] Unfortunately we have very little visual evidence for these more classical garden buildings and what survives remains very much in the tradition of medieval polygonal turrets.

Fountains

Illustrations of medieval gardens, from the most splendid manuscript illuminations of royal gardens down to simple woodcuts of peasants' gardens, show fountains in various sizes and shapes – some, great architectural tabernacles, others rustic basins. Medieval royal accounts include references to numerous fountains, some of which survived into the early sixteenth century and even longer.[31]

A fountain, made for Edward I, flowed 'day and night with red and white wine and the spiced drink known as pimento'.[32] The practice of substituting wine for water was continued in the Tudor period: a fountain inside the gatehouse at Theobalds, for example, was cleverly formed to look like grapes and ran with both red and white wine.[33] To create such marvels, one simply had to substitute wine for water in the cistern that fed the fountain. In the famous painting of the 'Field of the Cloth of Gold' (*c.* 1545, Royal Collection)

[28] Henderson, *Tudor House and Garden*, 155–64.
[29] Henderson, *Tudor House and Garden*, 76–7, 155–7.
[30] Henderson, *Tudor House and Garden*, 161–3.
[31] See references in Colvin (ed.), *King's Works*, Colvin (ed.), Vols. I and II (with an index).
[32] Colvin (ed.), *King's Works* I, 507. 'Pimento' or 'Piment' was a spiced, peppered drink, popular in medieval times.
[33] Henderson, *Tudor House and Garden*, 69–70.

there are two fountains shown: an hexagonal fountain decorated with gro-
tesques, with a figure of a blind Cupid at the summit; and a larger fountain
surmounted by a figure of Bacchus, quaffing red wine from a shell that
overflowed into the first basin, then out through lions' masks into the next
and so on, until it could be tapped by those nearby, who are shown in various
states of drunkenness around its base.[34] In the palace yard at Westminster was
another fountain that flowed with wine for the poor, but only 'when the Kings
of England are crowned'.[35] The fountain, shown in Hollar's seventeenth-
century etched view of Westminster, was a large architectural structure with
columns, an ogee roof, enclosing tiered basins. A small door in the lower wall
of the enclosure presumably allowed access. In Hollar's view, the fountain
dwarfs the figures around it and dominates the yard.

    This type of fountain – and the many examples like it – was meant to
impress by its size and prominent position in an open court or yard where, like
medieval conduits, it could also be used by the community.[36] The only surviving example is the fountain in the great court at Trinity College, Cambridge,
commissioned in 1601–02 by Thomas Neville, Master of the college, and fed
by a fourteenth-century conduit.[37] Inside the architectural surround are two
shell basins supported on a central shaft with four figures of 'antikeboyes'
(naked cherubs), through which the water flowed: first into the upper basin
and out through spouts in the mouths of the lion's heads, then into the lower
basin and out through more masks, and finally into the lead cistern at the
bottom, where the external taps supplied water to the community. Typical of
contemporary collegiate architecture itself, the fountain is a combination of
medieval forms and classical ornamentation.

    The imposing architectural fountain was a perfect vehicle for royal display.
Mary I built an impressive fountain in the outer ward at Windsor, raised on
steps with a lead cistern. Eight pillars (or columns) supported an ornamental
frieze, architrave and a lead canopy around which were coloured and gilded
heraldic animals, each holding up a cartouche with one of the royal badges. At
the top were a lion and an eagle (each almost six feet in height) holding
a 'great vane' with the English royal arms and those of Phillip II, Mary's

[34] Contemporary descriptions survive, as well, quoted in Charles Whibley (ed.), *The Lives of the Kings: The
Triumphant Reign of Henry VIII, by Edward Hall*, (London and Edinburgh: T. C. and E. C. Jack, 1904), 2 vols., Vol.I,
189–93.
[35] The etching of New Palace Yard by Hollar is reproduced in Colvin (ed.), *King's Works* I (Middle Ages), Pl.
36B.
[36] There were continental examples as well, including illustrations in the *Hypnerotomachia Poliphili* (Venice,
1499) and a domed fountain by Vredeman de Vries (see Elisabeth B. MacDougall (ed.), *Fons Sapientiae:
Renaissance Garden Fountains*, (Washington, DC: Dumbarton Oaks Colloquium on the History of Landscape
Architecture, No. 36, 1978), 72.
[37] Royal Commission on Historic Monuments (England), *An Inventory of the Historical Monuments of the City of
Cambridge* Part II (London: HMSO, 1959), 232–3. Robert Willis, *The Architectural History of the University of
Cambridge and of the Colleges of Cambridge and Eton* (Cambridge: Cambridge University Press, 1886), II, 627.

Fig. 7   Detail of John Norden's survey of Windsor Castle and park (© The British Library Board, Harl. MS 3749, fol. 3v)

husband.[38] The fountain rose more than thirty feet and is shown in John Norden's view of Windsor in 1607 (Fig. 7). It was finally dismantled in 1629.

In 1584, Elizabeth commissioned a similar fountain for Hampton Court, recorded in a drawing attributed to Cornelius Cure (Hatfield House) (Fig. 8).[39] The fountain was hexagonal, raised on three broad steps and a plinth and of two storeys: large Tuscan columns in the first level and flat pilasters in the second. At the summit a glittering figure of Justice with her sword and scales and standing on an open coronet. Within this architectural framework was the fountain itself: a gadrooned bowl raised on a central pillar with a figure of an 'antikeboy', again from which the water flowed into the bowl and basin. Foreign visitors noted that bystanders were sometimes caught unaware by water spurting from the marble columns, an early reference to *giochi d'acqua*.[40] The coloured stone used for Elizabeth's fountain, quarried in Kent, was in keeping with fashionable new trends for chimneypieces and monuments. The white marble used in the fountain had originally been intended for Henry VIII's tomb. Funerary monuments were the most impres-

---

[38] W. H. St John Hope's description, based on the accounts and Norden's view, is quoted in Colvin (ed.), *King's Works* III, 318.

[39] Described by John Norden in 1593 as '. . . a very bewtifull fountaine . . . erected . . . in the second court which graceth the pallace, and serveth to great and necessarie use, the fountaine was finished in Anno 1590, not without great charge'. John Norden, *Speculum Britanniae*, (London, 1593), 25–6. The fountain cost £1000. Colvin (ed.), *King's Works* IV, 143–4.

[40] G. W. Groos (trans.), *The Diary of Baron Waldstein: a traveller in Elizabethan England* (London: Thames and Hudson, 1981), 246–7.

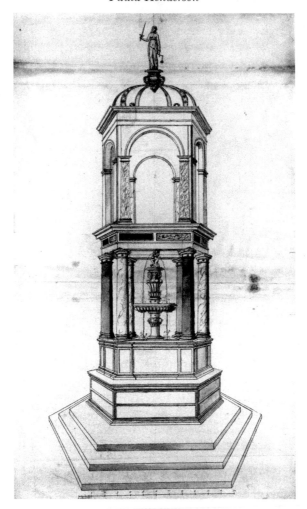

Fig. 8   Cornelius Cure (attrib.), drawing of a fountain for Hampton Court, 1584 (© The Marquess of Salisbury, Hatfield)

sive sculptural projects of the period and Cornelius Cure, Master Mason to both Elizabeth and later James, was among the most important of the South-wark School of carvers.

The link between funerary monuments and fountains is evident, too, in another form of fountain – the table fountain.[41] One of the earliest known examples was that of John Harington at Kelston (or Kilweston, Somerset),

---

[41] A contemporary tomb in a similar form is Lady Frances Bourchier at Chenies (Buckinghamshire). I am grateful to Adam White for information on table tombs.

Fig. 9 S. H. Grimm's drawing of the table fountain at Kilweston Hall, dated 1567 (© The British Library Board, Add. 15546, fol. 142)

whose wife Etheldreda was Henry VIII's illegitimate daughter. A drawing of Harington's fountain was made by Grimm in the eighteenth century (Fig. 9). Rising at the centre was an obelisk, surmounted by a rabbit (hare) with a ring on a barrel (tun), a rebus for Harington's own name. Water flowed from the barrel (on which the date 1567 was inscribed) into the basin, which then overflowed into the tank in the top of the table, ornamented with Tudor roses and portcullises, to celebrate Harington's family association with the monarchy. The water must have been fed and drained through the Tuscan columns that served as the table legs.

Similar table fountains are shown in the Lumley Inventory, made for John Lord Lumley in 1590 (Fig. 10).[42] Lumley had created one of the most cel-

---

[42] The Lumley Inventory, or Red Velvet Book, recorded the possessions of John, Lord Lumley, in 1590. It was originally published as 'The Lumley Inventories (1590)', Lionel Cust and Mary Hervey (eds.), *The Walpole Society* VI (1917–18), 15–50. The inventory has recently been published in full, see Mark Evans (ed.), *Art Collecting and Lineage in the Elizabethan Age: The Lumley Inventory and Pedigree* (London: The Roxburghe Club, 2010). The property of the Earl of Scarborough, it is currently on loan to the Victoria and Albert Museum.

Fig. 10   Table fountain from the Lumley Inventory, 1590 (© The Earl of Scarborough)

ebrated gardens of the late Elizabethan period at Nonsuch (a royal hunting
lodge that he leased from the crown).[43] The first of two table fountains
originally stood in the court at Lumley Castle (County Durham) and was
described as being '17 foote high with two bolls of white marble, standing
upon four great pillers of white marble'.[44] At the top of the fountain was the

[43] The most complete account on the garden at Nonsuch is in Martin Biddle, 'The Gardens of Nonsuch:
Sources and Dating', *Garden History* 27, No. 1 (Summer, 1999), 145–83.
[44] 'Lumley Inventory', f. 4, illustrated in Henderson, *Tudor House and Garden*, 189.

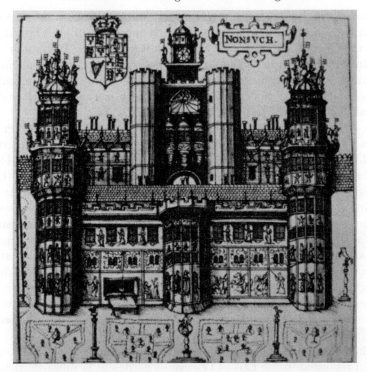

Fig. 11   View of the south front of Nonsuch Palace, attributed to Joducus Hondius, from Speed's map of Surrey, 1610 (© The British Library Board, C.7.c.5 [44])

Lumley popinjay on an orb supported by a small naked man (an Atlas or Atlante). Water poured from the orb into the first basin, then into the middle basin and, finally, into the top of the table itself, on which perched more popinjays, also spewing water.[45] The second table fountain was described by Paul Hentzner, who wrote of 'many columns and pyramids of marble, two fountains that spout water one round the other a pyramid, upon which are perched small birds that stream water out of their bills'.[46] The illustration in the inventory shows a dark table of black and red marble, supported on four columnar legs with a central column, the latter probably holding the pipes providing water to the fountain above. At the top is an obelisk with a small gilded ball finial flanked by three gilded popinjays who squirt the water into a white and black gadrooned bowl. This must be the same fountain shown

[45] Some of the columnar legs and bases, as well as one of the bowls of the fountain, survive in the gardens at Lumley Castle (County Durham).

[46] 'Lumley Inventory', f. 31; Hentzner, *A Journey into England*, 58–9.

projecting from the south front of Nonsuch in the view, possibly executed by
Joducus Hondius between 1584–93, that first appeared on John Speed's map
of Surrey, dated 1610 (Fig. 11).[47] A comparison between Harington's table
fountain and those of Lord Lumley show how an indigenous form could be
made more classical by the addition of Renaissance figures and especially by a
more refined use of architectural ornament. There has been a notable shift in
emphasis from heraldic to more classical motifs.

Even closer to contemporary continental classicism were two other fountains in the inventory in which heraldry played an even more limited role.
Instead, the fountains are dominated by classical figures: one, a full-length
nude female with a crescent moon in her hair pressing water from her breasts
into a large gadrooned bowl;[48] and, the second, another bare-breasted woman
emerging from a tapering base, divided into registers of lions' masks spewing
water into a quatrefoil basin.[49] Both fountains alluded to the chaste and
beautiful Diana (and, by implication, to Elizabeth I). Much has been made of
the classical nature of these fountains and it had been assumed that Lord
Lumley travelled to Italy. Recent research, however, has shown that he did not,
although his father-in-law, Henry Fitzalan, twelfth Earl of Arundel, did.[50]
Whether or not these fountains were designed or executed by a continental
artist, they were part of a garden that was notably classical in its ornament and
iconography.[51]

Similar in spirit to the figural fountains in the Lumley inventory was the
fountain recorded in the Earl of Leicester's garden at Kenilworth, described
in the contemporary letter by Robert Laneham.[52] Figures of Atlantes, supporting a globe, rose above an octagonal marble basin decorated with reliefs
depicting marine gods and goddesses. A recent reconstruction of this fountain
by English Heritage, based mostly on Laneham's letter, seems much too finely
modelled, particularly when we look at the one remaining fountain figure

[47] The most complete account is in Martin Biddle, 'The Gardens of Nonsuch: Sources and Dating', *Garden History* 27, no. 1 (Summer, 1999), 145–83.

[48] 'Lumley Inventory', f. 30, illustrated in *Henderson, Tudor House and Garden*, 190. Watson described the fountain as 'a shining column which carries a high-standing statue of a snow-white nymph, perhaps Venus, from whose tender breasts flow jets of water into the ivory-coloured marble, and from there the water falls down through narrow pipes into marble basins'; quoted in Biddle, 'Gardens of Nonsuch', 174.

[49] 'Lumley Inventory', f. 35.

[50] See Kathryn Barron, 'The Collecting and Patronage of John, Lord Lumley (*c.* 1535–1609)', in Edward Chaney(ed.), *The Evolution of English Collecting: The Reception of Italian Art in the Tudor and Stuart Periods* (New Haven and London: Yale University Press, 2003), 125–58.

[51] Another fountain, not recorded in the inventory possibly because it could not be transported, was referred to as an 'icy spring' or 'rocke welle', possibly a grotto, and included figures of Diana and Actaeon, bathed by 'pipes hidden in the rock'; cited in Groos (trans.), *Diary of Baron Waldstein*, 160. Platter described the fountain as 'a rock out of which natural water springs into a basin, and on this was portrayed with great art and life-like execution the story of how the three goddesses took their bath naked and sprayed Actaeon with water . . .'. Thomas Platter and Horatio Busino, *The Journals of Two Travellers in Elizabethan and early Stuart England* (London: Caliban, 1995), 62.

[52] On the bibliography and controversy surrounding 'Laneham's Letter', see Henderson, *Tudor House and Garden*, 249, n. 75.

Fig. 12   Fountain figure of the wild man, originally at Hawstead Hall, Suffolk, *c.* 1578 (photo: author)

from the period – the large (eight feet tall) of the Wild Man from Hawstead, Sussex (Fig. 12). The fountain was erected for a visit of the queen in 1578 (the date appeared on the original pedestal of the fountain) to Sir William Drury, whose crest and supporters appeared in the frieze above the fountain. The Hawstead fountain was placed at the entrance to the house/garden to welcome the queen, something that has been considered somewhat shocking because water flowed from the figure's 'urinary passage' (as it was described in a nineteenth century account) of the large (eight-foot) figure.[53] In fact, the wild man was a well-known medieval character, depicted in many art forms

---

[53] John Cullum, *The History and Antiquities of Hawsted and Hardwick* (London: J. Nichols, Son & Bentley, 1813), 156 and plate facing.

well into the late sixteenth century. In entertainments for the queen he was the embodiment of the darker side of human nature.[54] It would be through contact with the queen herself that the wild man could become civilized and enlightened, a reminder of her power and purity. The Hawstead figure – covered with hair and holding his club – represented that savage innocence that the queen would encounter on her arrival at Drury's house. Just why he was turned into a fountain is not clear, although he probably relates to *putto pissatore* (the figures of 'antikeboyes' already seen in fountains) and certainly to a later drawing of a fountain with urinating wildmen by John Smythson.[55] It must be assumed that the queen shared Drury's somewhat bawdy humour.

Evidence of fountains from the early Stuart period suggests more conventional classical figures. At Hatfield, the lower terrace of the garden was dominated by a marble basin supporting a figure of Neptune.[56] At Hadham Hall (Hertfordshire), each of the four compartments of the garden contained a fountain with lobed basins and water spurting from urn-like centrepieces, similar to fountains shown in drawings by Vredeman de Vries.[57] Figures from the fountains at Wilton survive, including Diana, Venus and Cleopatra, yet even these, made by the most admired sculptor of the period, Nicholas Stone, remain quite crude in execution.

Free-standing ornament

Unlike fountains, free-standing sculpture has not been associated with medieval gardens. The earliest known examples are the heraldic posts that filled the gardens at Hampton Court, emphasizing again the importance of heraldry in early gardens. As late as 1584 Leopold von Wedel noted 'thirty-four high columns, carved with various fine paintings: also different animals carved in wood, with their horns gilt . . . [all] set on top of columns, together with flags bearing the Queen's arms' at Whitehall.[58] This clutter of heraldry in early gardens gave way to something more imposing at Nonsuch, where Arundel and Lumley displayed their supporters (the prancing horse for Arundel and the popinjay for Lumley) on soaring columns and obelisks.[59] 'Pyramids', as obelisks were referred to in the period, became increasingly popular, both in gardens and as ornament on the house itself.

Other information about figural sculpture in gardens (that is, figures not associated with fountains) comes from documentary references to busts and

---

[54] On the wild man, see Bernheimer, *Wild Men in the Middle Ages* (Cambridge, Mass: Harvard University Press, 1952). Timothy Husband (assisted by Gloria Gilmore-House), *The Wild Man: Medieval Myth and Symbolism* (New York: Metropolitan Museum of Art exhibition catalogue, 1980). For a more complete discussion of this fountain, see Henderson, *Tudor House and Garden*, 204–5.

[55] Henderson, *Tudor House and Garden*, 191–3, Figs. 222, 224.

[56] Hatfield Cecil Papers, Box G/13 and Bills 69.

[57] Henderson, *Tudor House and Garden*, 191.

[58] Leopold von Wedel, *Transactions of the Royal Historical Society* N. S. IX (1895), 234.

[59] Henderson, *Tudor House and Garden*, 92, Fig. 114.

statues of Roman emperors: in the late sixteenth century, the Earl of Worcester built fine niches ornamented with shell work in the walk around the moat at Raglan Castle to hold statues of emperors and Lord Burghley displayed 'the twelve Roman emperors in white marble' on his summer-house at Theobalds.[60] Although the latter may have been imported from Italy, Burghley also displayed local archaeological finds. Camden referred to him as the 'Nestor of Britain', writing that he placed inscriptions from the Roman ruins at Silchester in his London garden.[61] Less explicable was the 'obelisk of alabaster surmounted by a figure of Christ...', noted by Baron Waldstein at Theobalds in 1600.[62] Religious figures were rare in any European garden and would seem even more incongruous in a post-Reformation English garden.[63] One possible explanation might be that the figure was 'Christ the gardener', a quasi-genre figure, similar to the rustic figures (usually of wood) noted in other gardens.[64]

By the time of Charles I, grand gardens included fine collections of antique statuary: Charles displayed his collection at St James's in a gallery designed by Inigo Jones; the Earl of Arundel at Arundel House; and the Duke of Buckingham at York House and in the gardens of his suburban house in Chelsea.[65] While some of the finest pieces survive – Giambologna's superb 'Samson and the Philistine', a gift that Charles passed on to Buckingham, now at the Victoria and Albert Museum, London – many have not. Exceptions include some of Nicholas Stone's sculptures for Wilton (the Bacchus and Flora from the Wilderness) and a Hercules for Oxnead Hall, Norfolk.[66] Again, these show how sharp the dividing line was between the quality of foreign imports and what was being produced locally.

NEO-MEDIEVALISM

The few descriptions we have of late Tudor gardens, like Theobalds and Nonsuch, suggest that strong classical themes were presented through architectural and sculptural decoration by the third quarter of the sixteenth century. At Kenilworth Castle, while the Earl of Leicester's garden had a

---

[60] Noted by many visitors to Theobalds, the quote is from Paul Hentzner, *A Journey into England*, 54–5. On Raglan Castle, see Elisabeth Whittle, 'The Tudor Gardens of St Donat's Castle, Glamorgan, South Wales', *Garden History*, 27:1 (Summer, 1999), 109–44. None of Burghley's or Worcester's sculptures survive.

[61] William Camden, *Britannia*, a facsimile of the 1695 edition published by E. Gibson (Newton Abbot: David and Charles, 1971), 296. See also Leslie W. Hepple, ' "The Museum Garden" Displaying Classical Antiquities in Elizabethan and Jacobean England', *Garden History* 29:2 (Winter, 2001), 109–20.

[62] Groos (trans.), *Diary of Baron Waldstein*, 83.

[63] Religious figures were rare even in Italian gardens; see Claudia Lazzaro, *The Italian Renaissance Garden: from the Conventions of Planting, Design, and Ornament to the Grand Gardens of Sixteenth-Century Central Italy* (New Haven and London: Yale University Press, 1990), 131.

[64] Henderson, *Tudor House and Garden*, 197.

[65] Henderson, *Tudor House and Garden*, 198–9. Many of the famous 'Arundel marbles' are at the Ashmolean Museum, Oxford.

[66] Both are illustrated in Henderson, *Tudor House and Garden*, Figs. 229, 234.

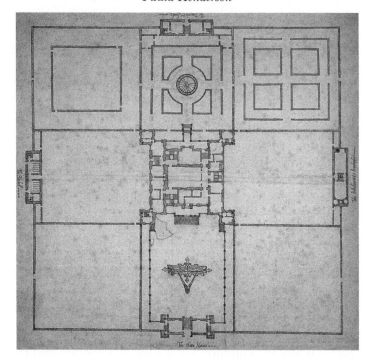

Fig. 13   Robert Smythson's plan of Wollaton Hall, *c.* 1580 (© RIBA Library Drawings and Archives Collection)

classical fountain and obelisks, the garden was full of heraldic references and
was enclosed within a space evoking the medieval *hortus conclusus*, apposite to
its position adjacent to the ancient castle. There were other gardens, like Sir
Thomas Tresham's ambitious 'moated orchard' at Lyveden with its enormous
mounts and deep canals, which related back to medieval water gardens.
Tresham's exquisite 'garden lodge', built in the form of a Greek cross and
ornamented with a Doric frieze, religious symbols and inscriptions and heraldic shields, was never completed. Whether Tresham would have added sculpture to his garden is not known, but it is difficult to imagine Ovidian or
mythological figures in a landscape created by so vehement a Roman Catholic.

But what about the garden at Wollaton, that paradigm of eclecticism? The
remarkable plan made by Robert Smythson of the house and its setting is
highly innovative, like the plan of the house itself (Fig. 13). Elsewhere I have
suggested that it was inspired by continental plans, particularly those published by Jacques Androuet du Cerceau.[67] Mark Girouard, however, has compared it to hypothetical plans and descriptions of the Temple of Solomon, as

---

[67] Henderson, *Tudor House and Garden*, 19–25.

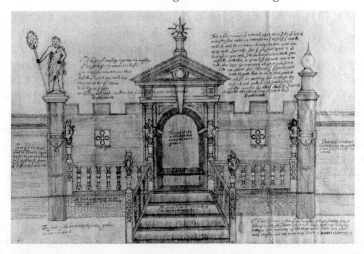

Fig. 14   Robert Lemyinge's design for a banqueting house or seat at Blickling Hall, Norfolk (Lothian Collection [National Trust] © NTPL/Angelo Hornak)

reconstructed by Anton Koberger in the late fifteenth century (and others).[68] If this is the case, what appears to be an attempt to classicize the landscape was, instead (or perhaps also), a recondite symbolic 'device' in keeping with the medieval aspects of the house itself. Unfortunately we have little information about the garden in Willoughby's lifetime.[69]

Two important early Stuart gardens do provide more concrete evidence of the introduction of archaic medieval elements into gardens. The first is a very detailed drawing by Robert Lyminge, the carpenter/architect of Blickling Hall (Norfolk), begun for Sir Henry Hobart in 1616. The drawing, inscribed 'the front of the banketting house to the garden', is not a proper enclosed building, but an elaborate garden seat set into the perimeter walls of the garden (Fig. 14).[70] The drawing is a fascinating and all too rare glimpse into the relationship between architect and patron, for Lyminge has annotated the drawing, giving advice and alternatives to the patron.

The recessed seat at the centre is set into an impressive classical aedicule beneath a triangular pediment surmounted by a 'fire ball' on a plinth. Heraldic beasts (not dissimilar to those in early Tudor gardens) stand on the newel posts of the steps up to the seat and at the ends of the balustraded

[68]   Originally in 'Solomon in Nottingham? Wollaton Hall', *Country Life*, Vol. 185 (3 October, 1991), 64–7, and more recently in *Elizabethan Architecture* (New Haven and London: Yale University Press, 2009), 242–5.

[69]   See Pete Smith, 'The Sundial Garden and House-Plan Mount: Two Gardens at Wollaton Hall, Nottinghamshire, by Robert (*c*. 1535–1614) and John (–1634) Smythson', *Garden History*, Vol. 31, No. 1 (Spring, 2003), 1–28.

[70]   The drawing is discussed in Caroline Stanley-Millson and John Newman, 'Blickling Hall: the Building of a Jacobean Mansion', *Architectural History* 29 (1986), 1–42, Figs. 5 and 6, including a full transcription of the inscription.

platform. Tall piers at either end support different figures: a ball finial on one; a large Hercules on the other. In the annotations, Lyminge explains that the ball finial can be used until figures (he recommends they 'bee of stone & as bigg as ye lyfe or els thay will mak no shew') are completed. Although showing a figure of Hercules, he leaves the final choice of figures to the patron. As classical as these elements are, the whole seat is set into crenellated walls punctured with quatrefoil loopholes. Similar loopholes were placed on the bridge at the entrance to the house, introducing a subtle defensive motif that seems to reappear throughout the house and garden.

The most dramatic evidence comes from the garden at Bolsover Castle (Derbyshire), itself a triumph of fantastic medievalism. Begun in 1612 as a private retreat for Bess of Hardwick's son Charles and completed by her grandson, William (later Duke of Newcastle), Bolsover was built on the site of an ancient castle, perched dramatically above the landscape.[71] Like Wollaton, the interiors are a skilful combination of classical and medieval ornament: Serlian chimneypieces stand beneath rib-vaulted ceilings and figures of Hercules hobnob with figures of wisdom and authority from the Old and New Testaments. To the south of the castle itself is the garden, an elongated circle, surrounded by high, battlemented walls with elevated walks leading from the main staircase (Fig. 15). Unlike its contemporary – Wilton House – the garden is not axially aligned with the house and even the fountain, which is the focal point of the garden, is off-centre. Although the figure of the nude woman that is the centrepiece of the fountain has traditionally been identified as Venus, I have argued elsewhere that she represents the Biblical heroine Bathsheba, clutching her sheet and emerging from the bath (the basin of the fountain was used for bathing). She averts her eyes from the window of William Cavendish's bedroom (the 'Elysium', painted with erotic scenes of classical gods and goddesses), the only room with a view of the garden (Fig. 16). David first saw Bathsheba from the roof of his palace and the effect of looking down on the statue of the young woman, modestly pulling her drape up to cover her naked body, must have aroused similar feelings in those who gazed down on her from Elysium or from the roof. Although in many ways the fountain appears to be classical, drawings by John Smythson suggest that he also considered Gothic forms, some of which were actually integrated into the final fountain. (Fig. 17). Bolsover is the culmination of the synthesis of romantic medievalism and sophisticated classism, leaving little doubt that conservative tendencies in the other arts were also reflected in gardens. That we have so little concrete evidence is simply typical of the problems of studying early English gardens.

Although the more serious classicism of Wilton would triumph over the fantastic medievalism of Bolsover, its foothold was not secure. Just over a

---

[71] The main family seat was at Welbeck Abbey, Nottinghamshire.

Fig. 15   View over the garden at Bolsover Castle, Derbyshire (photo: author)

century later, the Gothic style would be reintroduced into English gardens, sometimes in the form of ephemeral 'gothick' follies, but also as a highly charged political statement. The inscription carved over the door of the triangular, Gothic Temple of Liberty at Stowe (built by James Gibbs in the 1740s) reads, 'I thank the Gods that I am not Roman'.[72] For Lord Cobham, only the English Gothic style could evoke the associations of freedom and

---

[72] The inscription is written in French, *Je rends graces aux Dieux de nestre pas Romain*, from Corneille. See John Martin Robinson, *Temples of Delight: Stowe Landscape Gardens* (London: The National Trust, 1994), 103.

Fig. 16   The fountain at Bolsover Castle (photo: author)

ancient English liberties that he held so dear. The eighteenth-century return to medieval style, like that of Tudor and early Stuart periods, was linked to a fervent sense of national pride.

Independent scholar

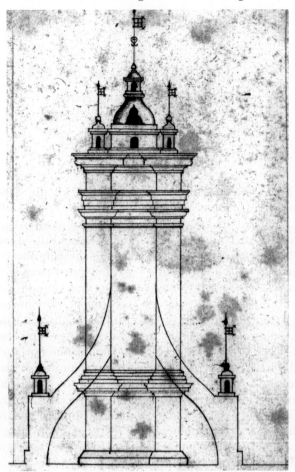

Fig. 17   John Smythson's sketch for a fountain, *c.* 1620 (© RIBA Library Drawings and Archives Collection)

3

River gods: personifying nature in sixteenth-century Italy

CLAUDIA LAZZARO

In January 1512, when a colossal ancient statue of the Tiber River was unearthed in Rome, many people gathered to see it (Fig. 1).[1] Pope Julius II immediately acquired the work for his sculpture garden in the Vatican, already famous for such antiquities as the *Laocoon* and the *Apollo Belvedere*. A year or two later, a second statue representing the Nile River (Fig. 2), also from the sanctuary of Isis, entered the Vatican Statue Court, and soon after a third river god. The *Tiber* and *Nile* led to a clear understanding of the ancient type, the identification of other statues, and ultimately the tremendous popularity in the sixteenth century of river gods in fountains, festivities and triumphal entries, political propaganda, and much more.[2] This essay examines selected early steps in this development to demonstrate how the Renaissance appropriated the ancient river god through installations, restoration, and the reinvention of the figure type. Over the course of the sixteenth century, the understanding of nature also developed in new directions, in part inspired by ancient texts. Artists explored how the human body could represent the natural world, how anthropomorphisms, rivers given human form, could function as personifications, figures who speak and act,[3] and how the human body could embody the meaning imprinted on it.[4] At the same time, patrons discovered the potential of river gods as vehicles for political messages about rule over territory. In particular, the Medici, especially Pope Leo X and later Duke Cosimo de' Medici, played important roles in some of the foundational stages of these investigations.

---

[1] Hans Henrik Brummer, *The Statue Court in the Vatican Belvedere* (Stockholm: Almqvist & Wiksell, 1970), 191–2.

[2] Ruth Rubinstein, 'The Renaissance Discovery of Antique River-God Personifications', in *Scritti di storia dell'arte in onore di Roberto Salvini* (Florence: Sansoni, 1984), 257–63; and Phyllis P. Bober and Ruth O. Rubinstein, *Renaissance Artists and Antique Sculpture* (London: Harvey Miller, 1986), 99–104.

[3] For the distinction between anthropomorphism and personification, see James J. Paxson, *The Poetics of Personification* (Cambridge: Cambridge University Press, 1994), 42.

[4] Gordon Teskey, *Allegory and Violence* (Ithaca: Cornell University Press, 1996), 19.

Locus Amoenus, First Edition. Edited by Alexander Samson. © 2012 The Authors.
Journal compilation © 2012 The Society for Renaissance Studies and Blackwell Publishing Ltd.

Fig. 1   *The Tiber*, Paris, Louvre (photo: Réunion des Musées Nationaux/ Art Resource, NY)

Fig. 2   *The Nile*, Vatican, Vatican Museums (photo: Scala/ Art Resource, NY)

ANCIENT SCULPTURE AND MODERN INSTALLATIONS

In Rome in the late fifteenth and early sixteenth centuries, families displayed their collections of ancient sculpture in the gardens and courtyards of their palaces and villas, and Pope Julius' Statue Court in the Vatican was likewise a garden with orange trees and flowering herbs.[5] Already in February 1512 the

[5] David R. Coffin, *Gardens and Gardening in Papal Rome* (Princeton: Princeton University Press, 1991), 17–27.

Fig. 3   Maarten van Heemskerck, view of the *Nile* and *Tiber* in the Vatican Belvedere Statue Court, 1532–33, drawing (photo: © Trustees of the British Museum)

pope brought there the *Tiber* (now in the Louvre), but by the time the *Nile* joined it, Julius was succeeded by the Medici Pope Leo X, who displayed the impressive pair together (Figs. 1 and 2). Observers were struck with the size of the statues – larger than life, colossal, even twice life-size, one estimated.[6] The Hellenistic type is clear in these two statues: bearded old men with scraggly hair and garlands, powerful bodies semi-reclining with the back leg raised and slightly bent and the front leg lying on the ground, the torso tilted toward the viewer and head turned away. Accounts of the statues noted the attributes, particularly the cornucopia, filled with fruits, bunches of grapes, and pine cones, to denote the abundance that the river brought to the territory through which it passed. The rivers were immediately identifiable by what they lean against – a she-wolf and Romulus and Remus for the Tiber, and for the Nile a sphinx, along with sixteen small putti, alluding to the height necessary to overflow and make the land fertile, a phenomenon that was of much scientific interest later in the century.[7]

A drawing of the statue court in 1532–33 by the Dutch artist Marten van Heemskerck hints at the commanding presence of the two great river gods in the centre of the court, raised on massive plinths (Fig. 3).[8] The intriguing

[6] Brummer, *Statue Court*, 191–204, 266–71.

[7] Bober and Rubinstein, *Renaissance Artists*, 99, 102; and Rubinstein, 'Renaissance Discovery', 259. For interest in the Nile overflowing, see Hervé Brunon, ' "Les mouvements des eaux de l'universe": Pratolino, jardin météorologique', in Hervé Brunon, Monique Mosser and Daniel Rabreau (eds.), *Les éléments et les métamorphoses de la Nature* (Bordeaux: William Blake & Co., 2004), 39, 42.

[8] Matthias Winner, 'La collocazione degli dei fluviali nel Cortile delle Statue e il restauro del Laocoonte del Montorsoli', in Matthias Winner, Bernard Andreae, and Carlo Pietrangeli (eds.), *Il Cortile delle Statue: Der Statuenhof des Belvedere im Vatikan* (Mainz: Philipp von Zabern, 1998), 119.

Fig. 4   Nicolas Beatrizet, *The Tiber*, c. 1540– c.1566, engraving (photo: © Trustees of the British Museum)

central position permitted viewing the statues from both front and back, as Heemskerck and others sketched them. The river gods faced each other, their bodies oriented in the same direction, as though in dialogue, the first of many such pairings through the century. The bases of the river gods are carved with rippling water, which Nicolas Beatrizet emphasized in prints of them. In his engraving, *The Tiber*, the back edge of the base is indicated at the right, but in the foreground Beatrizet continued the wavering lines to the edge of the sheet, suggestively transforming carved stone into a body of water (Fig. 4).[9] The engraving playfully evokes the actual installation, since the *Tiber* and *Nile* really did lie on beds of water, as the great platforms were also basins.[10] These beds were not still water, but moving, rippling, as in the engraving, from the streams emerging from these figures (or their bases) that Venetian ambassadors saw in 1523,[11] which associated the figures not just with the element of water, but with the idea of a river. The coat of arms on the monumental plinths, visible in Heemskerck's drawing, attributes to the Medici this novel linking of personification with natural element personified.

Ancient statues could also be appropriated by giving them new identities, in some cases through restoration, as in another river god discovered in Rome in the early sixteenth century, which was transformed into the *Arno*, a type that did not exist in antiquity (Fig. 5). The statue is a composite, or integration, as the practice became known. The sixteenth-century restorer completed the statue with both a modern head and a right arm from another antique sculpture, and he also carved a Medici diamond ring around the rim of the

---

[9] Michael Bury, *The Print in Italy 1550–1620* (London: British Museum, 2001), 137–8.
[10] Winner, 'Collocazione', 119.
[11] Brummer, *Statue Court*, 195 and 266, 'da questi escono due bellissime fontane'.

Fig. 5   *The Arno/Tigris*, Vatican, Vatican Museums (photo: Vanni/ Art Resource, NY)

vase and inside it the face of a lion.[12] The result is a subtle but clever conceit: the river's water emerges from the mouth of a Florentine lion. (The current designation as the *Tigris* dates from a late eighteenth-century misreading of the lion's face.) The sixteenth-century head is unmistakably Michelange-lesque in form and pathos, and a contemporary anecdote attributed to Mich-elangelo himself the idea for the unusual knotted beard.[13] In addition, Vasari credited its rustic setting in the Vatican to the Florentine sculptor. The date is uncertain, but one or the other Medici popes, Leo X or Clement VII, claimed the ancient statue as the Arno and as Florentine, with the stylistic 'signature' of Florence's most famous sculptor and with Medicean and Florentine emblems.[14]

Michelangelo's design for the installation of the restored statue in the Vatican, recorded in Heemskerck's sketch of the 1530s and more evocatively in a late eighteenth-century drawing by Anton Raphael Mengs, was another kind of integration, combining ancient and modern, art and nature (Fig. 6). The rough-hewn backdrop of the naturalistic setting Vasari described as made from *cipollaccio* in imitation of natural rocks.[15] The green and yellowish marble with black and white flecks, cut into rough, irregular shapes, must have

[12] Ruth Rubinstein, 'The Statue of the River God Tigris or Arno', in *Cortile delle Statue*, 275–85; and Brummer, *Statue Court*, 186–8.

[13] Rubinstein, 'Statue', 277, 282.

[14] Arnold Nesselrath, 'Il Cortile delle Statue: luogo e storia', in *Cortile delle Statue*, 10, dates the installation before Bramante's death in April 1514. Rubinstein, 'Statue', 277, 280–83, argues for the patronage of Clement VI, between 1532, when Michelangelo returned to Rome, and 1534, when the pope died.

[15] For the stone and Vasari's comments, see Rubinstein, 'Statue', 281 and nn. 17 and 19.

Fig. 6 Anton Raphael Mengs, *Study for the Sala dei Papiri*, Fermo, Biblioteca Civica Romolo Spezioli (photo: Biblioteca Comunale di Fermo)

appeared as moss- and vegetation-covered stones. Vasari explained that this marble was found buried among ruins, and his comment about it is equally applicable to the entire installation, that from ancient things modern works were fashioned, and these could be very beautiful. The installation not only links the anthropomorphic statue with water, but presents the river god as like a river itself lying amongst the rocks of its surroundings. The water pouring into the sarcophagus that served as a basin and cascading over it into a pool below would have added sounds of running water to evoke the sensation of a river. Later, shorn of all but the sarcophagus, the statue also lost the Renaissance affirmation of it as an image of the natural world.

In the Vatican Statue Court, the *Arno* in its rustic setting in the northwest corner complemented an ancient reclining female statue diagonally opposite, acquired by Pope Julius in 1512 and displayed in a similar natural rocky landscape (Fig. 7). Now known as *Ariadne*, in the sixteenth century the statue had two alternate identities, as Cleopatra, through a reading of her armband as a serpent and her body position as signifying death, and as a sleeping nymph, associated with a fresh water spring (the female counterpart of river gods), through her similarity with the recumbent pose of a popular Roman fountain type.[16] The juxtaposition of related yet contrasting poses of the two ancient statues would have been meaningful to contemporaries. Both are semi-reclining, but the *Arno* conveys a sense of promptness, emphasized by the modern additions, with the body supported by the arm, the torso emphatically tilted toward the viewer, and the sixteenth-century head, which appears awake

---

[16] Brummer, *Statue Court*, 154–84; and Leonard Barkan, *Unearthing the Past: Archaeology and Aesthetics in the Making of Renaissance Culture* (New Haven: Yale University Press, 1999), 233–43.

Fig. 7   *Cleopatra/Sleeping Nymph* (later *Ariadne*), Vatican, Vatican Museums (photo: Scala/ Art Resource, NY)

and alert, turned purposefully to the side. *Cleopatra*, on the other hand, seems immobile, with legs intertwined, drapery wrapped and criss-crossed, and right arm flung over her inclined head with closed eyes. The Renaissance, inspired by the ancients, understood the natural world as gendered, different parts of it having a male or female identity, which was represented in sculpture with appropriately masculine or feminine poses and gestures.[17] The setting of the *Cleopatra/Sleeping Nymph*, as we know it from Francisco de Holanda's drawing of 1538–39, refers to the story behind the popular statue type about a nymph sleeping in a cave to the murmuring sound of water (Fig. 8). The backdrop of striated rocks dripping water and fern-like vegetation evokes her woodland retreat, with again an ancient sarcophagus as a basin, giving the statue an identity unrelated to any that she had in antiquity. In his drawing, Holanda reinforced the association of the sleeping nymph with the spring that she personified, and also emphasized her femaleness, through subtle alterations to the statue. He inclined the figure toward the viewer, which enhanced the pose of abandon, and bared a second breast and more of her belly than in the ancient sculpture. Michelangelo's design for the *Arno* (Fig. 6), with its marble rocks, hard and masculine, and cascading water might be viewed similarly as reinforcing its designation as the (male) Tuscan river, whose source was in the Apennine Mountains north of Florence. The Renaissance installations, resto-

---

[17] Claudia Lazzaro, 'Gendered Nature and Its Representation in Sixteenth-Century Garden Sculpture', in Sarah McHam (ed.), *Looking at Italian Renaissance Sculpture* (Cambridge, Mass.: Cambridge University Press, 1998), 258–66.

Fig. 8   Francisco de Holanda, *The Fountain of Cleopatra/ Sleeping Nymph*, 1538–39, Antigualhas, fol. 8v, El Escorial, Library of San Lorenzo (Copyright Patrimonio Nacional)

rations, and coupling of these two figures gave them identities and associations that responded to contemporary concerns about both nature and gender.

RIVER GODS IN LEONINE IMAGERY

In the sixteenth century, river gods, inspired by the ancient statues, became obligatory in ceremonial entries and festivities and acquired new roles, as references to place, territories ruled, and alliances between states. The first such appearance occurred on the Capitoline Hill in Rome in September 1513 in the celebration organized by Pope Leo X soon after his election to commemorate the conferral of Roman citizenship on his brother Giuliano and his nephew Lorenzo de' Medici. The river gods Tiber and Arno featured both in paintings on the large temporary theatre and as characters in the spectacle, which introduced these images to a large audience at the event and in written descriptions. Both painted figures and living personifications borrowed their basic form from ancient sculpted prototypes – mostly nude and reclining, with white hair and beards to denote their age. The river gods, whether theatrical characters or images, stood for their respective geographical states through their association with symbols (Roman wolf and Florentine lion) and with personifications of the cities themselves. Together they presented the theme of the event – the unity of Rome and Florence. In the prelude to the comedy, the living river gods rise from their reclining positions to deliver brief and rambling speeches, which hint at future political uses.[18] Another event a few years later again connected the pope with the image of river gods: in 1517 Leo X transferred to the Capitol a second pair of classical statues – a different *Nile* with a *Tigris* – both of which had stood on the Quirinal through the Middle Ages.[19] These joined other ancient sculptures that Pope Sixtus IV had donated to the Roman people in the late fifteenth century.

We can imagine how the personifications might have appeared in the Capitoline festivities from their representation a couple of years later in the borders of the tapestries that Raphael designed for Leo X in 1515–16.[20] (These were destined for the lower walls of the Sistine Chapel and were displayed from late 1519.) In contrast to the grandiose scenes from the Acts of the Apostles in Raphael's tapestry designs, the horizontal borders below depict events in the life of Cardinal Giovanni de' Medici until his election as pope, in a style that imitates ancient Roman relief sculpture in fictive bronze.[21] Many of these pseudo-antique narrative scenes, with a progression of figures across a shallow space, entail the passage from one locale to another, among them Giovanni de' Medici riding from his investiture as cardinal at Fiesole toward Florence in the episode beneath *The Stoning of Stephen* (Fig. 9). At either side of the historical events are vignettes, little scenes representing various locations – Florence, Rome, Fiesole, and Mantua, designated through river gods as well as landscape features, architecture, and personifications of cities and at least one mountain. Ancient models inspired individual figures, among them the personification of Mantua in the form of the Vatican *Cleopatra/Sleeping Nymph.*[22] The vignettes indicate place, help to identify the episodes, and visually serve as a framing device, with symmetrical or comple-

[18] Fabrizio Cruciani, *Il teatro del Campidoglio e le feste romane del 1513* (Milan: Il Polifilo, 1968), LVII–LXIV, 7, 17, 26, 55, 57–9.

[19] Peter Partner, *Renaissance Rome 1500–1559: A Portrait of a Society* (Berkeley: University of California Press, 1976), 173.

[20] John Shearman, *Raphael's Cartoons in the Collection of Her Majesty the Queen and the Tapestries for the Sistine Chapel* (London: Phaidon, 1972), 3, 31, 37, 84, and Figs. 13, 17, 18, and 54. The existing tapestries are in the Vatican Museum, but the cartoons for the borders have not survived.

[21] Roger Jones and Nicholas Penny, *Raphael* (New Haven: Yale University Press, 1987), 142; Marcia B. Hall, 'Introduction to the Art History of Renaissance Rome', in Marcia B. Hall (ed.), *Rome* (Cambridge: Cambridge University Press, 2005), 142.

[22] Ilaria Romeo, 'Raffaello, l'antico e le bordure degli arazzi vaticani', *Xenia*, 19 (1990), 41–86, here 46.

Fig. 9   Pieter van Aelst after Raphael, *The Stoning of St Stephen Tapestry*, Vatican, Vatican Museums (photo: Musei Vaticani)

mentary poses of the river gods. Equally important, they bring the classical gods into proximity with Cardinal Giovanni. In his study of allegory, Gordon Teskey sees the role of the classical gods in the Renaissance as conferring legitimacy, through 'an aura of mysterious power', on the symbols of the state, most importantly, on the body of the prince.[23] The tapestry borders exemplify an early form of this, in which allegorical and narrative modes remain fairly separate.[24] Only the personified cities – female by tradition and according to linguistic gender – interact physically and emotionally with the historical scenes, as in the one beneath *The Miraculous Draught of Fishes* (Fig. 10). There the standing figure of Florence, who seems to emerge from the reclining Arno below her, extends her arm and points toward Cardinal Giovanni.

Raphael's river gods embody rivers, lying against hills and mountains, bearing overflowing urns, and sitting above the bodies of water that they personify. Likewise, the vignette representing Fiesole includes both a mountain

[23] Teskey, *Allegory*, 78–82, here 79.
[24] *Ibid*, 85.

Fig. 10 Pieter van Aelst after Raphael, *The Miraculous Draught of Fishes Tapestry*, detail of border, Vatican, Vatican Museums (photo: Musei Vaticani)

and seated astride it, the bearded male personification of Mount Falterona, at the left of the border below the *Stoning of St Stephen Tapestry* (Fig. 9). The six river gods in the surviving tapestries purposefully evoke ancient statues, reliefs, and gems, but none is an imitation. Rather, they display Raphael's inventiveness in creating variations on the theme of the reclining river god type, among them some completely nude, one grasping an urn with both hands, and the Arno seen from the back, as the Vatican *Tiber* and *Nile* could be viewed (see Fig. 10). Several represent the Arno, in diverse body types, poses, and attributes, once more inserting this river into the pantheon of river gods, and fixing the association of river deities with the body of Leo X.

NATURE AND CAPRICE IN *THE JUDGEMENT OF PARIS*

In Raphael's tapestry borders, the river gods serve as bookends of the stories, framing the narrative scenes, and as shorthand signifiers of place, independent of the historical episodes, but related and useful in identifying them. They also function as overt *all'antica* elements alluding to statues that Pope Leo X integrated into the Vatican display. In Raphael's design for *The Judgement of Paris*, engraved by Marcantonio Raimondi about 1517–20, an allegorical representation of place with explicit classical references frames a familiar mythological story (Fig. 11).[25] The classical tale concerns Paris, the seated

[25] For the engraving, see Wendy Stedman Sheard, *Antiquity in the Renaissance* (Northampton, Mass.: Smith College Museum of Art, 1978), cat. 90; and Innis H. Shoemaker and Elizabeth Broun, *The Engravings of Marcantonio Raimondi* (Lawrence, Kansas: Spencer Museum of Art, 1981), 146–7.

Fig. 11   Marcantonio Raimondi, after Raphael, *The Judgement of Paris*, c. 1517–20, engraving (photo: © Trustees of the British Museum)

nude shepherd in a Phrygian cap at the left, who is presented by Mercury, behind him, with the task of choosing the most beautiful of three goddesses, Juno with her peacock at the left, Venus with her son Cupid receiving the golden apple of victory, and Minerva at the centre of the composition, provocatively seen from behind. The large size, grandeur, and classical evocations announce the engraving's importance, but, as in the tapestry borders, the characters in the story fill no more than half the composition. The remaining space is taken up by the landscape setting with three nymphs at the left and a group of nymphs and two river gods at the right, famous from Manet's appropriation of them in his painting *Le Déjeuner sur l'herbe* of 1863. In his biography of Marcantonio, Vasari explained these figures as fantasies added 'per capriccio'.[26] About a century later, the French art theorist, Roland Fréart de Chambray, found them 'but a poetic accompaniment from the painter's genius that enriches the effect of his picture'.[27] While scholars have principally concerned themselves with the narrative and with Marcantonio's technical virtuosity, Hubert Damisch in his study of the theme of the Judgement of Paris attends to the capricious figures, the supplement or artistic premium that Raphael brought to his visual account of the myth, which contributed to the admiration of all Rome that Vasari reported.[28]

---

[26]   Giorgio Vasari, *Le vite de' più eccellenti pittori, scultori ed architettori*, ed. Gaetano Milanesi (Florence: G. C. Sansoni, 1906), 5: 411.

[27]   Both Fréart and Vasari are cited by Hubert Damisch, *The Judgment of Paris*, trans. John Goodman (Chicago: University of Chicago Press, 1996), 212–13.

[28]   Damisch, *Judgment*, 210–26; Vasari, *Vite*, 5:411.

Fréart understood the function of the nymphs and river gods as metaphorical embodiments of the landscape setting. He explained: 'for all these nymphs with their amphoras, and the two male figures holding reeds, seated and nude, paying no attention to what is happening, indicate nothing but that Mount Ida is abundantly provided with rivers and fountains.'[29] They were not entirely Raphael's invention, however, as he modelled his composition on two ancient reliefs in Rome, one in the Villa Medici, the other in the Villa Pamphili.[30] Raphael derived the number and general position of the personifications from their counterparts in each of the reliefs, and, as in his sources, he integrated them into a sequence of varied poses and *contrapposti* across the picture space. Nevertheless, he transformed both the individual figures and their compositional role. For example, the model for the seated nymph at the left in the Pamphili relief is seen from the back and turned slightly to the side, while in Raphael's design she sits at an angle and leans forward into her projecting knee, but rotates her head in the opposite direction. In contrast to the two reliefs, Raphael more emphatically differentiates the personifications from the characters in the story and gives them a greater prominence and visual interest. Damisch underlines Fréart's observation that the nymphs and river gods turn their backs to the narrative scene, ignoring it. They do, however, look back into the landscape, out to the viewer, off to the side, and at each other. Through their poses and gazes, they extend the picture space in depth and beyond the frame, a figural parallel to the naturalistic landscape around them. Because they have no story to tell, Raphael could exercise artistic license and create striking and novel figures and groups, which at the same time reveal a conception of the natural world as animate and alive.

Fréart identified the rivers as the Xanthus in the foreground at the right and behind the reeds he holds the Simois, both of which had their origins on Mount Ida. Their intersecting positions and overlapping attributes reflect the geographical reality, since the rivers join, as Fréart explained, 'after irrigating the Trojan countryside along their respective beds', which reminds us of the fateful aftermath of this episode in the Trojan War.[31] The Xanthus River is more youthful than his counterpart in the Villa Medici relief and in ancient statues. His youth, nudity, and fine physique perhaps convey the origins of the river on Mount Ida: the river is still young. Departing from the typical pose of the semi-reclining river god in ancient statues generally, Raphael instead borrows that of his own Heliodorus in the Vatican, with the front leg resting on the ground and the raised back leg supported by the foot, the two limbs alternately suggesting stasis and potential movement.[32] Unlike his biblical model, however, the river god sinks back languorously, his torso turned

---

[29] Damisch, *Judgment*, 212, 214.
[30] Both reliefs are illustrated in Bober and Rubinstein, *Renaissance Artists*, cats. 119 and 120.
[31] Damisch, *Judgment*, 213.
[32] Jones and Penny, *Raphael*, 179.

toward the viewer to display his superb anatomy. In contrast to the river god's open pose, his female counterpart, the androgynous seated nymph, is closed in on herself, elbow on raised knee, revealing only her curved back. She shifts her head, however, to gaze directly out at the viewer. The multi-directional body positions conceived in space and the suggestive and sensual poses exemplify the transformation of classical models in the sixteenth century as well as the Renaissance understanding of nature.

The inscription on *The Judgement of Paris* vaunts the power of beauty over intellect, virtue, kingdoms, and wealth.[33] This could be Paris speaking of his own choice of Venus and her promise of Helen of Troy, the most beautiful woman in the world. It is also Raphael and his amanuensis Marcantonio appealing to the judgement of the viewer and doing everything possible to move him or her with the beauty, sensuality, and nonchalance of all the figures. The aim, the inscription implies, is to arouse, not just through the figure of Venus, but with the whole, story and supplement equally. Why, then, does Minerva, goddess of wisdom, occupy the central position, more enticing than Venus with her rear view and the long curve of her nude body?

Since river gods must have been closely associated with Leo X in the second decade of the sixteenth century from the ancient statues in the Vatican, the Capitoline ceremonies of 1513, the tapestry borders of 1515–16, and the transfer of two river gods to the Capitol in 1517, perhaps this idyllic scene could also be read as a reference to Leonine Rome as another garden paradise like Mount Ida. In the *possesso* of 11 April 1513 (the ceremony in which a newly elected pope takes possession of the Lateran, the papal basilica), temporary triumphal arches ornamented with classical gods marked the route. One of them included the inscription, 'Once Venus had her time, Once Mars had his. Now Pallas [Minerva] has her time'. Alluding to his predecessors, the lascivious Alexander VI and the bellicose Julius II, the inscription suggests that Pope Leo X's reign would be guided instead by Minerva's wisdom.[34] Raphael did very well under Leo, and Rome may have seemed to him and to others a *locus amoenus* under the influence of the goddess.

RIVERS AND BODIES OVERFLOWING

A novel feature in Raphael's splendid river god is that, with no vase to overflow, water spurts instead from his own penis into the stream indicated by the reeds in his left hand (Fig. 12). (Although possibly ambiguous in reproductions, the straight lines against a light ground emerging from the penis clearly do not belong to the system of shading where leg meets lower torso.) The familiar

---

[33] SORDENT PRAE FORMA INGENIUM VIRTUS REGNA AURUM, roughly translated: Intellect, virtue, kingdoms and gold appear worthless compared with beauty.

[34] Olim habuit Cypris sua tempora, Tempora Mavors olim habuit, sua nunc tempora Pallas habet. I follow the translation of Ingrid D. Rowland, *The Culture of the High Renaissance: Ancients and Moderns in Sixteenth-Century Rome* (New York: Cambridge University Press, 1998), 212 and n. 42.

Fig. 12   Marcantonio Raimondi, after Raphael, *The Judgement of Paris*, detail, *c.* 1517–20, engraving (photo: ©
Trustees of the British Museum)

association of river gods with the fertility of the nearby land was traditionally
designated by a cornucopia filled with fruit and flowers. Raphael's image
instead evokes a rich tradition that linked urine, semen, and water in everything
from birth trays, large-scale oil paintings, and fountains with a pissing putto, to
bawdy jokes, euphemisms, word plays, and puns, as Patricia Simons has recently
demonstrated. In one well-known example, Lorenzo Lotto's *Venus and Cupid* of
the mid-1520s, Cupid urinates through a myrtle wreath onto Venus's torso,
alluding, in Simons' gloss, to 'fertilization, "watering", and ejaculatory desire'.[35]
The ubiquitous visual and verbal joking based on the interchange of liquids
made the quintessentially masculine image of a penile emission – 'making
water' or urinating available as an image of fertility, of a male river god both
'watering' and inseminating the surrounding land. The contemporary understanding of the processes of nature as analogous to human bodily and sexual
functions is what ultimately made this image of the river god legible.

While Raphael's Xanthus River reinforced the maleness of rivers as well as
the abundance of nature, other personifications indicated femaleness
through their poses. The historian of science, Katharine Park, discusses the
significance of the change in the personification of nature from a 'majestic,
clothed, and energetic' female in the literature and art of the Middle Ages
to a nude, lactating woman, or a many-breasted figure borrowed from the
ancient type of Diana of Ephesus. In contrast to the clothed medieval image of

[35] Patricia Simons, 'Manliness and the Visual Semiotics of Bodily Fluids in Early Modern Culture', *Journal of
Medieval and Early Modern Studies*, 32.2 (Spring 2009), 340–60, here 360.

Fig. 13   Giulio Romano, *The Quest for the Golden Fleece*, Mantua, Palazzo del Te, lunette in the Room of Psyche (photo: Scala/Art Resource, NY)

nature whose actions did not always conform to culturally feminine gender roles, the Renaissance Natura was defined in exclusively female terms by 'the anatomical attribute of breasts and the physiological attribute of lactation'.[36] Analogous to the water emerging from the river god's penis, milk spurts naturally and spontaneously from Natura's bare breasts. This image celebrates a nature conceived as effortlessly bountiful, indeed a 'regime of plenty', which Park sees as an expression of Europe's prosperity, fed by the natural resources of the fertile New World.[37] Both male and female images represent the over-flowing abundance of nature in allusive and suggestive terms.

Raphael's pupil Giulio Romano exceeded his teacher in devising an overt male counterpart to the lactating Natura in the Palazzo del Te in Mantua. The Room of Psyche, of about 1526–27, named after the story of Cupid and Psyche in the lunettes and vault, also celebrates love and pleasure in scenes of banquets and mythological couples. In one of the lunettes, story and frame, or artistic supplement as Damisch would have it, are inverted: a hoary river god dominates the scene, while in the right background a personified reed points toward Psyche, instructing her how to collect the golden fleece of sheep clinging to bushes (Fig. 13). Caricatured with bulging eyes and swollen belly, Giulio Romano's river god, positioned close to the picture plane, seems to tumble backward with spread legs into his rocky habitat. His flowing white hair, beard,

---

[36] Katharine Park, 'Nature in Person: Medieval and Renaissance Allegories and Emblems', in Lorraine Daston and Fernando Vidal (eds.), *The Moral Authority of Nature* (Chicago, University of Chicago Press, 2004), 50–73, especially 51 and 52. See also Lazzaro, 'Gendered Nature', 246–73.

[37] Park, 'Nature in Person', 61.

and moustache merge with the water cascading from his mouth and urn as well as from his penis. Giulio Romano's capricious fantasy is a witty, if indecorous, figure in keeping with the parody and salacious humour elsewhere in the room. At the same time this river god is an image of excess that speaks to the culture's concept of nature as abundance and spontaneous effusion, as well as its fascination with inexhaustible plenty, of commodities as well as natural resources.[38] More locally, it slyly alludes to the relevance of water to Mantua, surrounded on three sides by artificial lakes formed by the Mincio River, which made the region rich in both commerce and agriculture.[39]

WATER IN THE GARDEN AT CASTELLO

Sculpture, ancient along with modern, had long been displayed in gardens, but that in the Medici garden at Castello was unprecedented in incorporating all the personifications in Raphael's tapestry borders – mountains, rivers, and cities, distributed over space and integrated with the garden design. Duke Cosimo de' Medici's villa, a few miles northwest of Florence at the foothills of the Apennine Mountains, was celebrated in the sixteenth century for its abundant water, brought by aqueduct. The sculptor, architect, and hydraulic engineer, Niccolò Tribolo, designed the layout of the garden and its principal fountains from the spring of 1538, although several were completed only after his death in 1550.[40] In the original design, now much altered but recorded in a painting by Giusto Utens of 1599 (Fig. 14), the principal garden at the centre was subdivided into three terraces with two retaining walls. For the niches in the upper wall supporting the *bosco* or wood, which were encrusted with a surface of stalactites culled from the mountains beyond, Tribolo planned, but never completed, sculpted fountains of two local mountains, the Asinaio (now known as the Senario) and the Falterona. For the lower wall, in similar rustic niches directly below those intended for the mountains, Tribolo carved statues in sandstone of two local rivers, the Mugnone and Arno. Vasari was taken with the resemblance to the geographical and hydrographic reality. As in the garden, Monte Senario lies to the west of Monte Falterona and these two mountains are respectively the source of the Mugnone and Arno Rivers, which meet at Florence, just as the water conduits were to pass from the sculpted mountains to the river gods, then onto a fountain in the lowest terrace representing the city.[41]

[38] *Ibid.*; and see Richard A. Goldthwaite, *Wealth and the Demand for Art in Italy, 1300–1600,* (Baltimore: Johns Hopkins University Press, 1993).

[39] Christine Begley in Janet Cox-Rearick (ed.), *Giulio Romano: Master Designer* (New York: Bertha and Karl Leubsdorf Art Gallery, Hunter College of the City University of New York, 1999), 82, makes a similar point about another river god in the Room of Psyche, which is identifiable as the nearby River Po.

[40] For Castello, see Claudia Lazzaro, *The Italian Renaissance Garden* (New Haven: Yale University Press, 1990), 167–89.

[41] Vasari, *Vite,* 6: 77.

Fig. 14   Giusto Utens, *Villa Medici, Castello,* 1599, Florence, tempera on panel, Museo di Firenze com'era (photo: Scala/ Art Resource, NY)

Tribolo's river gods do not survive, but from considerable evidence for their appearance we can identify a reflection of them in two title pages to works by the Florentine historian and mathematician, Cosimo Bartoli. The colossal reclining *Arno* Vasari described as holding a vase against his thigh and leaning on a lion.[42] The raised and considerably bent front leg that is visible in Utens' lunette resembles that of the river god in the title page to Bartoli's *Opuscoli morali* of 1568, a translation of various texts of Alberti (Fig. 15). Vasari particularly praised the much smaller *Mugnone* (4 *braccia* or 2.3 metres long), in reality only a tributary of the Arno. With one hand on the ground, the other supported a vase on his shoulder, and the front (left) leg crossed over the back.[43] In the title page to Bartoli's 1550 translation of Alberti's treatise on architecture, based on a drawing by Vasari, the river god's legs assume the distinctive position of Tribolo's *Mugnone* (Fig. 16).[44] The pose recalls, but reverses, Michelangelo's *Dusk* and *Day*, in which the back leg is crossed over the front. Tribolo knew these figures well, as he worked on the Medici Chapel with Michelangelo and also made models of the Times of Day. In 1547, a river god representing the Arno was decreed the official emblem of the Florentine

[42] *Ibid.* 6: 78. For the river gods and *Fiesole,* see Bertha Wiles, 'Tribolo in his Michelangelesque Vein', *Art Bulletin* 14.1 (1932), 59–70.

[43] Vasari, *Vite,* 6: 77.

[44] For Vasari's drawing, see Paola Barocchi, *Mostra di disegni del Vasari e della sua cerchia* (Florence: Leo S. Olschki, 1964), 22. Vasari also used the pose of the *Mugnone* for the Tiber River in the Palazzo della Cancelleria in Rome in 1546, several years after Tribolo's statue. The second title page is a variation on this design. Bartoli's description, on which the drawing is based, was later published in his *Ragionamenti accademici* (Venice: Francesco de' Franceschi, 1567), 22v–26v.

Fig. 15   Alberti, Leon Battista (1404–1472), *Opvscoli morali di Leon Battista Alberti*, translated Cosimo Bartoli (Venice: Francesco de Franceschi, 1568), title page, woodcut (photo: Research Library, The Getty Research Institute, Los Angeles (84-B20717))

Academy, founded by Cosimo de' Medici and dedicated to the Florentine, vernacular language.[45] Bartoli displayed the emblem of the Academy on title pages to his publications that furthered the goals of the Academy by translating Latin texts into Italian.[46] His collaborator, Vasari, chose Tribolo's figures as models, perhaps because they embodied a visual language that was likewise distinctively Florentine.

[45] Claudia Di Filippo Bareggi, 'In nota alla politica culturale di Cosimo I: l'Accademia Fiorentina', *Quaderni storici*, 8.23 (1973), 569.
[46] Judith Bryce, *Cosimo Bartoli (1503–1572): The Career of a Florentine Polymath* (Genoa: Libraire Droz, 1983), 186 n. 2, 192 n. 17, and 274 n. 49. The figure also appeared in Bartoli's *Discorsi historici universali* and *Del modo di misurare*.

Fig. 16   Alberti, Leon Battista (1404–1472), *L' architettura di Leonbatista Alberti, tradotta in lingua fiorentina da Cosimo Bartoli* (Florence: Torrentino, 1550), title page, woodcut (photo: Research Library, The Getty Research Institute, Los Angeles (84-B6919))

The river gods in the title pages both represent the Arno, and although the legs differ, they follow Tribolo's *Arno* in leaning on a lion and holding a vase against the thigh. The position of the vase recalls that of the Vatican *Arno* (restored for one of the Medici popes), with its modern additions and

Fig. 17   Michelangelo Buonarroti, *River God*, *c*.1524–27, Florence, Casa Buonarroti (photo: The Bridgeman Art Library)

Michelangelo's installation, which Tribolo elaborated in his stalactite-covered niches (see Figs. 5 and 6). Michelangelo also planned river gods for the Medici Chapel, for which he made a large-scale terracotta model of 1524–27 (Fig. 17). Since the terracotta figure remained in the Chapel when Michelangelo left Florence and Tribolo later organized the statues strewn about, it surely inspired his own river gods, as it did many copies by other artists.[47] In ancient statues such as the *Arno*, the back leg is raised and the torso tilted forward, so that the body is essentially contained in a single plane (Fig. 5). In both Michelangelo's reclining model and Tribolo's statues, as is evident even in the woodcut images, the lifted front leg results in a torsion within the body, with much greater potential for expressiveness and movement. These artists remade the image of the river god, translating the ancient statue type into a new Florentine aesthetic.

The only one of Tribolo's sculptures at Castello to survive is the *Fiesole*, the personification of the hill town overlooking the Mugnone valley, which shared the river's niche, although in high relief rather than free-standing (Fig. 18). The contrapposto of her body is extreme, with leg facing one direction, head the opposite, projecting shoulder, twisted torso, and limbs extended back. Again the influence of Michelangelo is obvious, in the body's torsion as well as

---

[47] Jeannine O'Grody, 'Michelangelo: The Master Modeler', in Bruce Boucher (ed.), *Earth and Fire: Italian Terracotta Sculpture from Donatello to Canova* (New Haven: Yale University Press, 2001), 35–8.

Fig. 18   Niccolò Tribolo, *Fiesole*, Florence, Bargello Museum (photo: Ralph Lieberman)

in the resemblance to the master's unfinished sculptures. Tribolo must have begun with the *Arno*, progressed to the more adventuresome pair of *Mugnone* and *Fiesole*, and then turned to the mountains. Two terracotta figures in the Bargello attributed to Tribolo, identified alternately as rivers or mountains, may be prototypes for the unfinished statues. Both are in technically challenging, half-seated, half-crouching positions with hips off the ground, and with similar long beards and great urns (Fig. 19). Each body shifts multiple times in opposing directions, with no vestige of the planar, but rather energetic with muscular tension. Contemporaries understood such bent bodies or *figure sforzate* (bodies bent so that they faced in different directions), influenced by Michelangelo's radical innovations and fashionable in sixteenth-century Florentine sculpture, as manifestations of artistic license.[48]

[48] Michael Cole, 'The *Figura Sforzata*: Modeling, Power, and the Mannerist Body', *Art History*, 24.4 (September 2001), 526–33.

92   *Claudia Lazzaro*

Fig. 19   Niccolò Tribolo, *Models for Rivers or Mountains,* Florence, Museo Nazionale (photo: Alinari/ Art Resource, NY)

Tribolo's personifications of rivers and mountains, far from empty displays of artistry, produced human bodies that conveyed the character of the entity they personified. The humanist Niccolò Martelli, who visited Castello in 1543, explained that the *Mugnone* had one foot over the other to denote that he had departed quite a bit from his old path (Fig. 16).[49] The pose signified that the river had changed course over time, as in fact it did many times.[50] Martelli also found the *Mugnone* colder and more austere than the *Arno,* but his austerity tempered by the softness of *Fiesole* (Fig. 18). The river god's angular limbs would have contrasted with her full thighs and round breasts, demonstrating contrasting male and female aspects of nature, and the city fertile and flourishing through the nourishment of the river's waters. Another innovation in Tribolo's sculpted fountains, developing further the Vatican installations, is the integration of water with the statues' actions. Utens' lunette confirms Vasari's account that water poured from the vases of the river gods. The Monte Asinaio pressed his beard, as one of the terracotta models does, and water emerged from his mouth, perhaps running down the beard, to demonstrate that the mountain is a source of water.[51]

The replacement for Tribolo's unfinished mountains, a bronze statue of the Apennine Mountains by Bartolomeo Ammannati, was added to the pool at the

[49] Niccolò Martelli, *Dal primo e dal secondo libro delle lettere di Niccolò Martelli* (Lanciano: R. Carabba, 1916), 22–3.
[50] Pasquino Pallecchi, 'Hydrografia', in Gabriella Capecchi (ed.), *Alle origini di Firenze: dalla preistoria alla città romana,* (Florence: Edizioni Polistampa, 1996), 19–20.
[51] Vasari, *Vite,* 6: 77.

Fig. 20   Bartolomeo Ammannati, *Appennino*, 1563–65, Castello, Villa Medici (photo: Claudia Lazzaro)

centre of the *bosco* in 1563–65, and perhaps already conceived by Tribolo in some form (Fig. 20).[52] Water pours over his body from an outlet on top of his head, and he shivers. Hervé Brunon discusses various competing ideas in the sixteenth century about the origins of water, among them the Aristotelian understanding that cold permits subterranean air to transform itself into water.[53] Ammannati's personification, shivering and dripping, performs the natural action of the mountain, producing water through the cold within its depths. At Castello, the fountains in sequence on the hillside replicate the passage of water in the Tuscan state; they also hint at a larger theme, the origins of water in the natural world, which was later fully developed in the Medici garden at Pratolino, as Brunon explains.[54] Tribolo worked as a hydraulic engineer for two Medici gardens and also for the Florentine state, but Vasari regretted that he wasted his time wanting to straighten rivers rather than making sculpture.[55] His skill at hydraulics made the sequence of garden fountains possible, and his novel sculpted images reflect both his artistic skill and his practical understanding of the movement of water in nature.

In the sixteenth century, river gods became vehicles for contemporary notions about natural science, artistic creativity, and political hegemony. Renaissance installations of the newly discovered ancient statues, along with the related *Cleopatra/Sleeping Nymph*, emphatically associated them with

---

[52] Giorgio Galletti, 'Tribolo maestro delle acque dei giardini', in Elisabetta Pieri and Luigi Zangheri (eds.), *Niccolò detto il Tribolo: tra arte, architettura e paesaggio* (Poggio a Caiano: Comune di Poggio a Caiano, 2001), 154, demonstrates that the water conduits were put in place under Tribolo.

[53] Brunon, 'Mouvements des eaux', 39.

[54] *Ibid.*, 33–53.

[55] Brunon, 'Da Castello a Pratolino: Buontalenti e l'eredità del Tribolo', in *Niccolò detto il Tribolo*, 168.

nature, while none of the other antique sculptures in the Vatican were supplemented with fountains and naturalistic settings. The installations logically led to sculpted river god fountains, with the water integrated into the figure's action. Renaissance artists invented new river god types for local rivers, which allowed them to signify not just aspects of nature – gendered, animate, abundant – but also particular places and together with other personifications of nature, a region in microcosm. They could confer legitimacy on a prince or demonstrate the effects of his good rule (in natural abundance, flood control, aqueduct construction, and so on) in triumphal entries, garden fountains, and much more. Ancient statues supplied a model for a powerful nude body in a reclining pose, but the variations and new types that soon appeared conveyed characteristics of a particular river – its course or relative age and size, or expressed graphically the idea of abundance in specifically male terms. Unlike characters charged with telling a story, river gods demonstrated artistic license, but artistic style was also inflected with place. Raphael's Xanthus River in the pose of his Heliodorus in the Vatican carried Roman associations, and Tribolo's were indisputably Florentine, following Michelangelo's artistic innovations and his precedents in the *Arno* installation and the river god designs for the Medici Chapel. At the same time that the river god became ubiquitous in the sixteenth century, it was also intimately bound up with the image of Michelangelo, the Florentine Academy, the Medici, and Florence.

Cornell University

4

Dissembling his art: 'Gascoigne's Gardnings'

Susan C. Staub

'When court had cast me off, I toyled at the plowe . . .'[1]

In 1573 George Gascoigne published his *Hundreth Sundrie Flowres bounde up in one small Poesie. Gathered partely (by translation) in the fine outlandish Gardins of Euripides, Ovid, Petrarke, Ariosto, and others: and partly by invention, out of our owne fruitfull Orchardes in Englande: yelding sundrie sweete savours of Tragical, Comical, and Morall Discourses, both pleasaunt and profitable to the well smellying noses of learned Readers.* In doing so, he became one of the first professional imaginative writers in England and risked what has come to be known as 'the stigma of print' by publishing his collected works.[2] For years, scholars have pondered the elaborate subterfuge Gascoigne created in constructing his volume: presenting it as a poetic anthology in the tradition of Tottel's *Miscellany*, hiding his authorship of the whole, prefacing it with letters that detail his reluctance to publish, including titles that suggest the social circumstances that occasioned the poetry, and adding an intruding narrator/editor who interprets and comments on some of the individual pieces. Poised on the cusp of manuscript and print culture, the volume is ambivalent about its very existence. It is a contradiction: a pseudo-coterie poetic collection in print, it replicates private textual circulation even as it clearly casts its lot with the 'vulgar sort' who actively sought a wider readership through publication.

When Gascoigne repackaged *A Hundreth Sundrie Flowres* as *The Posies* in 1575 after the negative reception the original volume received,[3] ostensibly taking

---

[1] George Gascoigne, 'The Greene Knights Farewell to Fansie' in *The Posies of George Gascoigne Esquire* in *The Complete Works of George Gascoigne*, ed. John W. Cunliffe, 2 vols. (1907; repr. New York: Greenwood Press, Publishers, 1969), Vol. 1, 380. I use Cunliffe's edition throughout and hereafter will note page numbers in the text.

[2] The classic essay detailing this so-called 'stigma' is John W. Saunders, 'The Stigma of Print: A Note on the Social Bases of Tudor Poetry', *Essays in Criticism*, 1 (1951), 139–64. More recent scholars have developed this argument in various ways. See, for example, Richard Helgerson, *The Elizabethan Prodigals* (Berkeley: University of California Press, 1976); Arthur F. Marotti, 'Patronage, Poetry, and Print', *Yearbook of English Studies* 21 (1991), 1–26; and Wendy Wall, *The Imprint of Gender: Authorship and Publication in the English Renaissance* (Ithaca: Cornell University Press, 1993).

[3] Although literary historians have generally accepted the idea that the volume was banned and was thus one of the first state suppressions of a non-religious text, more recent scholars have begun to question that assumption. See, for example, Cyndia Susan Clegg, who argues that *A Hundreth Sundrie Flowres* was likely not

Locus Amoenus, First Edition. Edited by Alexander Samson. © 2012 The Authors.
Journal compilation © 2012 The Society for Renaissance Studies and Blackwell Publishing Ltd.

on the persona of a reformed prodigal and professing sorrow for his younger transgressions, he nonetheless mocked the 'curious Carpers' and 'Ignorant readers' (10) who, he claimed, misinterpreted his intentions. Where the earlier collection was published as the works of 'sundrie authors', but with clear indicators that Gascoigne was actually the author of the entire anthology, in the revised book he claims authorship of both the previous and the current volume, and presents the texts as *The Posies of George Gascoigne Esquire. Corrected, perfected and augmented by the Authour.* Identifying himself simultaneously as 'Esquire' and 'Authour', Gascoigne here seems to flout the convention that separated gentility and publication.[4] Freighted with prefatory apparatus that establish his authority as a publishing author – three letters to various types of readers that take up the first seventeen pages of the volume, twenty commendatory poems in praise of the author, followed by 'The opinion of the author himself after all these commendations' – Gascoigne seems to leap feet first into print culture. Marotti sums it up well, 'Whereas the presentation of *A Hundreth Sundrie Flowres* foregrounds the reader's convenience and use, this second edition of Gascoigne's work is designed to dignify, even monumentalize its author.' Even the title page suggests something important; the bibliographic information is enclosed in an architectural border, 'enshrining the work as a literary monument'.[5] And the book no longer hides its commercial worth, enticing buyers with the advertisement that it is 'new and improved'. The title page even points to the text's value as a monetary commodity: 'These Bookes are to be solde at the Northwest dore of Paules Church'. Although Gascoigne changed the content of his book in this second edition less than he claims, the new presentation is actually quite remarkable, vividly illustrating a reconfiguration of authorship in response to the changing marketplace of print and his desire to enter that marketplace. Recent scholarship has argued that as writers began to court publication and make their works available to a wider readership than manuscript circulation afforded, they of necessity challenged the standard pose of writer as literary amateur and created new ways to enhance their cultural authority.[6] The title page, prefatory letters and commendatory poems certainly help to renegotiate Gascoigne's role as author, but perhaps the most striking device Gascoigne uses to authorize his writing, and the one on which I will focus this essay, is his development of the garden analogy only hinted at in the earlier volume. In this 'improved' edition, the poems are more fully structured as a garden, with each placed under an

banned, but instead was self-censored by Gascoigne in 'George Gascoigne and the Rhetoric of Censorship: *A Hundreth Sundrie Flowres* (1573) and *The Posies* (1575)', in *Press Censorship in Elizabethan England* (Cambridge: Cambridge University Press, 1997), 103–22.

[4] See Arthur F. Marotti, *Manuscript, Print, and the English Renaissance Lyric* (Ithaca: Cornell University Press, 1995), 225.

[5] *Ibid.*, 223–5.

[6] Wall, *The Imprint of Gender*, 3–4.

appropriate category: flowers, herbs, and weeds.[7] Where *A Hundreth Sundrie Flowres* highlighted the alleged editor's role in gathering the disparate 'flowers' of the poetic garden and made no differentiation among the various poems, the new volume shifts attention to the author and to the reader's right use of the text. Gascoigne's development of the garden analogy implies a restructuring and expansion of audience and thus his volume can be read in conversation with another kind of text finding a growing readership during the period, gardening manuals and herbals. My intent here is to consider the effect of the gardening trope on Gascoigne's enterprise: What exactly were the meanings of the garden in the sixteenth and early seventeenth centuries and what were the implications of Gascoigne metaphorically casting himself as a gardener, and even imagining himself walking and sitting in his own garden in several of the poems? I am not concerned so much with actual gardens here, but with garden rhetoric, with the ideology and justifications for gardens as presented by garden writers from the period.

In one of the letters preceding the various poems and plays in *The Posies*, as Gascoigne elaborates on the rationale for this reorganization, he guides his readers, offering evaluative judgments about the value of each poem:

> I have here presented you with three sundrie sortes of Posies: *Floures, Hearbes,* and *Weedes.* In which division I have not ment that onely the Floures are to be smelled unto, nor that onely the Weedes are to be rejected. I terme some Floures, bycause being indeed invented upon a verie light occasion, they have yet in them (in my judgement) some rare invention and Methode before not commonly used. And therefore (beeing more pleasant than profitable) I have named them Floures.
>
> The seconde (being indeede morall discourses, and reformed inventions, and therefore more profitable than pleasant) I have named Hearbes.
>
> The third (being Weedes) might seeme to some judgements, neither pleasant nor yet profitable, and therefore meete to bee cast away. But as many weedes are right medicinable, so may you find in this none so vile or stinking, but that it hath in it some vertue if it be rightly handled. Mary you must take heede how you use thē. For if you delight to put Hemlocke in your fellowes pottage, you may chaunce both to poyson him, and bring your selfe in perill. But if you take example by the harmes of others who have eaten it before you, then may you chaunce to become so warie, that you will looke advisedly on all the Perceley that

---

[7] I think the original volume is much more complex and sophisticated; despite the fact that Gascoigne conceals his authorship of the whole, it is very much a book that interrogates authorship and writing. Though he pretends to follow the protocol of the courtier poet in hiding his authorship, the book also allows non-coterie readers, that is, any reader who could afford to buy the volume, to participate in the game. In that volume, Gascoigne plays at the role of coterie poet, knocking out trifles, displaying *sprezzatura*, but also poking fun of the disingenuous strategies authors use to deflect responsibility for publishing their works. Since the prefatory letters to *A Hundreth Sundrie Flowres* seem clearly a fiction, there is reason to believe that the letters in *The Posies* are just as much a ruse and the moralizing in the revised volume is part of the pose. I agree with Cyndia Susan Clegg's argument that the letters in *The Posies* should be read sceptically. Furthermore, it is hard to take Gascoigne's categories seriously when there often seems little logic for specific poems being placed where they are.

you gather, least amongst the same one braunch of Hemlock might anoy you.
(12–13)

The extended explanation of the placement of the various poems suggests a
text that is more ordered and controlled by its author – and perhaps less sure
of its readers – and thus moves it away from the miscellaneous, privately
circulated pseudo-manuscript Gascoigne mimicked in *A Hundreth Sundrie
Flowres*. This strategy would also seem to broaden the audience from the
coterie reader he appeared to cultivate in the earlier edition. Here he writes
to the reverend divines and to the young gentlemen of England, but also to
readers generally. But more importantly for my analysis, Gascoigne's extension of the garden analogy connects it with the garden manuals that emerged
in the sixteenth century. Although garden books were practical for the most
part and would thus seem to have a completely different intent than poetry,
their rhetoric often sounds very much like that of poetic collections from the
period and betrays the same social aspirations that Gascoigne's text exhibits.
Both Gascoigne and garden writers extend the network of readers in what had
previously been a privileged, exclusive world, whether of poetry or landscape.
In *The Posies*, potentially more readers are exposed to the poetic practices of
courtly writers and readers and are granted 'privileged access into a cultivated
private world'.[8] Published anthologies thus 'market exclusivity'.[9] Garden writings also appeal to their readers' social ambitions, to what Rebecca Bushnell
has called 'green desire'.[10]

   Like the poetic miscellany, the garden manual began as an assemblage of
bits of knowledge, but became more structured and hierarchical as the form
developed. Bushnell argues that this increasing organization reflects the
growing professionalization of gardening; we witness the same progression in
Gascoigne's movement from the random assortment of poetry in *A Hundreth
Sundrie Flowres* to his value-laden arrangement in *The Posies*, a change that
suggests his growing sense of himself as a professional writer. As Bushnell
describes it, 'The earlier books let the gardener-readers delight in finding
their own way through the book and the garden', much like Gascoigne's
reader in *A Hundreth Sundrie Flowres* is instructed to wander seemingly at
random through the poetic flowers, dipping in and out like the bee and
'gather[ing] hony from even the most stinking weede'.[11] 'The later books',

[8] I quote Elizabeth Heale's description of Tottel's *Miscellany*, a description that holds for both Gascoigne and
garden writers as well. Heale, 'Songs, Sonnets and Autobiography, Self-Representation in Sixteenth-Century
Verse Miscellanies', in Henk Dragstra, Sheila Otway, and Helen Wilcox (eds.), *Betraying Our Selves: Forms of
Self-Representation in Early Modern English Texts* (New York: St Martin's Press, 2000), 61.

[9] Wall, *Imprint of Gender*, 96.

[10] This is the first part of the title of Rebecca Bushnell's important study of garden writing, *Green Desire:
Imagining Early Modern English Gardens* (Ithaca: Cornell University Press, 2003). My analysis has been very much
informed by Bushnell's work.

[11] 'The Printer to the Reader', *A Hundreth Sundrie Flowres*, ed. George W. Pigman, III (Oxford: Clarendon
Press, 2000), 3. The image is repeated in *The Posies* as well.

Bushnell explains, 'present readers with an ordered garden and book, rather than trusting them on their own. This order, it is implied, is "natural", mimicking nature's seasons and hierarchies, not requiring more than that the gentle reader see him- or herself in the text as lord of what he or she surveys.'[12] Gascoigne's ordering also creates a hierarchy with moral signposts derived from nature – flowers, herbs, and weeds.

There is no way to know if Gascoigne had these manuals in mind when he revised *A Hundreth Sundrie Flowres*, or if he even read any of these texts. (At least one reader from the period, Gabriel Harvey, connects Gascoigne with this writing when he cites him, along with Thomas Tusser, a popular sixteenth-century horticultural writer, as one of the 'vulgar writers' among whom 'many things are commendable'.[13]) What we do know is that these books were extremely popular. Martin Hoyles notes that nineteen gardening books were published in the sixteenth century, 'eleven concerned with herbs and eight on horticulture'. The numbers remained constant through the first half of the seventeenth century, but the later half of the century witnessed a 'fivefold' increase in these publications.[14] It is tempting to argue that the popularity of garden literature affected Gascoigne's choice of trope in *The Posies*, but in all likelihood, he is simply developing a traditional literary analogy. We can, however, recognize resonances in both *The Posies* and garden writings from the period that illustrate a changing cultural landscape. Both defend their work as imaginative labour; both share similar intellectual and social concerns; and both suggest a desire for self-display and social advancement. Both are forced to negotiate authorship and redefine their readership as their texts cross social boundaries through publication. The same concerns that permeate so much of Gascoigne's work are evident in the gardening manuals of the period with their interrogation of profit and pleasure, art and nature, the reliability of sources – and with their obsession with the vulgarity of men who wrote or gardened for profit. Recent scholarship also suggests the connection between the garden manual and notions of nationhood, the history of the book, and the burgeoning print marketplace – all issues apparent in Gascoigne's work. These writings suggest that Gascoigne's analogy can be read as more than just a convention and is fundamentally connected to the ways that he fashions his identity as gentleman, author, and Englishman.

Michael Leslie and Timothy Raylor posit that economic developments during the period resulted in changing concepts of land and landscape; for one, sufficient wealth increased the number of people who gardened for aesthetic and/or productive reasons rather than for subsistence. By 1575, they argue, 'both the ability to order the landscape according to sophisticated intellectual motives, and the desire to do so, had spread widely through the

---

[12] Bushnell, *Green Desires*, 51.

[13] Gabriel Harvey, *Pierces Supererogation*, quoted in Meredith Skura, *Tudor Autobiography: Listening for Inwardness* (Chicago: University of Chicago Press, 2008), 139.

[14] Martin Hoyles, *Gardeners Delight: Gardening Books from 1560–1960* (Boulder: Pluto Press, 1994), 9.

English gentry.' In turn, the increased involvement with the land beyond 'manual drudgery' turned the 'cultivated landscape' into a 'key metaphor, and more than a metaphor, in the intersecting realms of national, religious, and individual identity'. Referring to the entertainments Gascoigne wrote for Queen Elizabeth later in the same year, Leslie and Raynor go so far as to suggest that 'Gascoigne's entertainments and those of other Elizabethan and Stuart writers are unthinkable without a number of changes in the cultural context in which the land was conceived.'[15] As greater numbers of the gentry became landowners, the idea of land as private property meant that land might be used for personal economic gain and/or for individual pleasure. Perhaps this change in zeitgeist emboldened Gascoigne to stake out his poetry as his own property as well.[16]

In titling his work *A Hundreth Sundrie Flowres* (with its echo of Tusser's popular *A Hundreth pointes of good Husbandrie*) and later revising it as *The Posies* (with its pun on poesy/posy, poetry/flowers), Gascoigne is playing with the literal meaning of the word 'anthology'. According to the *Oxford English Dictionary*, an anthology is a collection 'of the flowers of verse, that is, small choice poems, especially epigrams, by various authors'. Etymologically, the word derives from the Greek phrase for 'flower collection', and like its synonym from Latin, 'florilegium' (meaning flower culling), it emphasizes the gathering aspect of poetry collections. Such imagery provides an apt analogy for the poetic activity of invention. Clearly, Gascoigne was tapping into conventional ideas about poetry and rhetoric. But my particular concern in this essay is the way Gascoigne's gardening trope resonates with changing ideas about literal gardens in the period as reflected in husbandry and gardening books.

Of course, likening poetry to flowers and books to gardens *was* conventional. By comparing his volume to a garden, Gascoigne may well be simply using a traditional trope for a literary collection of poetry and legitimizing his work by connecting it with classical authors. The metaphor of the book as garden and poems as flowers was a common one during the period, perhaps originating with *The Greek Anthology* and continuing in the sixteenth century with such works as *Flowres of Epigrams*, *A Small Handfull of Fragrant Flowers*, *A Paradise of Dainty Devises*, *A Posie of Gilliflowres*, *Brittons Bowre of Delights*, and *A Sweet Nosegay*, to give just a random sampling.[17] Richard Newton argues that collections that present themselves as gardens, bowers, and bouquets 'draw upon organic metaphors to imply their unity, thus suggesting to readers a

---

[15] 'Introduction', Michael Leslie and Timothy Raylor (eds.), *Culture and Cultivation in Early Modern England: Writing and the Land* (Leicester: Leicester University Press, 1992), 3.

[16] On the connection between textual property rights and land ownership, see Elizabeth Eisenstein, *The Printing Press as an Agent of Social Change: Communications and Cultural Transformations in Early-Modern Europe* (New York: Cambridge University Press, 1985), 120–21.

[17] For a full discussion of the idea of the book as garden, see Randall L. Anderson, 'The Metaphor of the Book as Garden', *The Yearbook of English Studies* 33 (2003), 248–61.

special, studious attention to their parts in order to discern their structural function, moral use, or poetic value'.[18] Gascoigne himself states as much when he instructs his readers at the beginning of *The Posies*, 'Smell every poesie right and you therein shall finde,/ Fresh flowers, good hearbes, and holsome weedes to please a skilfull minde' ('The opinion of the aucthor himself after all these commendations', 33). The comparison of poet to gardener recurs in Renaissance poetic theory. In a section of *The Arte of English Poesy*, entitled 'That the good poet or maker ought to dissemble his art, and in what cases the artificial is more to be commended than the natural, and contrariwise', Puttenham argues that poetry is

> an aid and coadjuter to nature . . . as the good gardener seasons his soil by sundry sorts of compost . . . and waters his plants, and weeds his herbs and flowers, and prunes his branches, and unleaves his boughs to let in the sun; and twenty other ways cherisheth them, and cureth their infirmities, and so makes that never, or very seldom, any of them miscarry, but bring forth their flowers and fruits in season.[19]

Puttenham's extended metaphor shows just how interwoven the discourses of poetry and gardening were at this time. Both gardening and poetry 'surmount' and 'alter' nature, but in Puttenham's view, the poet's art is greater because the poet's art comes from the imagination; as Sidney would have it, the poet creates 'golden worlds'.[20] Admittedly, Puttenham concedes, the gardener too might create things yet unknown:

> the gardener by his art . . . will embellish the same in virtue, shape, odour, and taste, that nature of herself would never have done, as to make the single gillyflower, or marigold, or daisy, double, and the white rose red, yellow or carnation; a bitter melon, sweet; a sweet apple, sour; a plum or cherry without a stone; a pear without a core or kernel; a gourd or cucumber like to a horn or any other figure he will – any of which things nature could not do without mans help and art.[21]

Both poetry and the garden highlight the power and authority of the men who created them. Although Gascoigne did not develop the concept with an eye toward real organization, the garden analogy provides a rationale for the

---

[18] Richard C. Newton, 'Making Books from Leaves: Poets Become Editors', in Gerald P. Tyson and Sylvia S. Wagonheim (eds.), *Print and Culture in the Renaissance: Essays on the Advent of Printing in Europe* (Newark: University of Delaware Press, 1986), 250.

[19] George Puttenham, *The Art of English Poesy, A Critical Edition*, eds. Frank Whigham and Wayne A. Rebhorn (Ithaca: Cornell University Press, 2007), 382–3.

[20] 'Nature never set forth the earth in so rich a tapestry as divers poets have done; neither with so many pleasant rivers, fruitful trees, sweet-smelling flowers, nor whatsoever else may make the too much loved earth more lovely', Philip Sidney, *A Defence of Poetry*, 1579–80, ed. Jan Van Dorsten (Oxford: Oxford University Press, 1966), 24.

[21] Puttenham, *The Arte of English Poesy*, 383.

disparate contents he includes: sonnets and other lyric poetry, prose, comedy and tragedy. Most broadly, the garden image sanctions the variety of poems and poetic devices contained in such volumes, often a variety not only of genres but in *The Posies* of personae as well. The insistence on variety derives at least in part from the rhetorical tradition of *copia* filtered through Erasmus from Quintilian. In this tradition, variety is considered a necessary corollary to achieving pleasure in spoken and written discourse: 'The end of poetry is pleasure and profit, and the aim of poetry is attained by variety, for the greatest poems contain every phase of art and life', Renaissance poetic theorists tell us.[22]

Furthermore, copiousness was an essential element in humanist educational theory, as the frequency with which books are likened to gardens attests. As Rebecca Bushnell explains, 'This metaphor conveyed the idea of a book as a collection of elements, each with its individual interest and value, ordered in pleasant contiguity and available for consumption.' Readers, then, were analogous to farmers ploughing a field or harvesting valuable crops.[23] Or, they were likened to bees, flitting in and out of the book, making honey from the 'flowers' they encounter. In an echo of Erasmus, who compares the student to a 'diligent bee', Gascoigne elaborates on the image, insisting that 'the industrious Bee may gather honie out of the most stinking weede, so the malicious Spider may also gather poyson out of the fairest floure that growes' (12).[24] His spider-bee analogy deflects responsibility for his poems onto reader, and challenges them to read correctly.

As the analogy of the garden suggests, the principle of variety has as its rationale not just a display of the writer's virtuosity; its true source is nature. Erasmus explains, 'Variety everywhere has such force that nothing is so polished as not to seem rough when lacking its excellence. Nature herself especially rejoices in variety; in such a great throng of things she has left nothing anywhere not painted with such wonderful artifice of variety.'[25] Interestingly, in describing nature as 'painted with some wonderful artifice of variety', Erasmus inverts the commonplace that links nature and art: here, nature performs the task of the artist. More typically, the variety expressed in the work of art mirrors the plenitude of nature. The garden itself perfectly commingles nature and art since the garden represents nature improved by art. Variety is important not only because it creates pleasure; it expresses a fundamental tenet of the Renaissance conception of the world itself.

---

[22] Joel Spingarn, *A History of Literary Criticism in the Renaissance* (New York: Harcourt, 1963), 16.

[23] Rebecca W. Bushnell, *A Culture of Teaching: Early Modern Humanism in Theory and Practice* (Ithaca: Cornell University Press, 1996), 135.

[24] In Erasmus' terms, the student-bee flies through the authors' gardens and lights 'on every small flower of rhetoric, everywhere collecting some honey that he may carry off to his own hive', *On Copia of Words and Ideas*, trans. Donald King and H. David Rix (Milwaukee: Marquette University Press, 1963), 90.

[25] *Ibid.*, 16.

The emphasis on variety carried over from the rhetorical tradition to the Renaissance garden as well. In garden writer Gervase Markham's estimation, 'The adornation and beautifying of gardens is not onely divers but almost infinite, the industry of mens braines hourely begetting and bringing forth such new garments and imbroadery for the earth, that it is impossible to say this shall be singular, neither can any man say that this or that is the best, sith as mens tastes so their fancies are carried away with the varietie of their affections, some being pleased with one forme, some with another.'[26] Here, as in poetic gardens, the artistic power of the maker is emphasized. The fashion at this time, a fashion that was beginning to spread from aristocratic gardens to those of the middling sort, was to include as many diverse types of plants, and hence, colours as possible. The shapes were also varied: in aristocratic gardens topiary works pruned to resemble animals, geometric shapes, even man himself were frequent elements. And the plenitude of the garden was not just limited to the sense of sight; flowers were chosen for their smells as well as their colours. Water splashing from fountains and other water works and birds chirping from trees completed the sensory overload afforded by the garden.[27] In poetry and gardening alike 'variety and abundance' held a higher value than 'brevity and simplicity'.[28]

There seem to have been three dominant types of books on gardening: husbandry manuals, which gave instructions on gardening for food and maintaining the land; aesthetic garden manuals, which appeared later and described gardening for pleasure;[29] and finally herbals, the last form to develop, which were more scientific in intent and were often much more elaborate books with a more systematic ordering of plants. It is difficult to gauge the actual readership of these texts, and the readership must surely have differed depending on the kind of gardening being described. Although the books on husbandry seem to have the broadest reach and cost only a penny, Andrew McRae believes even at a penny only the gentry could have

---

[26] Gervase Markham, *The English Husbandman* (London, 1613), 120. Early English Books Online (EEBO hereafter) http://0-gateway.proquest.com.wncln.wncln.org/openurl?ctx_ver=Z39.88-2003&res_id=xri:eebo& rft_id=xri:eebo:citation:99847322 (accessed November 2009). The idea of individual taste as an indicator of value is expressed in Gascoigne as well.

[27] Eugenio Battisi, 'Natural Artificiosa to Nature Artificialis', in David Coffin (ed.), *The Italian Garden: First Dumbarton Oaks Colloquim on the History of Landscape Architecture* (Washington, DC: Dumbarton Oaks, 1972), 3–4. Battisi describes the Italian garden, but recent scholars, such as Elizabeth Woodhouse have shown similar elements in the English aristocratic garden. See 'Spirit of the Elizabethan Garden', *Garden History* 27 (1999), 10–31. See also, Michael Leslie, 'Spenser, Sidney, and the Renaissance Garden', *English Literary Renaissance* 22 (1992), 3–36.

[28] Bushnell, *A Culture of Teaching*, 121.

[29] Subsistence and pleasure gardening were not mutually exclusive; in fact, in the sixteenth and early seventeenth centuries the ideal garden served both ends. In *The English Husbandman*, Gervase Markham speaks of the importance of mingling 'commoditie' and 'comliness', and he finds this blending to be a distinctly English skill. See Rebecca Bushnell, *Green Desires*, 97.

afforded them.[30] Yet while some of these texts were clearly meant for elite readers, most seem to envision a broader readership. Many, like Gascoigne's text, are presented with elaborate prefatory material – multiple letters to various types of readers, decorative borders, and even portraits of the authors.[31] On the one hand, there is Thomas Tusser's extremely popular *A Hundreth pointes of good Husbandrie*, 1557 (originally published by Tottel in the same year as *Songes and Sonettes* and later revised as *Five Hundreth Points of Good Husbandry*), which McRae cites as best illustrating 'the populist intentions of this emergent native tradition' with its 'practical and moral advice' for the 'husbandman and "huswife" '. Structured as a calendar with a programme of activities for each month and written in doggerel verse, the format 'is surely consistent with an attempt to fix information in the minds of the literate or semi-literate'. 'The book was intended for the use of small farmers unaccustomed to books, rather than for the entertainment of the gentry', McRae believes.[32] Laura Stevenson, on the other hand, sees the appeal to simplicity as a pose and places the book in the georgic tradition of Hesiod and Virgil. Noting its wit and wordplay as well as its dedications to Lord and Lady Paget, Stevenson argues that it was intended to 'teach the value of simple, industrious living to aristocratic men who had retired from the army or politics and wished to become gentlemen farmers'. Whatever its intentions, the book was popular, going through twenty editions between 1573 and 1638, making it one of 'the fifteen most popular books in Elizabethan England'.[33] Other texts seem clearly to have an elite audience in mind, but they too are deceptive. Henry Lyte's *A Niewe Herball, or Historie of Plantes*, published in 1578, for example, is an illustrated folio of almost 800 pages with front matter that includes the author's coat of arms and a dedicatory letter to Queen Elizabeth in which he explains his reasons for translating into English – his love and admiration of all learning and virtue and 'to profite our Countrie and to please so noble and loving a Princesse'. But in his letter 'To the friendly and indifferent Reader', he explains his desire to educate 'the meanest of [his] Countriemen (whose skill is not so profounde that they can fetche this knowledge out of strange tongues . . .)', implying a broader readership as well.[34] Likewise, Thomas Hill's 1558 *A most briefe and pleasante treatise, teachyng howe to dresse, sowe, and set a garden*, often considered the first book on aesthetic gardening published in England, addresses the 'gentle reader' but also expresses the author's wish that

[30] Andrew McRae, *God Speed the Plough: The Representation of Agrarian England, 1500–1660* (Cambridge: Cambridge University Press, 1996), 139.

[31] In looking at these texts, I was struck in particular by the similarity of the portraits of John Gerard, *Herball* (1597) and John Parkinson, *Paradisii in Sole* (1629) with that of Gascoigne in *The Steele* Glasse (1576).

[32] McRae, 146–7.

[33] Laura Caroline Stevenson, *Praise and Paradox: Merchants and Craftsmen in Elizabethan Popular Literature* (New York: Cambridge University Press, 1984), 140–41.

[34] Henry Lyte, *A Niewe Herball, or a Historie of Plantes*, (London, 1578), ii, iii. EEBO <http://0-gateway.proquest.com.wncln.wncln.org/openurl?ctx_ver=Z39.88-2003&res_id=xri:eebo&rft_id=xri:eebo:citation:99843065> (accessed November 2009).

the knowledge [in the book] shall move the simple and unlettered to whom I write this my boke not only to bestow the more diligence in the dressying, sowying, and setting of these and other herbes in their gardens, but to be carefull also how to avoyde noyous wormes, beastes and flyes, that commonlye harme gardens.[35]

Bushnell provides a nice summation: most garden manuals, she concludes, 'experimented in some way with defining and expanding their readership, appealing most often to men but sometimes to women, to the rich and poor, and to those seeking profit as well as entertainment'.[36] Joan Thirsk traces the development of this literature to translations of classical writers on horticulture in the fifteenth century because Latin texts were readily available to English gentleman readers. But English garden writers almost immediately adapted their writing to suit their English audience. As Thirsk explains, writers strove 'for a homely style of writing that was readily intelligible to all. This had far-reaching consequences, for the literature became more effective, reaching a wider circle of readers.'[37] Gascoigne expresses this same impulse when he talks about the importance of English and the benefit writing in his native language has to his countrymen: scorning what he calls words that 'smell of the Inkhorne' (that is, overly bookish words) or words that are foreign, he says, 'I have alwayes bene of the opinion, that it is not unpossible eyther in Poemes or in Prose too write both compendiously, and perfectly in our Englishe tongue' (5). He later elaborates, 'Yet hope I that it shall be apparant I have rather regarde to make our native language commendable in it selfe, than gay with the feathers of straunge birds' (6). Garden writers repeatedly emphasize the importance of writing in the vernacular, a necessary component for creating a true English author. And they further stress the need to adapt gardening practices to English plants and climates. *Foure Bookes of Husbandry, collected by M. Conradus Heresbachius* (1577) advertises itself on the title page as 'Newely Englished by Barnabe Googe, Esquire';[38] Thomas Hill notes that he provides information 'as the lyke heatherto haue not bine published in the Englishe tungue'.[39] Several decades later when Gervase Markham contrasts his writing with those who translate foreign manuals, he more fully articulates the importance of a native tradition:

[35] Quoted in Bushnell, *Green Desires*, 41.

[36] *Ibid.*

[37] Joan Thirsk, 'Making a Fresh Start: Sixteenth-Century Agriculture and the Classical Tradition', in Michael Leslie and Timothy Raylor (eds.), *Culture and Cultivation in Early Modern England: Writing and the Land*, (Leicester and London: Leicester University Press, 1992), 18–19, 20.

[38] In 'The Epistle to the Reader', Googe notes that he puts the text in English for the reader's 'further profite and pleasure', *Foure Bookes of Husbandry, collected by M. Conradus Heresbachius* (London, 1577), sig.iij. EEBO http://0-gateway.proquest.com.wncln.wncln.org/openurl?ctx_ver=Z39.88-2003&res_id=xri:eebo&rft_id=xri:eebo:citation:99839716 (accessed November 2009).

[39] Thomas Hill, 'The Preface to the Reader', *The Proffitable Arte of Gardening, now the third tyme set fourth* (London, 1568). EEBO <http://0-gateway.proquest.com.wncln.wncln.org/openurl?ctx_ver=Z39.88-2003&res_id=xri:eebo&rft_id=xri:eebo:citation:99839833> (accessed November 2009).

when . . . I beheld that every man was dumbe to speak anything of the Husbandry of our own kingdom, I could not but imagine it a work most acceptable to men, and most profitable to the kingdome, to set down the true manner and nature of our right English Husbandry.[40]

This impulse, what Wendy Wall calls 'the new business of Englishing print', served to counteract the idea that print was stigmatizing, instead illustrating the necessity of publication for the 'preservation and dissemination of the nation's distinctive qualities'.[41]

Not only did they see their goal as educating by writing in the vernacular, but they also began to 'preach the benefits of gardening as a means to improve the English land and the English people'.[42] Although the practical purpose of these manuals might be to instruct their readers in the intricacies of horticulture, with topics ranging from growing various plants, to improving the soil and guarding against canker worms, green flies, great moths, and snails with shells, they also frequently express an additional moral concern as well: like literature, they sought to profit as well as delight.[43] The gardener's job was to improve nature, either of the land, or of his readers and himself. Honest labour was thought to contribute to the social and moral well-being of the nation. Thus the 'cultivated landscape becomes the supreme expression – national, political, and religious – of the "country", and the most powerful figuration of the cultivation of the human spirit'.[44]

When Gascoigne explains his rationale for republishing his works in the prefatory letters to *The Posies*, he offers them as a negative exemplum or mirror to the 'youthful gentlemen of England':

Beware therefore, lustie Gallants, how you smell to these Posies. And learne you to use the talent which I have highly abused. Make me your myrrour. And if hereafter you see me recover mine estate, or reedify the decayed walls of my youth, then beginne you sooner to builde some foundation which may beautifie your Pallace. If you see me sinke in distresses (notwithstanding that you judge me quick of capacitie) then lerne you to mainteyne your selves swimming in prosperitie, and eschue betymes the whirlepoole of misgovernment. (14)

He also admits several times that he seeks preferment, though even there as a benefit to his country:

as I seeke advauncement by vertue, so was I desirous that there might remaine in publike recorde, some pledge or token of those giftes wherwith it hath pleased

---

[40] Markham, sig. A1v.

[41] Wendy Wall, 'Renaissance National Husbandry: Gervase Markham and the Publication of England', *Sixteenth Century Journal*, 27 (1996), 770–72.

[42] Bushnell, *Green Desires*, 29.

[43] Here I am citing headings from Hill's *The Profittable Arte of Gardening*.

[44] Leslie and Raylor, *Culture and Cultivation*, 4.

the Almightie to endue me: To the ende that thereby the vertuous might bee incouraged to employ my penne in some exercise which might tende both to my preferment, and to the profite of my Countrey. (5)

His contention that he brought forth his second edition so that 'all men might see the reformation of my mind' reveals just how fitting the pose of gardener was for Gascoigne, a man who had earlier been accused of being 'a common Rymer and a deviser of slaunderous Pasquelles againste divers persons of greate callinge' and a 'notorious Ruffiane and especially noted to be bothe a spie; an Atheist and godless person'.[45] Like the gardener who benefits from his labour in the garden (even if vicariously), Gascoigne offers the work he performed in creating his poetic garden as proof of his reformed status.[46] Here Gascoigne seems at least partially to abandon the dissembling that Puttenham recommends – the idea, that is, that the gentle-man must not show that he labours to write or that he writes for reward or profit. In fact, the word 'toyle' appears several times in the commendatory poems to *The Posies*.

The importance of labour and its moral profit recur in garden writings. To Markham, for example, the perfect gardener is known for his 'Diligence, Industry, and Art'. By 'Industry' Markham means 'labour, pain and study'.[47] This 'discourse of improvement' is everywhere present in garden writings of the period.[48] Gardening even takes on a more direct spiritual component in some of these texts; through his cultivation of the soil, man might return to a prelapsarian state of grace.[49] One writer, speaking of the 'lovely, honest and delightful recreation of planting', expresses hope that 'men might regain some of the lost splendour of Eden'.[50] An accepted place for spiritual reflection (ironically, also for sexual dalliance, though not in garden

---

[45] Charles Taylor Prouty, *George Gascoigne: Elizabethan Courtier, Soldier, and Poet* (New York: Columbia University Press, 1942), 61.

[46] Sometimes, it seems the gentleman gardener benefits vicariously because he depends on the work of others: William Lawson, describing how to hire a good gardener, says he should be honest, and certainly not 'an idle, or lazie lubber'. If the gentleman manages to find such a worker, 'God shall crowne the labours of his hands with joyfulnesse, and make the clouds droppe fatnesse upon your Trees', *A New Orchard and Garden* (London, 1618), 2–3. EEBO <http://0-gateway.proquest.com.wncln.wncln.org/openurl?ctx_ver=Z39.88-2003&res_id=xri:eebo&rft_id=xri:eebo:citation:99842495> (accessed November 2009). See Bushnell for a discussion of this contradiction, *Green Desire*, 88–9. There is at least some contradiction in Gascoigne's worthy gardener pose, as well. The courtly poet who sought to showcase the ease of his writing – its lack of labour – in *A Hundreth Sundrie Flowres*, now suggests his reformation through labour as he shifts attention to the didactic importance of his poems.

[47] Bushnell, *Green Desire*, 85.

[48] I borrow this term from McRae, *God Speed the Plough*. See, especially, Chapter 5.

[49] Anthony Low argues that this is the purpose of the georgic, which he defines as redeeming labour for the gentleman. *The Georgic Revolution* (Princeton: Princeton University Press, 1985).

[50] William Hughes, quoted in Keith Thomas, *Man and the Natural World: Changing Attitudes in England 1500–1800* (New York: Oxford University Press, 1996), 236.

manuals), the garden brought men nearer to God. Even the most mundane activities, such as pruning a tree, took on spiritual importance. William Lawson explains,

> Such is the condition of all earthly things, whereby a man receaveth profit or pleasure, that they degenerate presently without good ordering. Man himselfe lefte to himselfe, growes from his heavenly and spirituall generation, and becommeth beastly, yea devilish to his owne kinde, unlesse he be regenerate. No marvaille then, if trees make their shootes, and put their sprayes disorderly. And truely (if I were worthy to iudge) there is not a mischiefe that breedeth greater and more generall harme to all the Orchard . . . than the want of the skilfull dressing of trees.[51]

In Lawson's and other garden writers' views, gardening controls the 'rampant sensuality' and 'wantonness' of Eden.[52]

Nonetheless, the sensuality of the garden still posed a problem, as Gascoigne himself learned from the reception of his first lascivious flowers. Echoing the language of Renaissance poetics, garden writers constantly assert the double benefit of the garden as delightful and useful. While gardens are extolled as being 'delectable' and 'delightful', making 'all our sences swimme in pleasure', the pleasurable aspect of the garden is always counterbalanced with its utility.[53] John Gerard, for instance, insists on the transformative power of beautiful flowers, which, he says, 'do bring to a liberall and gentlemanly minde, the remembrance of honestie, comelinesse, and all kindes of vertues.' 'For it would be', he continues, 'an vnseemely and filthie thing . . . for him, that doth looke vpon and handle faire and beautifull things, and who frequenteth and is conuersant in faire and beautifull places, to haue his minde not faire, but filthie and deformed.'[54] Here Gerard seems very much like Gascoigne as he puts the onus for the proper perception of the garden on its viewer rather than its maker. He also makes a not too veiled appeal to social class; the appropriate response is the mark of a 'gentlemanly minde'. Nonetheless, in these estimations pleasure seems to hold its own value. Because these texts manage to resolve the dilemma created by aesthetic pleasure, the discourse of gardening provides an ideal defence of poetry.[55]

While garden writers struggled to define the delights of the garden as morally profitable, they also sought to profit financially despite their protests to the contrary. One way they did both was by titillating their readers with

---

[51] Lawson, *A New Orchard and Garden*, 32–3.

[52] Bushnell, *Green* Desire, 96.

[53] Lawson, *A New Orchard*, 56.

[54] John Gerard, *The Herball or Generall Historie of Plantes* (London, 1597), 698–9. EEBO <http://0-gateway.proquest.com.wncln.wncln.org/openurl?ctx_ver=Z39.88-2003&res_id=xri:eebo&rft_id=xri:eebo:citation:99857504> (accessed November 2009).

[55] Christine Coch, 'The Woman in the Garden: (En)gendering Pleasure in Late Elizabethan Poetry', *English Literary Renaissance* 39 (2009), 114.

promises of unknown, new, and rare information. These writers had to find
a way to market their books to their enlarged readership, and the presentation of the information in these works as novel and secret was another way
to do so. Thomas Hill repeatedly uses the word 'secret' in his works – 'of the
ordering, care and *secretes* of . . . lettuce', 'of the order, care and *secretes* of
the poppy', 'certaine helpes and *secretes* against the Garden wormes', and on
and on. And when he revises the work as *The Gardener's Labyrinth*, he entices
his readers with the rarity and worthiness of his book: these 'instructions are
rare secretes' and 'laudable secretes in Garden matters'.[56] As with books,
novelty became a major factor in the commercial value and appeal of individual flowers, but as Keith Thomas explains, the choice of flowers one
planted also became a sign of social class. One garden writer, in fact, recommends certain species specifically for their social desirability, stressing
that there was 'no lady or gentlewoman of any worth' who did not like
tulips. The garden thus works as an organic display with socially and eco-
nomically differentiated spaces of pleasure and profit. But garden fashions
seemed to be a precarious thing. Flowers followed social trends much as
clothing did, and as access to them descended the social scale, they tended
to fall out of fashion and lose their commercial value. Thomas goes on to
detail the resulting frenzy to keep up:

> This constant desire to keep ahead of the fashion (or at least to profit by selling
> to those who wished to keep ahead) was one of the chief stimuli to horticultural
> innovation. It underlay the preoccupation with rarity, novelty and hybridization.
> It encouraged the gentry to spend large sums of money on improving new
> varieties from overseas; and it forced them to install stoves and greenhouses in
> which tropical plants could be housed and abnormally early or late flowering
> achieved.[57]

Although he refers specifically to formal aristocratic gardens, Roy Strong
describes a similar impetus: the garden was 'a symbol of pride and an expression of royal and aristocratic magnificence'.[58] But, as Bushnell has shown, the
social status afforded by the garden crossed aristocratic boundaries, providing
a way for the gentry and merchant class alike to aspire upwards and to show
their respectability.

When Gascoigne imagines himself walking and writing in his garden in the
poems entitled 'Gascoigne's Gardnings', the poetic garden coalesces with the

---

[56] Thomas Hill, *The Proffitable Arte*, Sigs. Bii-Biiii, and Didymus Mountain [Thomas Hill], *The Gardener's
Labyrinth* (London, 1594), second part, 3. EEBO <http://0-gateway.proquest.com.wncln.wncln.org/
openurl?ctx_ver=Z39.88-2003&res_id=xri:eebo&rft_id=xri:eebo:citation:99839854> (accessed November
2009).
For further discussion of this aspect of garden manuals, see Bushnell, *Green Desire*, 55–6. Gascoigne also calls
attention to 'the depth and secrets' of his conceits in *The Posies*. And earlier, *The Adventures of Master F. J.* created
the illusion of insider and secret knowledge of an aristocratic world.
[57] Keith Thomas, 231–34.
[58] Roy Strong, *The Renaissance Garden in England* (London: Thames and Hudson, Ltd, 1979), 11.

literal garden. He at once suggests his status as a gentleman and a garden owner at the same time that he refashions himself as an author. He invites the visitor to partake in the pleasures of both gardens, concluding with a posy inscribed in Latin, '*Quoniam etiam humiliates amœna delectant*', which Prouty translates as 'Pleasant places delight even those of humble station'.[59] With those parting words, Gascoigne presents his *Posies* to the world.

In titling his work *A Hundredth Sundrie Flowres* and later organizing it as a garden in *The Posies*, Gascoigne was drawing on conventional ideas about poetry, rhetoric and education. But by considering Gascoigne's collection in conjunction with gardening books from the period, a form growing in popularity throughout the sixteenth and early seventeenth centuries, we can see more clearly the issues Gascoigne confronts, issues that seem inextricably involved with print culture and changing social values. The rhetoric of these manuals suggests an attempt to reconfigure social relationships, authorise the authors, and fashion their readership. In *Green Desires*, Rebecca Bushnell shows how garden writers sought to elevate gardening 'to the status of both profession and recreation, and thus to remake themselves'. 'Even in their most banal prose', she concludes, 'they fashioned the image of the gardener as a sensualist, man of wit, lover of God, and creator of wealth.'[60] Gascoigne does the same with his garden of verse.

Appalachian State University

---

[59] Charles Taylor Prouty (ed.), *A Hundreth Sundrie Flowres* (Columbia: University of Missouri Press, 1970), 287. Pigman translates this motto, 'Since pleasant things delight even those who have been brought low [or humiliated]', (667).

[60] Bushnell, *Green Desires*, 16.

5

'My innocent diversion of gardening': Mary Somerset's plants

JENNIFER MUNROE

Mary Somerset, first Duchess of Beaufort, was respected in her day as a collector and cultivator of plants, both exotic and common, on her estate in Badminton. And yet, when she writes to Sir Robert Southwell in 1694,[1] she is surprisingly humble about her achievements, calling hers an 'innocent diversion of gardening'.[2] The duchess's attention to plant collecting and botanical knowledge, though, was hardly just an 'innocent diversion', as characterized by J. E. Dandy, editor of the massive *Sloane Herbarium*, when he concludes, 'Considering the importance of the gardens at Badminton and the position which they evidently hold in the history of English gardening, it is remarkable that published references to them [or to the Duchess herself], other than those by contemporaries, should be so few and so slight' (209).[3] That Mary Somerset was an important figure in gardening history seems abundantly clear. This essay, however, demonstrates how Somerset's work with plants blurs the line between 'gardening' and the twin fields of horticulture and botany; hers was an endeavour that crossed over into what we might see as more than just plant collecting and is indicative of scientific thinking about plants as well.

It is clear from the many papers preserved by Sir Hans Sloane, long-time President of the Royal Society and Somerset's regular correspondent, from the respect her contemporaries had for her growing skills at Badminton estate,[4] and from the many men and women who relied on her for the plants they grew in their own gardens, that Somerset's work with plants was impressive and influential. The duchess was an ambitious collector, as demonstrated by the variety and sheer number of plants she grew, and by the extensive space

---

[1] Sir Robert Southwell was elected President of the Royal Society in 1692.

[2] Badminton Estate (hereafter BE) MS FmF 1/5/9.

[3] James Edgar Dandy (ed.), *The Sloane Herbarium* (London: The British Museum, 1958), 209. Subtitled, 'An Annotated List of the Horti Sicci; With Biographical Accounts of the Principal Contributors', the *Sloane Herbarium* represents a significant corpus of writings about plants from the period in Sloane's possession and the men and (some) women whose work he valued.

[4] I would like to extend a note of gratitude to the current Duke of Beaufort for allowing me to work on Mary Somerset's manuscript letters and catalogues in the Muniments Room of the Badminton Estate. I wish also to thank Elaine Milsom, his gracious assistant, for helping me navigate these materials and for delicious hot chocolate on a cold, rainy afternoon among the musty family papers.

Locus Amoenus, First Edition. Edited by Alexander Samson. © 2012 The Authors.
Journal compilation © 2012 The Society for Renaissance Studies and Blackwell Publishing Ltd.

the plants occupied on the grounds at Badminton. Drawings made by Somerset found in the collections at the British Library and elsewhere demonstrate that she was invested in making a bold architectural statement with the plants she grew that would be as memorable as the architecture of the house her husband maintained. In one drawing in particular, we see extensive garden tree-lined alleys radiating out from a centre, with plants at the end of each. While it is not clear precisely how much actual acreage these alleys cover, it is sizeable.[5] Moreover, household accounts document the vast sums of money Somerset spent on improvements to various areas of the house, including the gardens: 'The accompt of the building of dry walls planting fensing trees and buying Elms for planting the walks' (1664–78), for example, totaling £24,702; by 1690, these expenses reached £29,760, and the list of expenses suggests that, even though these figures include expenses in addition to plants, the investment she made in the plants themselves was considerable. Still, it might be easy to assume that even a woman with her impressive horticultural skills in late seventeenth-century England would hardly have been thought to have made a more systematic contribution to the burgeoning disciplines of botany and horticulture than that.

However, Somerset's work with plants represented more than just an impressive acquisition of domestic and foreign species; it also resembled that of the foremost natural philosophers, the early scientists, of her day. In what reads as an experimental journal akin to what we might see in the hand of John Ray or Sir Hans Sloane, two of the most prominent seventeenth-century natural scientists, Somerset's papers detail both the product and, importantly, the ongoing process of her work: 'Dake-leaved Solanum sow'd in April 1691 it grows very well of cutings, it hath produced ripe seed, it is 4 foot 2 inches high, grows very well in any warme place in the garden in the summer.'[6] And in an entry that demonstrates exacting detail about planting the 'scarlet and black bean', Somerset expounds,

> The scarlet and black bean to be put wth the scarlet an upwards the egg shall first halfe fill'd wth the sheeps dung and then a pretty deal of bay salt, then fill it up wth sheeps dung thrust very hard put sheeps dung round the egg shell and fill the pott wth earth and put it in the hott bed.[7]

Such descriptions most obviously call to mind the kind of work so many early modern women did in their gardens at this time, and Somerset was clearly a woman who not only gardened with great enthusiasm, but who also took the time to record her ideas about gardening, a move that in itself suggests that

---

[5] British Library (hereafter BL), Sloane MS 4071, fol. 204. See also Chambers, who includes a copy of the drawing. Douglas Chambers. '"Storys of Plants": The Assembling of Mary Capel Somerset's Botanical Collection at Badminton', *Journal of the History of Collections* 9 (1) 1997.

[6] BL Sloane MS 4070 fols. 39v–65r.

[7] BL Sloane MS 4071 fol. 202.

she saw her skills with plants as potentially benefitting others, not just herself. Then what makes the way she describes her plants indicative of more than just good gardening? What makes her work more 'scientific' than that, and what does it matter that such work with plants is so frequently partitioned – as *either* gardening *or* science – in this way, for early modern men and women as well as for scholars today?[8] In revaluing the kind of work Somerset did and the knowledge it embodied, we can reposition her (and potentially, other women like her) as a player in the early fields of botany and horticulture, as a woman who saw herself as contributing to bodies of knowledge in significant and lasting ways.

'STORYS OF PLANTS': SOMERSET'S COLLECTIONS

Somerset's attentiveness to the growing process makes her endeavour not just one of planting practice but also of plant study. As such, what she characterizes as an 'innocent diversion of gardening' unfolds as reflection and experimentation inherent to her garden work and links hers to the work of the early horticulturalists and botanists of England. When Somerset writes of her experience with plants, for instance, 'this I proned [pruned]', 'this to be inquired into', and 'the biggest will blow the next yeer they must be kept under some pent house in the winter', she details a process of testing and hypothesis familiar to us today as the scientific model.[9] Like the seventeenth-century men who sought to understand and articulate the complex workings of the natural world, who used their own senses as well as rational thought as their guiding principles, so too does Somerset describe here, as she does similarly elsewhere, how her experience pruning and planting is cause for future testing – 'this to be inquired into' – and hypothesis, or speculation on cause-and-effect relationships of the past, present, and future – the proper conditions to allow the plants to 'blow' the following year. Such comments suggest that she saw the work she did with plants as not only specific to her estate conditions, since her instructions read as not strictly limited to these conditions alone, but also to the broader questions of how one might best cultivate in general contexts the species she identifies as well.

Somerset also regularly engaged in an exchange of ideas and plants with Royal Society Fellows, respected natural philosophers of the day (or, as we would know them today, horticulturalists and botanists proper) like Sir Hans Sloane, James (or Jacob) Petiver, William Sherard, Robert Southwell, and Jacob Bobart, all of whom engaged in a reciprocal exchange of horticultural

---

[8] The omission of work like Somerset's in such important and otherwise illuminating works in the history of science as Bruno Latour's *Science in Action* is telling. See Bruno Latour, *Science in Action: How to Follow Scientists and Engineers Through Society* (Cambridge: Harvard University Press, 1987). This essay calls for a revaluing of such work, in conjunction with the recovery of women scientists in the period, in order to evaluate more fully how bodies of knowledge are socially constructed and women's (often invisible) role in their construction.

[9] BL Sloane MS 4071, fols. 37–38.

advice and plants with her. Despite her marginalization from the annals of science, Somerset was clearly part of the inner circle.[10] These many letters suggest that they saw her as their equal who wielded power as both patron and proven horticulturalist in her own right. As part of this inner circle, Somerset's lists of plants, directions for growing, and regular correspondence with these male scientists can tell us much about how she regarded herself and how she was regarded by them as a trusted botanical authority. From these letters, for example, we can surmise that the duchess regularly accepted seeds from Gresham College, academic home to many of the Royal Society activities, with the idea that she would experiment with the seeds they sent her, then report on her successes and failures and compare them with plants she raised from seeds she collected from her own garden:

> I had indifferent good succes wth the seeds you gave mee, severall of them have produced large plants wch I hope will prove trees, I cannot brag of the number that I have rais'd of those from the colledg, 2 of them are blowne, I have sent you one leake, to shew you the colour tho indeed it is too its prejudice being much more beautiful upon the plant, the silke cotton thrives very well, & so does the Gourd but that do's not yet put out a flower, I have severall plants rais'd from y^r Shaddock that are more then seven inchs high, this hot summer brings on my plants to such a height that I am forc't to top plants that are in the ground again the wall in the orengree [orangerie] wch is 18 foot high . . . I shall be very impatient till you performe y^r promis of affording mee one of the books you are publishing, I must not forget to thanke you for the transactions wch I have constantly receav'd the paper enclos'd is what seeds of the colledge ones that are yet come up.[11]

Somerset writes to Sloane again, a letter in which she links her knowledge about plants to his as she describes various fruits, seeds, flowers, and leaves she sends him, which makes her think about his soon-to-be-published botanical book.

> I send leavs & flowers of what are rais'd of the colled'g seeds, they are so few not worth their sending them, I have kept some of all the sorts of seeds, perhaps I may have better sunes [sun?] next year, they were so few that I have fill'd the small booke wth some others that I thinke were not in the former . . . I inquire often how y^r book that you writ mee word was in the presse went on, when it is finish'd y^r promis will bee claim'd by [me].[12]

---

[10] We must keep in mind that many of the duchess's correspondents were also regular correspondents of prestigious scientists of the day, including John Ray, John Evelyn, and Hans Sloane. For further discussion, see especially (with respect to how these scientists played a role in Mary Somerset's life in particular) Chambers, 'Storys of Plants', 50, and (for general discussion) Shapin, *The Scientific Revolution* (Chicago and London: The University of Chicago Press, 1996).

[11] BL Sloane 4062 fol. 25 (Badminton, 10 July, likely in the late 1690s).

[12] BL Sloane MS 4061 fol. 21 (Badminton, 13 December).

Not only does it seem that Somerset is engaged in a regular practice of testing the seeds that come from Gresham College and her own estate, but her references to the 'Transactions' and Sloane's book tell us that she saw her efforts as potentially contributing to the formally codified knowledge about plants associated with the Royal Society Fellows themselves. It appears that Sloane thought highly enough of her to readily send her copies of the 'Transactions' at a time when few women were assumed to have an interest let alone an ability to comprehend the mysteries of the natural world that the 'Transactions' presumed to illuminate; and Sloane's apparent 'promis' of giving her a fresh copy of his new book, still at the press, demonstrates that her skills with and understanding of plants was extensive enough to warrant her having access to the most up-to-date scientific claims about the vegetable kingdom.

These and the other many manuscripts preserved in the British Library, the Botany Library at the Natural History Museum (London), and in the Muniments Room at the Badminton estate all clearly show that Somerset imagined herself as more than just one who used others' advice for growing; she saw herself as one who worked to create new knowledge as well.[13] Historian Douglas Chambers praises Somerset's accomplishments, suggesting that Somerset indeed made contributions to the developing fields of botany and horticulture. But while he writes that she successfully expanded 'both its vocabulary and its subject' and that her work represents 'the very process of empiricism and abstraction' that Locke outlined in his *Essay on Human Understanding*,[14] he also characterizes her copious lists of plants as merely 'collections of collections'.[15] We know from her references that Somerset had clearly been reading some of the most influential botanists of the day: Gerard, Lyte, Dodoens, Parkison, Plukenet, Lyden, Ray, Boyle, and from the encyclopedic *Hortus Malabaricus* (which she refers to throughout as 'HM').[16] Yet, even the great John Ray, in one of his frequent letters to Sir Hans Sloane, characterizes his own writings as a 'Collection': 'the greatest part of my Supplement being only a Collection of such names & Titles gathered out of Books'.[17] Even as Chambers goes far to recuperate Somerset's status as a plant collector, gardener, and even to a large extent horticulturalist and botanist, then, I would argue that we need still to go further. To claim that the duchess's work represented merely 'collections of collections', as he does, ultimately underplays the new knowledge about plants and plant classification to which Somerset saw herself as contributing. Her manuscripts clearly document more than just 'collections of collections'.

---

[13] BL Sloane MS 4071: catalogue of Plants at Badminton, and some of plants in Chelsea garden; some in the duchess's hand, some not. These detail her elaborated instructions (as opposed to just a list) or revisions.
[14] Chambers, 'Storys of Plants', 58, 59.
[15] *Ibid.*, 50.
[16] See, for example, BL Sloane MS 4071 fol. 218.
[17] BL Sloane MS 4036 fol. 289 (10 March 1696).

As part of her effort to create new knowledge based on her own cultivating practice, the duchess certainly drew from men's books (the 'collections' so well documented by Chambers), but she draws particular attention to the plants in her care that she cannot find in others' books, indicating that she saw herself as one who identified what she believed might be new species (or species new to England), one who was on the cutting edge and not just who implemented others' teachings. In some cases, she writes of plants she grows that she does not believe are already identified in her books, as she does in 1693, when she says, 'These plants I can find no figures of in any of my books, they are therefore to be described as they grow now at Badminton 1693: Sugar Apple, Adinofrle (?) or Bixa Ov no figure, described in Ray, Anhena or Senna hexaphylla Leyden described 577.'[18] Or, in 1702, when she insists, 'These are in none of my books, March [1702]: the marks of blew paper in any of my books, are marks I put of plants, that I am doubtfull whether they bee amonge my plants, upon this paper the number & the letter.'[19] Similarly, she writes of the 'Adinostle or Bixa Ovieda or Manaw or Roncon tree', that

> The leafe is shaped and the colour of the leafe like the leafe of the Judas tree it grew the first year [1?] foot inchs it had no branchs but the leavs grew out of the body the leavs shed in March; and then it begun to put out new buds, I cannot yet find any figure of it in any of my books.'[20]

In other cases, though, Somerset directly revises the work of her male sources to correct their mistakes and reflect what she saw as more accurate information, citing her horticultural successes at Badminton as authorizing her to do so. She counters the opinion of her own gardener, Mr Adams, for instance, in an entry from 1692, when she remarks, 'That in the stone called so by Adams [her gardener] is some other plant.'[21] And she questions the accuracy (or at least the universal applicability) of great botanical works and writers when, in seeming frustration, she insists, 'none of the Lyrium in Parkisons H are like those plants of mine that Mr Bobart calls so to send to Mr D[oody?] for seeds of these things they being seeds used by the Apothecary' and 'HM 1:39, Balam Pulli; Parkison 237 Tamarind; Pluknet 64:4 not well described by any of them the plants I have being more beautifull then any of these prints.'[22] For the Duchess of Beaufort, her personal growing experience trumps that of the foremost botanists and writers of her day, as her regular revision of their ideas and observations about plants demonstrates that she regarded herself as their equal. In effect, the duchess identifies incorrect information from her books and demands that her information should replace theirs. Somerset elsewhere calls attention to the

---

[18] BL Sloane MS 4070, fol. 79v.
[19] BL Sloane MS 4072, fols. 1–2.
[20] BL Sloane MS 3343, fols. 173–174r.
[21] BL Sloane MS 4071 fol. 142 (21 September 1692).
[22] BL Sloane MS 4070 fols. 64–64v and BL Sloane MS 4070 fol. 59, respectively.

fact that certain trees in Plukenet's book (a highly respected source for plant classification and description) were miscategorized. She writes, 'Pluk 140:3 Spanish Ash, should have been wth the Trees'; 'Pluk 185:1 Callameter, or Milkwood in Pluk is Galactoxylon, this should have been amongst the trees'; and 'Pluk 185:1 Wild Callabash and Wild Cashe trees, should have been wth the trees.'[23] Not only do her descriptions demonstrate that she privileges her experience with growing and plant identification above Plukenet, but she also inherently places her personal standing as a horticulturalist over his and, elsewhere, over others' as well.

MAKING EXPERIMENT MATTER: WRITING AND THE DIFFERENCE IT MAKES

The question remains, then, how did Mary Somerset, Duchess of Beaufort, go from being among the horticultural elite in post-Reformation England to relative obscurity today as either a premiere gardener or as a woman who demonstrated an impressive knowledge about plants? In a recent biography of Mary Somerset and her husband, Henry, Molly McClain highlights the duchess's achievements and collections of plants, a forty-year enterprise that resulted in the 'largest collection of exotic plants in England'.[24] And yet, McClain almost exclusively emphasizes the duchess's reliance upon 'friends and relatives', as well as upon male authorities (including at times her own husband) and professionals, for the information she had about them.[25]

One possible reason for Mary Somerset's accepted reputation as a good gardener while being marginalized from the annals of science may relate to the fact that the disciplines of horticulture and botany were themselves still in the process of being defined,[26] determined in large part by one's ability to conduct public experiments and publish accounts of them. As Adrian Johns argues in *The Nature of the Book*, the New Science mobilized by the work of Francis Bacon and later others was codified in the latter half of the seventeenth century by Fellows of the Royal Society, whose published experiments and works on natural philosophy established them as professional 'scientists'

---

[23] BL Sloane MS 3343 fol. 265.

[24] Molly McClain, *Beaufort: The Duke and His Duchess, 1657-1715* (New Haven and London: Yale University Press, 2001), 120.

[25] Historian Londa Schiebinger similarly positions Mary Somerset as something of a contradiction. On the one hand, Schiebinger sees Somerset as 'no amateur gardener' (despite Schiebinger's inclusion of her in the section on 'Armchair Botanists'). On the other, Schiebinger frames Somerset's contributions as a subset of the great Sir Hans Sloane's, subordinating the Duchess's twelve-volume herbarium to just one among many in Sloane's 'stockpile of specimens' which, she argues, 'catapulted *him* into the top echelons of British science' (my emphasis). See Londa Schiebinger and Claudia Swan (eds.), *Colonial Botany: Science, Commerce, and Politics in the Early Modern World* (Philadelphia: University of Pennsylvania Press, 2005), 59, 58.

[26] While the disciplinary differences between horticulture and botany are more defined today, with the former being more related to cultivation practices and the latter to the scientific study of plants, these disciplinary boundaries were by no means clear in the seventeenth century in England. Rather, a more general boundary between amateur and professional pertained in these and other domains.

rather than amateur observers of the natural world.[27] Women, for whom circulation in the public venues where experiments were conducted and discussed (such as coffee houses and universities) or public modes of idea exchange (the print marketplace – books, newspapers, etc), had inherently limited access to such ways of establishing their claims to knowledge;[28] and though she was an elite woman with options other women would not have had, Mary Somerset was similarly limited. Women may not have had the opportunities of their male contemporaries to assert their knowledge in such ways, but a concerted effort to uncover the ideas they preserved in manuscript commonplace books, letters, and catalogues can help us rethink the importance of their work and its bearing on the development of early modern science.

One significant obstacle to such recovery and re-evaluation work is that, unlike the men of the time (like Sloane), whose ideas about natural philosophy dominated the print marketplace, Somerset's legacy, like that of most early modern women who may have done similar work, and like the very gardens they planted, exists almost exclusively in ephemera. As McClain writes in summation of Somerset's life:

> Mary died in January 1715, leaving behind little evidence of her life. She exists now only in the silvery fragments of letters and well-worn account books, in fading silk embroidery and catalogues of exotic plants. While her husband's achievements were preserved in the façade of Badminton, her legacy – the blossom of a scarlet hibiscus or the narrow leaf of a China Sumack – died and slowly faded into dust.[29]

McClain's characterization of Somerset's work and knowledge demonstrates the need to reorient how we trace such legacies of anyone, male or female, as they inform our understanding of the creation of bodies of knowledge. To say that Somerset 'only' survives in the fragments that remain of her correspondence and other manuscript collections undermines the importance unpublished writings can play in reconstructing the extent to which her ideas were valued by others then or might deserved to be valued today. After all, Somerset's steadfast record-keeping culminated in her assembling her ideas into an experimental edition of her botanical and horticultural knowledge, a twelve-volume herbarium she painstakingly compiled and had bound. This herbarium represents the collective knowledge in the copious catalogues and myriad hours spent caring for flowers, shrubs, and trees on the grounds at her

---

[27] Adrian Johns, *The Nature of the Book: Print and Knowledge in the Making* (Chicago and London: The University of Chicago Press, 1998), 444–542.

[28] See Steven Shapin, 'Houses of Experiment', *Isis* (79), 1988, 373–404. Shapin discusses how the various spaces of experiment that helped legitimate work as 'scientific', though he does not address the fact that women's work with plants typically occurred in quite different places. By not looking at alternative spaces and alternative practices that may otherwise be scientific in nature, I would argue, we further the gendered division in the sciences more broadly.

[29] McClain, *Beaufort*, 215.

estate and in the hothouses where she nurtured seedlings and cared for ailing plants. To see Somerset's influence as extending only so far as the lifespan of the plants she herself accumulated or tended, then, is to underestimate the importance of these bound volumes, despite or perhaps even because they were never published.[30] And in fact, the very ways in which McClain laments Somerset's increasingly less visible contributions to early modern science reinforce the split between amateur and professional, between manuscript and print culture that in turn further disallows women's recognition as makers of knowledge across periods and disciplines.

This seemingly easy split between manuscript and print in terms of how each is ascribed relative permanence,[31] however, is complicated by the case of Somerset's herbarium. She writes Hans Sloane about a 'parcell' of plants, most likely part of what ultimately became the twelve-volume herbarium still in the Sloane holdings in the Botany Library at the Natural History Museum in London.[32] On the one hand, as when she calls hers an 'innocent diversion of gardening', Somerset seems to undervalue the contributions she seeks to make in her herbarium. Somerset similarly requests Sloane's approval of her descriptions, many of which she cross-references with botanical authorities such as Parkinson, Petiver, and Ray, as she does, for instance, in 1699/1700, when she writes,

> I return you many thanks good Docter for giving y^r selfe the trouble of getting mee a booke bound for my Parchments, when they are just into the booke, I will have loose papers put into the booke wth those names, I think belong to them if you will bee troubl'd wth them, to see the faults before they are in the booke, to send it to you, it being pitty to have them after so much charge to bee false nam'd wch may easily bee done by mee, most of them being rais'd by seed wch came wthout names.[33]

The humble stance Somerset takes in this letter to Sloane is not unique to her (or to those who might regard themselves as professionals rather than amateurs), and yet it bears a striking to resemblance to a similar letter from the prominent philosopher, John Locke, when he writes Sloane asking that he review his work on natural history as well:

---

[30] This herbarium was originally preserved by Hans Sloane in his collections in the British Museum and is now located in the Botany Library of the Natural History Museum in London.

[31] For a more lengthy discussion about the relationship between manuscript and print, and amateur versus professional work supported by the division between them, see Roger Chartier (ed.), *The Culture of Print: Power and the Uses of Print in Early Modern Europe* (Princeton: Princeton University Press, 1987) and Elizabeth Eisenstein, *The Printing Press as an Agent for Change* (Cambridge: Cambridge University Press (hereafter CUP), 1979). For discussion of this question as it relates specifically to natural philosophy, see Elizabeth Spiller, *Science, Reading, and Renaissance Literature: The Art of Making Knowledge, 1580-1670* (Cambridge: CUP, 2004) and Marina Frasca-Spada and Nick Jardine (eds.), *Books and the Sciences in History* (Cambridge: CUP, 2000).

[32] See Natural History Museum, Botany Library (hereafter NHM BL) HS 235.

[33] BL Sloane MS 4061 fols. 17–17r (25 September 1699/1700).

And if y^u thinke the history of them worth the publishing to the world with a cut of then y^u know y^u may command me in greater matters than that, only I thinke what I write for my owne private memory ought to be verified & corrected a little before it appear in the world. To wch possibly I may finde something to adde, for if I misremember not I visited this yonge man a second time, & tooke some farther notes, these I will looke out amongst my papers & bring to town with me & then y^u shall dispose of the whole as y^u think fit.[34]

Locke looks to Sloane as an advisor about what of his materials should be printed (and the accuracy of what he has written) in much the same way as Somerset does. So, while she is humble about how much of the work she has got right, Somerset readily sees her work as in dialogue with Sloane's own botanical studies, a conversation in which she is an authority over as well as a student of knowledge not entirely different from that which took place between respected male scientists.

In two separate letters, though, Somerset's discussion of her herbarium conveys a sense of its permanence, even if it is still a compilation in manuscript, and she never suggests she believes it will be printed and sold; in it, she translates a lifetime of plant experimentation into bound volumes to be collected and reviewed by others. A letter in secretary hand to a 'Mr. Gosline' is clear about the parameters of the binding process, suggesting that she wanted to retain a great deal of control over the process by which her knowledge became codified in bound books. In July 1706, her amanuensis writes from Badminton,

My Lady Dutchesse comands me to lett you know that her Grace desires you will goe to Mr Beale [?] and know the Booke-binders name that bound the last Philosophicall Transactions for her Grace and let him binde these, and if there be any wanting to add to them the last of her Graces is December 1704:

Her Grace desires you will deliver the inclos^d Box with your owne hand to Mr Robert Child Goldsmith at Temple Barr: and that you'l goe to Doctor Sloane and give her Graces service to him and let him know she requests him to assist her Grace in haveing her Draught of Plant's bound and she desires you'l show him the inclos^d paper which is the exact measures of the Parchments.

There is also some very good Prints that her Grace has which she desires to have bound in Bookes that they may be preserved, she desires you would also advise with the Doctor who may be trusted with them that they may not be chang'd (there being her Grace says, so little honesty in the world, [ ]) have enclos^d a list that the Doctor may direct whith or these in 2: or 3: volumes or may be bound in one.[35]

---

[34] BL Sloane MS 4036, fol. 294 (22 March 1696/97).
[35] BL Sloane MS 3343, fol. 115r.

As demonstrated by this and the previous letter, Somerset saw herself as an authority who disseminated as well as received knowledge about plants. In this way, she was much like Sloane and the other scientists she corresponds with, as their letter too, allowed them to share and challenge each other's ideas.[36] Somerset insists that the contents of her 'Draught of Plant's' 'not be changed', even by the likes of the illustrious Sir Hans Sloane. In fact, her precise instructions about the 'exact measure of the Parchments' they be fitted to, demonstrates her desire to control not just the content, but also the parameters of their binding into books. Moreover, the consistency of the parchments in the herbarium suggests that the duchess may well have sent the dried plant species already affixed to the very parchments that became part of the herbarium's pages. And, by sending her parchments and plants to the same book binder who bound Sloane's own 'Philosophical Transactions', much as she refers to them, just as she clearly has read the 'Transactions' personally sent to her by Sloane as I discussed earlier, Somerset associates the horticultural and botanical knowledge her work represents with that of the Royal Society fellows, for whom the 'Philosophical Transactions' were a regular venue for legitimizing their ideas.

Well preserved in the Botany Library of the Natural History Museum in London, Somerset's herbarium (second only in the library to the extensive plant collections and horticultural ruminations of a Mr Biddle, vicar) we find plants and some seeds that are familiar from her lists of plants in the Sloane manuscripts.[37] Assuming a reader familiar with botanical descriptions, the plants included in these volumes typically refer to the corresponding entries in published authorities, such as Plukenet, Parkinson, Ray, and the *Hortus Malabaricus*; and while her work indicates a clearly pre-Linnaean system (and her entries do not have a defined taxonomic classification, but are instead more a random assortment of plants), the specimens she includes are, as the entry on the inside cover declares,

> very well preserved and flourishing there better then in any garden of Europe I ever saw; Her Grace having what she called an Infirmary or small green house, to which she removed sickly or unthriving plants, and with proper culture by the care of an old woman under her Grace's direction brought them to greater perfection then at Hampton court or anywhere. Most of the plants are referred to [by] Mr. Ray.[38]

[36] See, for instance, BL Sloane MS 4036, especially fols. 43, 55, 63, 289, and 294, all among members of the Royal Society Fellows, including John Ray, Sir Hans Sloane, John Locke, and Jacob Bobarts.

[37] Mark Spencer, curator at the Botany Library, likens what Somerset does in compiling the information contained in the many published books of her respected, well-known counterpart and correspondent, Sir Hans Sloane. I would like to offer my deepest gratitude to Dr Spencer for giving up an afternoon to go meticulously through the herbarium and to assist me in contextualizing its significance.

[38] NHM BL HS 66.

While Somerset's methods of plant classification may not in themselves be considered 'scientific' today any more than they were in the seventeenth century, details present in the herbarium itself demonstrates that these bound volumes were valued enough by Sloane for them to become a permanent part of his library. Not only does Somerset's herbarium represent an impressive body of work that resembles the sort of assembling of plant specimens by Sloane himself and others, but we also know that Sloane loaned the duchess's herbaria to John Ray, noted botanist, who made various annotations on them, including some (though not many) revisions to her descriptions.[39] For Ray to borrow the volumes shows that he took Somerset's work seriously. Judging from the notations he makes, on the rare occasions when he does make them, it seems that Ray was checking her work. At times, Ray does correct Somerset, but he writes nothing, even in instances when the herbarium seems to seek identification of certain plants, suggesting perhaps that the plants unknown to the Duchess were also unknown to Ray.[40] And, it suggests as well that he approved of her work. He ultimately concludes, 'the specimens . . . are very fair ones, and curiously dried and preserved.'[41] To have that sort of recognition from Ray is akin to an endorsement of the ideas Somerset's herbarium forwarded.

Somerset's herbarium exists in only one copy; it was never printed to be circulated in the public marketplace like the work of the natural philosophers who sought to make a name for themselves as they demonstrated their knowledge of plants in their own writings. It might be easy to disregard the importance of such a massive collection of dried plants and their descriptions, or at least to assume that if this work mattered, it (or at least the ideas in it) would more directly have found its way to print. It might also be easy to dismiss Somerset's knowledge about plants as only the amateur musings of a woman who may well have known a great deal about growing plants, but who made no significant or lasting contributions to formalized scientific discourse about plants. However, Sloane's careful preservation of Somerset's herbarium in his personal collection suggest that he saw the ideas in it as worth saving, as material to reference in his and others' own study of the vegetable kingdom. And the fact that the male professionals of her day not only sought Somerset's feedback about the practical aspects of growing plants, but that they also engaged with her ideas in a serious manner and saw her writings as worth preserving, warrants a re-evaluation of how we think about her ideas and writings today.

If we are truly to understand the contribution women made to botany and horticulture in the early modern period, we might take a lesson from Somerset's own books and the process of knowledge acquisition, experimentation,

[39] As per discussion with Mark Spencer, curator of the Botany Library.
[40] NHM BL HS 235.
[41] See Ray *Correspondence* 437 (NHM BL HS 131–42); see also Dandy, 211.

and engagement with the circulation of ideas they represent. The case of Mary Somerset demonstrates one example of how women actively sought status as both consumers and producers of botanical knowledge, that they were regarded as authorities in their own right. That is, Somerset did more than simply act as an intermediary, practicing the authoritative wisdom about plants in books by men; she created new knowledge about the plants she grew by using her experience with the plants themselves to augment the information about them in authoritative accounts found in books. By quantifying her plants and directions for planting in such a systematic way (even if not to a clear taxonomic classification, as would emerge under Linnaeus), and by putting her knowledge down in writing (and multiple books), Somerset declared her horticultural endeavour as more than just an informal pastime. Her manuscript books detail a woman who saw herself as a kind of amateur botanist, one who contributed to bodies of knowledge and whose experience with plant cultivation authorized her writing. And revaluing Somerset's engagement with and potential contributions to horticulture and botany may help us in turn to revalue the copious work of so many women like her, whose ideas, penned in manuscripts rather than put into print, seemingly disappear like the gardens they planted.

University of North Carolina at Charlotte

6

Outdoor pursuits: Spanish gardens, the huerto *and Lope de Vega's* Novelas a Marcia Leonarda

ALEXANDER SAMSON

Climate and geography shaped the ways in which landscape was enjoyed as well as the form taken by Spanish gardens. Although there were attempts to imitate the great formal gardens of Italy and northern Europe, Castilian and Andalusian riverbanks continued to figure prominently in the outdoor pursuits of the nobility and in literary evocations of the *locus amoenus*. The lexis of gardens in early modern Spain reflected the imprecision and differences between the unbounded, informal and shady retreats from the city in the south, and the verdant, enclosed worlds of gardens in the north. Lope de Vega's short stories, the *Novelas a Marcia Leonarda*, are one of numerous fictionalizations of these liminal spaces that play on their moral ambivalence and contrast pleasure in their openness and informality with their hidden and public dangers.

Pliny the Elder as procurator of Hispania Tarraconensis had devoted attention in his *Naturalis Historia* to Spain's plants, describing the apples, figs, plums and pomegranates, the ornamental box, broom, juniper, rose, yew and others that abounded in Iberia.[1] Garden culture in the peninsula had been definitively shaped by the Muslim and Islamic gardens of the Syrian Ummayads, who adapted the aqueducts and irrigation left behind by the Romans.[2] Numerous plants that were cultivated in Spain from as early as the tenth century were not introduced into northern Europe until the sixteenth, everything from spinach and apricots to the caulifower and white jasmine.[3] Plants from the New World, on the other hand, often found their way whether as images or seeds, all over Europe from nurseries in southern Spain, such as

---

[1] See Pliny the Elder, *Naturalis Historia*, 12.7, 14.30 and 71, 16.32 and 198, 17.166, 170 and 249, 18.336, 25.84ff.

[2] The best known Islamic gardens of pre-modern Spain include the Alhambra (Generalife) in Granada, Real Alcázar in Seville, Palacio de Galiana in Toledo and Alcázar in Córdoba. The primacy of Arabic achievements in the field of gardening and agriculture can be gleaned from the 'Andalusian Georgics', *Ibn Luyun: Tratado de Argicultura*, trans. Joaquina Eguaras Ibáñez (Granada: Patronato de la Alhambra, 1988), *Libro de Argicultura, su autor el Doctor excelente Abu Zacaria Iahia*, trans. José Antonio Banqueri, fac. ed. Expiración García Sánchez and Esteban Hernández Bermejo (Madrid: Ministerio de Argicultura Pesca y Alimentación, 1988) and Ibn Bassal, *Libro de agricultura*, trans. José Maria Millás Vallicrosa and Mohamed Aziman (Tetuan: Instituto Muley el-Hasan, 1955).

[3] See John Harvey, 'Garden Plants of Moorish Spain: A Fresh Look', *Garden History* 20 (1992), 71–82, here 72.

Locus Amoenus, First Edition. Edited by Alexander Samson. © 2012 The Authors.
Journal compilation © 2012 The Society for Renaissance Studies and Blackwell Publishing Ltd.

Seville's famous botanic garden founded by Simón Tovar, a long-standing correspondent of the botanist Clusius.[4] A botanic garden had also been founded at the University of Valencia as early as 1567. The garden history of the peninsula is still unfurrowed ground with almost no survivals from the early modern period.[5] One exception, El Buen Retiro, was given by Olivares to Philip IV in 1631; its gardens designed by the Florentine, Cosme Lotti, part of the team that had worked on the Bóboli gardens. Lotti had arrived in Madrid in 1628, accompanied by a carpenter and two gardeners.[6] The inauguration took place in 1632 and was celebrated in verse by Lope. There is also a description in a letter by the English ambassador Walter Aston, about some festivities in 1636 involving new watersports.[7] The gardens blended Italian Renaissance influences with Baroque exuberance (see Fig. 1).[8]

Another famous garden from this period in Madrid belonging to the Flemish nobleman Jean de Croy, Count of Solre, was depicted on Pedro de Texeria's city plan from 1656. De Croy also had a vegetable garden on the banks of the Manzanares acquired from the Marquise of Villareal in 1628, which included a pavilion with paintings by Juan van der Hamen, an irrigation pump, numerous orange, lemon and lime trees, fields of barley, asparagus and artichokes. Van her Hamen's painting *Offering to Flora* (1627), owned by de Croy and depicting more than fifty different varieties of flower, typical of Madrid gardens of the early seventeenth century, may portray elements of de Croy's *huerto* (see Figure 2).[9] Flowers are scarce in paintings of the sixteenth century and where they appear in pastoral novels, it is more as a literary device and evocative backdrop than a rural reality. However, a fashion for flowers led painters like Pérez Sierra to specialise in them, to such an extent that Palomino doubted whether he produced more beautiful specimens in his garden in the calle de las Infantas or on canvas. The poet Luis de Góngora insisted in a contract following an unfortunate period under the stewardship of Cristóbal de Heredia that whoever rented his Cordoban house have a gardener to look

[4] Peter Mason, 'A Dragon Tree in the Garden of Eden: A Case Study of the Mobility of Objects and their Images in Early Modern Europe', *Journal of the History of Collections* 18 (2006), 169–85, 175.

[5] A number of valuable books on Spanish garden history have appeared in the late twentieth century: María Teresa de Ozores y Saavedra, Marquesa de Casa Valdés, *Jardines de España*, (Madrid: Aguilar, 1973) was the first substantial, richly illustrated book on its subject. Later scholarly books have included Consuelo M. Correcher, *The Gardens of Spain* (New York: Harry N. Abrams, 1993) and Carmen Añón Feliú, Monica Luengo Añón, and Ana Luengo Añón, *Jardines artísticos de España* (Madrid: Espasa Calpe, 1995). However, much remains to be done and the documentation of Spain's historic gardens is sparse. Nor has garden archaeology been pursued with vigour. At Madinat al-Zahra, one of the most important garden sites in Europe, archaeological investigation has been carried out spasmodically since the early twentieth century – but only 10 per cent of its area had been excavated by 2001.

[6] Ozores y Saavedra, *Jardines de España*, 127.

[7] Gregorio Marañon, *El Conde-Duque de Olivares* (Madrid: Espasa Calpe, 1958), 127.

[8] See Jonathan Brown and John H. Elliott, *A Palace for a King: the Buen Retiro and the Court of Philip IV* (London and New Haven: Yale University Press, rev. ed. 2003), 34, 56, 64 and 65, for images including the Casa del Campo, Pardo, El Escorial and Buen Retiro. See also Velazquez's recently restored *La tela real* for an image of landscape in the vicinity of El Pardo.

[9] See Felix Scheffler and Luis Ramón-Laca, 'The Gardens of Jean de Croy, Count of Solre, in Madrid and the "Offering to Flora" by Juan van der Hamen', *Garden History* 33 (2005), 135–45; esp. 135–7 and 141.

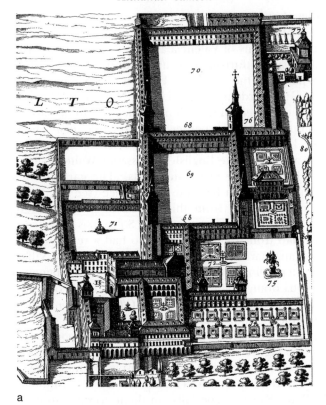

a

Fig. 1a   Pedro Teixeira Albernaz, detail from *Topographía de la villa de Madrid (El Buen Retiro Palace)* (Antwerp: 1656), 20 sheets of paper 45 x 56cm, Madrid, Museo Municipal de Madrid

after the plot.[10] Lope de Vega invoked gardens as metaphor, real and imagined spaces, in a series of poems, letters, plays and prose fictions, describing actual gardens and landscapes, imagined pastoral arcadias, as well as his own garden and horticultural activity in the Calle de Francos in the heart of Madrid. He was familiar with Andrés de Laguna's translation of Dioscorides, whether or not it played a part in his own practical experience as a gardener. He made full use of the resonances of the garden as an Edenic, georgic space redolent with allegorical possibilities, both political and sexual, and *hortus conclusus*, symbolic of virginity.

Castilian climate shaped the particular form taken by the *locus amoenus* in the literary imagination as well as the kinds of outdoor pursuit that were represented there, leisure activities that blurred the boundaries between

[10]   Emilio Orozco Díaz, *Temas del barroco de poesía y pintura* (Granada: Universidad de Granada, 1989), 'Ruinas y jardines su significación y valor en la temática del barroco', 121–76, here 141 and 143.

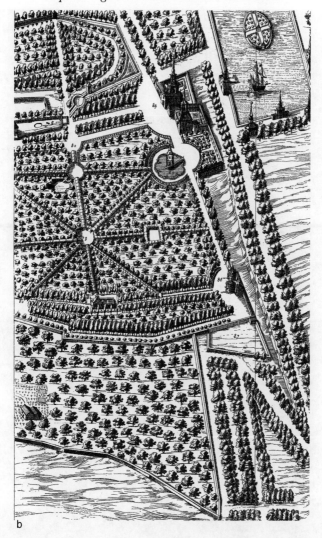

Fig. 1b   Pedro Teixeira Albernaz, detail from *Topographía de la villa de Madrid (gardens of the El Buen Retiro Palace)* (Antwerp: 1656), 20 sheets of paper 45 × 56 cm, Madrid, Museo Municipal de Madrid

public and private and saw Spain's great formal gardens becoming tourist attractions for throngs of people, high and low. The Spanish 'huerta' or 'huerto' (cultivated natural spaces created for leisure with trees and flowers) often found besides a river was tied to specific social practices, outdoor pursuits whose public nature was peculiar to early modern Castile. The language for describing these spaces is confused and ambiguous in a way that reflects their liminal status. Gardens, particularly those parks and meadows

Fig. 2   Juan van der Hamen, *Offering to Flora*, 1627, oil on canvas, 216 × 140 cm, Madrid, Museo del Prado

next to riverbanks, play a central role in the literary representations in early modern Spain of amorous intrigue and the leisure pursuits of the nobility; from *La Celestina* with its medieval walled garden at the heart of the plot both literally, morally and metaphorically, to the *escudero*'s assignations with prostitutes in *Lazarillo de Tormes*, the compusive liar Don García's banquet speech in the Mexican Juan Ruiz de Alarcón's play *La verdad sospechosa* and Cervantes' innocent hidalgo family in 'La fuerza de la sangre' from his *Novelas ejemplares*, torn apart returning from a day in the cool shade of the bank.[11] Other great cities also of course had riverside gardens.[12] However, the particular form that the *locus amoenus* took in the Spanish literary imagination was shaped by the climatic conditions that determined the plants, forms and uses of gardens and outdoor spaces in the different parts of the Iberian penninsula. The heat and aridity of the parched Castilian plains encouraged literary evocations in which the characteristic shade and water figure prominently.

Garcilaso de la Vega gave definitive form to the Spanish *locus amoenus* in his *Third Eclogue* and established the model for a host of imitators,[13] with its blend of mythological, classical and Italianate themes, focusing on loss and death transformed through art.[14]

> Cerca del Tajo, en soledad amena,
> de verdes sauces hay una espesura,
> toda de hiedra revestida y llena
> que por el tronco va hasta el altura
> y así la teje arriba y encadena
> que'l sol no halla paso a la verdura;
> el agua baña el prado con sonido,
> alegrando la hierba y el oído. (ll. 57–64)[15]

---

[11] The speech in Alarcón's play is a model of *conceptista* ekphrasis: 'Entre las opacas sombras/ y opacidades espesas/ que el soto formaba de olmos,/ y la noche de tinieblas,/ . . . / Llegó en su coche mi dueño,/ dando invidia a las estrellas,/ a los aires suavidad,/ y alegría a la ribera', *La verdad sospechosa*, ed. Alva Eversole (Madrid: Cátedra, 2006), 65–7.

[12] See the vivid descriptions of some in London in C. Paul Christianson, *The Riverside Gardens of Thomas More's London* (London: Yale University Press, 2005). See also Anton van den Wyngaerde's view of London, in Howard Colvin and Susan Foister (eds.), *The Panorama of London circa 1544* (London: London Topographical Society, 1996) and Franz Hogenberg, *Civitas orbis terrarum, c.* 1572, Guildhall Library, Corporation of London.

[13] Garcilaso's vision of nature derived from Sannazaro, Ariosto, Theocritus, Virgil and Caesar. He was imitated by amongst others Diego Hurtado de Mendoza, particularly *Melibeo-Damón* and *Fábula de Adonis* in *Poesía*, ed. Luis Díaz Larios and Olga Gete Carpio (Madrid: Cátedra, 1990), 65–72, 167–93, and Luis de Góngora in his *Fábula de Polifemo y Galatea*, ed. Alexander A. Parker (Madrid: Cátedra, 2007).

[14] See Trevor Dadson, 'Rewriting the Pastoral: Góngora's *Fábula de Polifemo y Galatea*' in Isabel Torres (ed.), *Rewriting Classical Mythology in the Hispanic Baroque* (London: Tamesis, 2007), 38–54.

[15] The imaginary landscape of Garcilaso's *Egloga tercera* can be compared with descriptions in the chorographies of Pedro de Alcocer, *Historia o descripcion de la imperial ciudad de Toledo* (Toledo, 1554) and Pedro de Medina, *Libro de las grandezas* (Seville, 1548). Translation from *Selected Poems of Garcilaso de la Vega*, ed. and trans. John Dent-Young (London: University of Chicago Press, 2009), 125.

[Close by the Tagus, in pleasing solitude, there is a stand of willows, a dense grove all dressed and draped with ivy, whose multitude of stems goes climbing to the top and weaves a canopy thick enough to exclude the sun, denying it access to green leaves below; the sound of water fills this place making both plants and human ears rejoice.]

The Venetian ambassador Andrea Navagero, who had initially persuaded Garcilaso and Boscán to experiment with Italianate metres such as the 'octava real' of this poem, had been impressed in 1526, attending the wedding of Charles V and Isabel of Portugal, by the ordinary houses' gardens in Granada with pools of water, myrtle, rose and 'mosquetas', musk roses, celebrated throughout Spanish literature.[16] This type of 'Moorish' garden, whose epitome, the Generalife at the Alhambra, was the honeymooning royal couple's destination, went on influencing Spanish gardens throughout the sixteenth century. The Casa de Pilatos in Seville testifies to the survival of the Islamic garden, with its tiles and fountains, patios and running water, and its *convivencia* with imported Italian Renaissance styles.[17] The dialogue of Antonio de Torquemada's *Jardín de flores curiosas* is carefully situated in a space that mirrors that of the eglogue, a 'ribera del río' [riverbank] where 'paseándonos debajo destos árboles, gozando del frescor del aire y del río . . . debajo de esta sombra, para que el sol no nos toque; y aquí podremos oír el regocijado sonido que el agua' [walking beneath the trees, enjoying the freshness of the air and river . . . beneath this shadow, so that the sun does not touch us, here we can listen to the joyful sound of the water].[18] This escape from the heat of the day frames their philosophical contemplation of nature's diversity and variety, their consideration of the size of the world and its novelties.

The medieval, walled, female pleasure garden in *La Celestina* built for Melibea symbolizes the vanity of her father Pleberio's worldy dreams, the breaching of its walls and the loss of her virginity their end. The lovers first meet in this 'huerta', as Calisto retrieves his ironically straying bird of prey, their illicit liaison is consumated there, and in a symbolic re-enactment of the Fall from Eden, both will meet their deaths; Calisto falling after one of their trysts from the ladder propped up against the high, protective walls, spattering his brains on the cobbled street below, while Melibea commits suicide leaping from a tower overlooking the garden.[19] The plants referred to in *La Celestina*

---

[16] John H. Harvey, 'Spanish Gardens and Their Historical Background', *Garden History* 3 (1974), 7–14, here 7.

[17] On the Casa de Pilatos see Philippa Joseph, 'Travel, Acquisition, Display: Concerning Don Fadrique Enríquez de Ribera (1476–1539) and the Casa de Pilatos, Seville, *c.*1520–1540', PhD Thesis, Oxford Brookes 2010. For a general account of Spanish gardens see Constance Villiers-Stuart, *Spanish Gardens: Their History, Types and Features* (London: Batsford, 1929).

[18] Antonio de Torquemada, *Jardín de flores curiosas*, ed. Giovanni Allegra (Madrid: Clásicos Castalia, 1982), 102.

[19] Despite the fact that the word 'jardín' does not figure in the text, rather Melibea refers to her 'huerto', a word that occurs fifteen times in the text, the exhibition held in the Monasterio de San Juan, Burgos, commemorating the 500th anniversary of the publication of the first known edition was entitled *El jardín*

are herbs, roots and twigs with medicinal properties used by healers or witches, or applications in manufacturing beauty products.[20] In *Lazarillo de Tormes*, the garden is a space of sensual enjoyment and sexual temptation, his master's poverty and lack of virility exposed by the inability of his rhetoric to substitute for the food he lacks:

> en una huerta vi a mi amo en gran recuesta con dos rebozadas mujeres, al parecer de las que en aquel lugar no hacen falta, antes muchas tienen por estilo de irse a las mañanicas del verano a refrescar y almorzar sin llevar qué por aquellas frescas riberas.[21]

> [I ... perceive my master in a garden over the water, in great talk with two comely women, which by their countenance seemed to be some of them, whereof in Toledo a number are rifely found; and many of them take a use of going abroad early in the morning in summer time, to take the air in those gardens, and to break their fast without provision of their own under trees and shadows, near that pleasant river.]

In exactly the same spot on the banks of the Tagus in Toledo half a century later the family in Cervantes' *Novela ejemplar* 'La fuerza de la sangre' [The force of blood] 'Una noche de las calurosas del verano volvían de recrearse del río en Toledo ... el paso, tardo, por no pagar con cansancio la pensión que traen consigo las holguras que en el río o en la vega se toman en Toledo' [In a hot summers night, there returned from recreating themselves at the river of Toledo ... their pace slow, that they might not loose through wearines, those pleasures which the meadowes lying along the river side of Toledo, did afford them].[22] The social practice common throughout the sixteenth century of seeking refuge from the heat in landscapes cultivated specifically for public leisure, outdoor spaces and particularly riverbanks where there was a lack of clearly defined boundaries, was commented on by English visitors. The contrast between the verdant north and parched south provoked Sir Richard Wynn to make typically slighting comments about the outdoor facilities at the Alcázar palace in Madrid where Charles lodged in 1623 during his visit:

> About three in the afternoon, the Prince, as usually is his wont, went down into the garden, such a one as hardly deserves the name; so nasty and ill-favouredly

---

de Melibea (Sociedad Estatal para la Conmemoración de los Centenarios de Felipe II y Carlos V, 2000). The word 'huerta' is used in the plot summary introducing the opening dialogue.

[20] See Auto VI.

[21] *Lazarillo de Tormes*, ed. Roy O. Jones (Manchester: Manchester University Press, 1963), 33–4. The wordiness of David Rowland's *c.* 1568–9 translation underlines the difficulties of translating the references to the 'huerto/a' in the original, from Keith Whitlock (ed.), *The Life of Lazarillo de Tormes* (Warminster: Aris & Phillips, 2000), 117.

[22] Miguel de Cervantes, *Novelas ejemplares*, ed. Harry Sieber, 2 vols (Madrid: Cátedra, 1992), Vol. 2, p. 77. Translation is James Mabbe's *Exemplarie nouells in sixe books* (London: John Dawson, 1640), sig. Aa2r, 179.

kept that a farmer in England would be ashamed of such another: yet this he must walk in, or mew himself up in two little rooms all day long.[23]

Returning to the ambassadorial residence in the evening Wynn 'met at least five hundred coaches; most of them had all women in, going into the fields (as usually they do about that time of the day) to take the air.'[24] Even for households wealthy enough to possess gardens, recreational trips to the country and riverside were an established custom in early modern Madrid.

The lexis for describing landscape and garden, the spaces of aristocratic outdoor pursuits in early modern Spain was ambiguous in a way that reflected these culturally specific uses of space. Despite the definitions in Sebastián de Covarrubias' *El tesoro de la lengua Castellana* (1611), where 'jardín' was defined as 'Huerto de recreación de diversas flores y yerbas olorosas, con fuentes y cuadros repartidos con muchos lazos, y obra que llaman los latinos topiaria' [Huerto for leisure with diverse flowers and fragrant herbs, with fountains and parterres with many knots, and examples of what the Latins call topiary], the language of gardens meant that the terms 'huerto', 'huerta' and 'jardín' were used interchangeably.[25] The 'huerto' or 'huerta' were defined as 'lugar o en el campo o la ciudad o poblado en el cual se crían árboles frutales y hortaliza . . . el que tiene agua de pie y está en la ribera, ordinariamente llamamos huerta; los que son de flores y recreación se llaman jardínes' [somewhere in the country, city or town where fruit trees and garden produce are cultivated . . . those which have running water at their feet and are on a riverbank are normally called a *huerta*; those that have flowers and are for recreation are called gardens].[26] The fact that the definitions are made in terms of each other and the precise nature of distinctions underline that the difference is concerned with scale and function, as well as audience and genre. In his poetry collection *La Filomena* (1621), Lope referred to his 'jardín' in the 'Epístola octava' to the Sevillian poet Francisco de Rioja: 'Que mi jardin, mas breue que cometa/Tiene solos dos arboles, diez flores,/Dos parras, vn naranjo, vna mosqueta,/Aqui son dos muchachos Ruiseñores,/Y dos calderos de agua forman fuente' [my garden briefer than a comet has got two trees, ten flowers, two vines, an orange tree, musk rose, two male nightingales and two cauldrons full of water that make a fountain].[27] References in his letters to the garden at his house in the calle de Francos, however, refer to a 'huerto',

[23] Sir Richard Wynn, *A brief relation of what was observed by the Prince's servants in their Journey into Spain, in the Year 1623*, ed. Dámaso López García (Santander: Proases, 1996), 97.

[24] *Ibid.*

[25] Sebastián de Covarrubias Orozco, *Tesoro de la lengua castellana*, ed. Felipe Maldonado (Madrid: Castalia, 1995), 679.

[26] *Ibid.*, 651.

[27] Lope de Vega, *La Filomena con otras diuersas Rimas, Prosas, y Versos* (Madrid: viuda de Alonso Martin, a costa de Alonso Perez, 1621), 'El jardín de Lope de Vega. Al Licenciado Francisco de Rioja en Seuilla. Epistola octaua', fols. 150–61, fol. 160v–161r. The first of the so-called *Novelas a Marcia Leonarda* ('Las fortunas de Diana') appeared in this collection. Marcia Leonarda was the pseudonym of Lope's lover, the actress Marta de Nevares.

although it was not simply a vegetable patch, but rather for flowers 'Eternos incensarios de mi casa' [eternal censers of my home] and fruit trees, including the tulips sent to him by his friend, the Fleming Emmanuel Sueyro.[28] 'Huerto' is the term most commonly found in the early modern Spanish reinventions of the pastoral and eclogue, perhaps connoting rusticity and less formality than the French 'jardín', although different usages do not exclusively follow more elite forms and audiences. Spain's climate shaped the nature of the outdoor spaces used by the social elites and the kinds of activity that these landscapes and backdrops lent themselves to. The confusing lexis and semantics of this area demonstrate Castile's difference from other parts of Europe. The 'jardín' or formal garden was clearly distinct from the traditional patio or courtyard garden, similar although not identical to the 'huerto' or 'huerta' – an orchard, cultivated plot, vegetable patch, kitchen garden or parkland grounds next to a riverbank. Other common terms like 'vergel' ('huerto ameno especialmente plantado para la recreación') [a pleasant *huerto* especially planted for recreation], 'pensil', strictly a hanging garden but by extension any 'jardín delicioso' [delightful garden] and the Toledan term 'cigarral' ('huertas cercadas, donde hai arboles frutales, y tambien sus casas') [enclosed *huertas* where there are fruits trees and houses] also form part of this semantic nexus.[29] Lope made use of the garden, as a metaphor and space in a variety of different ways from his short stories like the *Novelas a Marcia Leonarda*, to his religious poetry, the *hortus conclusus* symbol of virginity, invoking its resonances as a *locus amoenus*, an Edenic or georgic space, playing with its potential as political allegory as part of a discourse of household economy. Lope himself was also a gardener and employed a series of horitcultural conceits in references to his 'huerto'. The protagonist of 'La prudente venganza' falls in love with his rival's bride in an orchard and is drowned by him away from prying eyes as he swims in the same river. These spaces, like the flowers they contained, symbolized beauty – the shaping power of art but also death.[30]

When Philip II travelled to England to marry Mary Tudor in 1554, the accounts of his courtiers assimilated their experience of landscape through the popular romances of chivalry, like *Amadís de Gaula* and *Palmerín*, whose

[28] Lope de Vega, *La Filomena con otras diuersas Rimas, Prosas, y Versos*, fol. 152v. See note 61 in the introduction.

[29] See Maryrica Ortiz Lottman, 'Dramatizing Garden Imagination in Baroque Spain', in Michael Conan (ed.), *Gardens and Imagination: Cultural History and Agency*, Dumarton Oaks Colloquium on the History of Landscape Architecture 30 (Cambridge, MA: Dumarton Oaks Research Library and Collection, 2008), 224–42 and 'The Real and Mystical Gardens of Teresa of Avila' in Hilaire Kallendorf (ed.), *Companion to Hispanic Mysticism* (Leiden: Brill, 2010), 323–42. I would like to thank Maryrica for all her assistance with this chapter.

[30] The famous Calderonian sonnet in *El príncipe constante*, 'Éstas que fueron pompa y alegría' unfolds a complex conceit comparing the stars with flowers, harbingers of changing fortune, the brevity of life and power of fate. Other versions of this theme are found in the work of Lope where flowers compete with the infinity of stars and paintings of spring's carpets, see *Arcadia* (Madrid: Luis Sanchez, 1598), sig. A1v–A2r: 'quiso que la tierra compitiesse con la hermosura de las estrellas del cielo, en la variedad de las flores, y alli descogio la primauera/ de las fabulas, sus pintadas alombras'. The British Library copy C.96.a.13 is inscribed Diego Derrobles.

northern European settings had established a pre-existing pattern for their ideal imaginary landscapes.[31] The lackey Andrés Muñoz, in an account published in Zaragoza the same year as the marriage, described how 'parescian que se hallaban en algo de lo que hauian leído en los libros de cauallerias, segun se les represento aquella hermosura de fuentes, y marauillosos arroyos vertientes, y diuersidades de olorosas flores y arboles y otras lindezas de verduras' [they appeared to have found themselves in something akin to what they had read of in books of chivalry, in light of the beauty of the fountains, marvellous bubbling streams, and diversity of sweet-smelling flowers and trees and other lovely foliage that appeared before them].[32] Their response to England's gardens contrasted the 'florestas de Amadís' [leafy glades of Amadis] with the 'rastrojos de Toledo' [stubble of Toledo], even though they had soon come to long for the latter again.[33] While on his northern European tour in 1549–51, before the journey to England, Philip had begun the process of creating magnificent gardens in Spain to rival those in Italy, Germany and the Low Countries, dictating detailed instructions for the planting of trees in Aranjuez as early as 1550. These instructions were reiterated in Brussels in 1556 and in 1557, despite the scale of business confronting him while in London, Philip worried enough about the gardens of his palace to issue additional instructions.[34] Influenced perhaps by his sojourn as king of England, he introduced the English elm, along with the Oriental plane, at the heart of the planting scheme at Aranjuez, which one traveller claimed later in the century had more than 200,000 trees.[35] Even before this first important horticultural project of Philip's reign began in earnest in October 1561 under the direction of Juan Bautista de Toledo, the king had commissioned reports from royal gardeners Gaspar de Vega and Jerónimo Algora. The report by Gaspar de Vega signed on 16 May 1556 described a visit to Fontainebleau: 'no me pareció tan gran cosa, como tiene la fama; el es grande edefiçio y ay en el cosas muy ricas de pinturas y tallas, especialmente dos galerias que tiene, que la una es mas grande que la grande de Londres' [it did not seem to me to be as great as it is esteemed; it is a large palace with many beautiful paintings and sculptures, especially two galleries that it has, one of which is bigger than the big one {probably the Privy Gallery in Whitehall} in London], about which Philip commented in a marginal annotation 'Que hizo bien en escrevirme todo esto . . . la de Xanburg [Chambord] dexo, que dicen que es la mejor, como lo dira alla el marques de Cortes' [he did well to write to me of all of

---

[31] See Glyn Redworth, 'Nuevo mundo u otro mundo?: conquistadores, cortesanos, libros de caballerías y el reinado de Felipe el Breve de Inglaterra', *Actas del I Congreso Anglo-Hispano*, 3 vols. (Madrid: 1994), Vol. 3, 113–25.

[32] Andrés Muñoz, *Viaje de Felipe II a Inglaterra (Zaragoza, 1554) y Relaciones Varias Relaivas al Mismo Suceso*, ed. Pascual de Gayángos, (Madrid: La Sociedad de Bibliofilos Españoles, 1877), 70. [sig. e i v].

[33] *Viaje de Felipe II*, 77. [sig. e v v].

[34] Agustín de Amezúa y Mayo, *Opúsculos Histórico-Literarios*, 3 tomos (Madrid: Consejo Superior de Investigaciones Científicas, 1951–3), Tomo 3, 'Felipe II y las Flores', 376–412, 382.

[35] Francisco Iñiguez Almech, *Casas reales y jardines de Felipe II* (Madrid: Consejo Superior de Investigaciones Científicas, 1952), 128 and 393.

this . . . I will leave aside Chambord which they say is the best, the Marques Cortes will tell me about it].[36] The report continued with an assessment of the state of the royal works in Spain, covered with Philip's comments 'Que se haga asi', 'Que huelgo mucho dello', 'Esta bien' [Let it be done thus, I am most pleased about this, That's fine]. His architect Juan de Herrera sent the royal gardener Jerónimo Algora to inspect French, English, Dutch and Italian gardens and wrote in a letter on the horticulturalist's death in 1567 that amongst his books, one on Italian gardens by the Italian architect Serlio, who worked on Fontainebleau for Francis I, was 'bueno de tomar' [worth holding on to].[37] Philip as king of England and head of the Habsburg empire took time to inform himself and carefully plan in person every aspect of Spain's horticultural transformation.

The leading classical authority on botany, Dioscorides was published in a fresh Latin translation by Andrés Laguna in 1554 and dedicated to Philip's secretary Gonzalo Pérez. Laguna complained that the original text had been perverted, mutilated and truncated in as many as seven hundred places by previous translators.[38] A vernacular translation was published in Antwerp in September 1555, this time dedicated to Philip himself who had just crossed the channel to Brussels, alleging that Spanish 'por nuestro descuydo, o por alguna siniestra constelacion, ha sido siempre la menos cultiuada de todas, con ser ella la mas capaz, ciuil, y fecunda de las vulgares' [as a result of our carelessness or for some malign heavenly influence has always been the least cultivated, despite being the most able, civil and fertile modern language] and as a result despite translations into many other tongues, the lack of medical knowledge in Spain was having serious adverse consequences.[39] He is silent about the journeys he has made and amount he has expended bringing plants from Greece, Egypt and Berbery 'muchos simples exquisitos y raros, para conferirlos con sus historias' [many simple, exquisite and rare specimens to corroborate with their descriptions], however, he hopes that after his refusal by the Imperial ambassador in Venice Francisco de Vargas that: 'vos nos allanareys de tal arte el camino, que podamos como por nuestras casas, hollando aquellas naciones barbaras, caminar por todo el Oriente, y contemplar, y aun traher por vuestros Reynos en triumpho, aquellas Diuinas plantas' [you will smooth the way for this art, so that we are able as if we were in our own homes to set foot in barbarous kingdoms and traverse the Orient, contemplate and even bring in triumph into

[36] Iñiguez, *Casas reales y jardines de Felipe II*, 166. The report is reprinted as Appendix 1, 165–74.
[37] Ozores y Saavedra, *Jardines de España*, 120.
[38] Andrés de Laguna, *Anotationes in Discoridem Anazarbeum, per Andream Lacunam Segobiensem, Medicum* (Venice: Gulielmum Rouillium, 1554), sig. a2r– a3r: 'Quo labore dum fungerer, annotaui septingentos, vel plureis locos, in quibus autor ille, partim peruersus ab interpretibus Latiis, partim mutilus ac truncus, partim genuina sua priscaque destitutus dictione, conspiciebatur'.
[39] Andrés de Laguna, *Pedacio Dioscorides Anazarbeo, acerca de la materia medicinal, y de los venenos mortiferos, traduzido de lengua Griega, en la vulgar Castellana, & illusrado con claras y substantiales Annotationes, y con las figuras de innumeras plantas exquisitas y raras por el Doctor Andres de Laguna, Medico* (Antwerp: Juan Latio, 1555), sig. ¶2v.

your kingdoms those divine plants].[40] Botanical research is here drawn into an equivalence with military expansion. Plants are then discussed through their anthropomorphic virtues: justice, in remaining as they do always in their correct spot; charity, allowing other plants to grow on them; strength, the palm tree bending but never breaking; conjugal love, with the female palm dying away in the absence of the male tree; religion, heliotropic plants following the sun; liberality, with their fruit – and so on. He ends his dedication calling on Philip to establish great gardens in Spain:

pues todos los Principes, y las universidades de Italia, se precian de tener en sus tierras, muchos y muy excellentes jardines, adornados de todas las plantas que se pueden hallar en el vniuerso: tambien V. M. prouea y de orden, que a lo menos nos tengamos uno en España, sustentado con estipendios Reales.[41]

[all the princes and universities of Italy pride themselves on having in their territories many most excellent gardens, adorned with all the plants that can be found in the universe: may your Majesty provide and give order that at least we may have one in Spain paid for from royal revenues.]

Whether or not Laguna's treatise followed the king's known interest or was responsible for stimulating it, there is no doubt that Philip II became a serious subscriber to flower power. As one critic has commented by 1559, Philip 'traía una afición poco frecuente, pero muy noble y simpática, por los árboles, flores y jardines' [was possessed of an uncommon but most noble and pleasant affection for trees, flowers and gardens].[42] The horticulturalist Gregorio de los Rios, who as we saw underlined the licit and improving nature of cultivation 'aparta los hombres de todos los vicios' [it removes men from all manner of vice][43] dubbed him 'Antófilo' [Flower-lover] in his horticultural treatise, *Agricultura de jardines* (1592), three years after he was made a chaplin of the Casa del Campo, an estate purchased from the royal secretary Fadrique de Vargas in 1562 by Philip.[44]

A series of Flemish and French gardeners began to arrive in Spain from 1561 onwards: Juan Holbecq from Tournai (260 florins a year); Héctor Henneton; Juan Bordiau; Daniel and Joos Van Honele; Guillermo Coluens; Guillaume de Voos; Estienne and Marthurin Rouet; Juan Lengle; Juan Rebondí; and Rugel Patien.[45] According to the traveller, Lamberto Wyts in 1571, Holbecq or Hollebecke, had been joined by his brother to oversee the

[40] Andrés de Laguna, *Pedacio Dioscorides*, sig. ¶3r.
[41] *Ibid.*, sig. ¶4v.
[42] Amezúa y Mayo, 'Felipe II y las Flores', 379.
[43] Gregorio de los Rios, *Argicultura de jardines, primera, y segunda parte* reprinted in Alonso de Herrera, *Agricultura general que trata de la labranza del campo y sus particularidades* (Madrid: viuda de Alonso Martin, 1620), fols. 244–69, fol. 245.
[44] Lope described the Casa del Campo in his play *La gallarda toledana* and inserted two sonnets, ekphrastically alluding to Boticelli's spring, in *Lo que pasa en una tarde*, see Amezúa y Mayo, 'Felipe II y las Flores', 395.
[45] *Ibid*, 385.

Fig. 3   Jardines de la Isla, Palacio de Aranjuez (photo: author)

creation of the gardens.[46] Even an Englishman figured in the accounts. A huge shipment of plants from Flanders arrived in Laredo in 1566 with willows, osiers, and cammock.[47] Philip's new young bride Isabel de Valois shared his enthusiasm. Madame Clermont's diary about the French queen's life in Spain for her mother, Catherine de Medici, described in 1560 the isle in the gardens

---

[46] Ozores y Saavedra, *Jardines de España*, 120.

[47] Iñiguez, *Casas reales y jardines de Felipe II*, 128 and *ibid.*, 121. Original documents are in Archivo de Zabálburu, caj. 146, n. 51 and 85 (docs. 25, 35 and 48). See also Archivo del Instituto de Valencia de Don Juan, envíos 61, 95, 99.

at Aranjuez as unfinished and their eagerly awaiting the arrival of 'votre jardinier', the place as whole however was 'un fort beau lieu' (see Fig. 3).[48] The gardens at Aranjuez were celebrated in a series of poems, including Gómez de Tapia's *Egloga pastoril en que se describe el bosque de Aranjuez* [*Pastoral Eclogue describing the woods at Aranjuez*] of 1582, published as part of a treatise on hunting from the fourteenth-century reign of Alfonso XI:

> En medio deste nueuo Parayso
> vn ancha huerta esta en quadro traçada
> de rojo y odorifero Narciso
> y blanco Lirio a trechos esmaltada,
> en torno todo esta con tal auiso
> de la Nimpha[49] a quien Pan siguio cercada
> que puesto que alos pies haga reparo
> alos ojos permite entrar de claro.[50]

[In the midst of this new paradise, a wide orchard-garden is set out in a square with red, sweet-smelling Narcissi, flecked here and there with white lilies, all around besieged with reminders of the nymph pursued by Pan which make feet think twice, but which draw in the eye with their clarity.]

The ambivalent language around Spanish gardens is again present with the use of the term 'huerta' to describe what is clearly a formal pleasure garden, although the commonplace image of a 'new paradise' may point away from the more artificial connotations of 'jardín'. The white and red invoke the prosopopeia in invocations of the the beloved in courtly poetry, while the classical allusion populates the garden's planting with a mythological schema. It alludes to avenues, pictures created out of flowers, figures artificially sculpted from myrtles, i.e. topiary, and garden buildings from which the crystalline waters of the river can be touched: 'puede bien desde un bajo aposento/ tocar la mano al agua cristalina' [a hand can well trail in the clear water from a chamber on the banks'.[51] It is full of theatrical effects testifying to art's ability to transcend and outdo nature:

> Pomone allí, con mano delicada
> lo natural con arte aderezando,
> está en la planta a Venus dedicada

---

[48] Iñiguez, *Casas reales y jardines de Felipe II*, 155.

[49] Pitys, who was transformed into a pine tree, but more likely Syrinx who was turned into a water reed from which Pan fashioned his famous pipes.

[50] *Libro de la montería que mando escreuir el muy alto y muy poderoso Rey Don Alonso de Castilla, y de Leon, vltimo deste nombre. Acrecentado por Gonçalo Argote de Molina. Dirigido A la S. C. R. M. del Rey Don Philipe Segundo* (Seville: Andrea Pescioni, 1582), 'Egloga pastoril en que se descriue el Bosque de Aranjuez, y el Nascimiento de la Serenissima Doña Ysabel de España. Compuesto por Don Gomez de Tapia Granadino,' sigs. ¶¶5r–¶¶¶3v, fos. 22–5, Sig. ¶¶6 r.

[51] *Ibid.*, fol. 23r, sig. ¶¶¶¶1r.

siempre [sic] varias figuras estampando,
cuál de ave, cuál de fiera denodada,
de tal manera al vivo remedando,
que habrá quien a las aves red tendiese
y de las fieras quien temor hubiese.

[Pomona there, with delicate hand adorning nature with skilled art, is pattern-
ing a variety of figures with the plant sacred to Venus,[52] here a bird, there a
tireless wild beast, her mimicry so lifelike that there will be those who cast a net
over the birds and fear the wild animals.][53]

The garden's mimesis is such that it reverses the Ovidian transformations
commonly thematized in Renaissance gardens. One of the most surprising
aspects of Gómez de Tapia's poem is its reference to the garden's use by all
estates of society, its attraction as a site of pilgrimage for tourists: 'De gente
está la estancia siempre llena/ que de apartada parte y de vecina,/ cuál de
obscuro linaje, cuál de claro,/ a ver concurren el milagro raro' [the estate
is always full of people, from far and wide, of illustrious lineage and low,
who gather to witness this strange miracle].[54] This natural space like the
miracle is universal and egalitarian in its significance and appeal. In addition to this Arcadian version of Aranjuez, as an image of political harmony,
Gonazalo Argote de Molina incorporated in his edition of the Alfonsine
hunting treatise, a very different description of the royal palace of El Pardo
near Madrid:

en torno [de la casa] vna ancha caua, y en el fondo della munchos compartimien-
tos, Vasos y Macetas de yeruas medicinales, y Flores estrañas, traydas con mucha
curiosidad de diuersas regiones, adornadas las paredes de la Caua con Iazmines,
Yedra y Rosas, en cada esquina vna fuente de agua que por Maxcarones de Piedra
sale.[55]

[around the house a broad ditch, at the bottom of which were many compartments, urns and pots with medicinal herbs, and strange flowers, brought with
great curiosity from diverse regions, adorning the walls of the hollow jasmines,
ivy and roses, at each corner a fountain of water spouted from stone figure-
heads.]

This is a more traditional palace garden with privileged views from the house
of the parterres, a mixture of the medicinal and floral – a variety of planting
that reflected the reach of Habsburg power, its imperial exoticism.

While Gómez de Tapia's eclogue merely alluded to Aranjuez's variety
of trees, some native, others imported ('árboles de especies diferentes,/ parte

---

[52] Presumably the rose.
[53] *Ibid.*, fol. 22r, sigs. ¶¶5r.
[54] *Ibid.*, fol. 23v, sig. ¶¶¶¶1v.
[55] *Ibid.*, Capitulo XLVII 'Descricion del Bosque y Casa Real del Pardo', sig. ¶¶¶4 r–v.

plantados, parte allí nacidos' [trees of different species, some born there, others transplanted]), the poet Lupercio Leonardo de Argensola treated the same landscape as a botanical garden, dwelling on its role in acclimatization, as an agricultural laboratory for 'injertos' [grafts], where art and technical skill overcome the shocks of transplantation from distant, foreign climes.[56] For Argensola, Aranjuez was a political metaphor for the harmony of an ethnically, naturally and climatically diverse, multicultural empire:

> Cualquiera aquí su condición aplica,
> aunque su origen traiga de otra parte,
> do el sol menos o más se comunica.
> Suple la falta de la tierra el arte,
> y del calor con límite y del hielo
> aquello que conviene les reparte.[57]

[whoever here strives to fulfill their nature, although their origins may have brought them from another place where the sun imparts more or less heat. The lack of the soil is supplemented by art, heat with limit and cold with that which it is convenient to share out.]

The co-operation and equilibrium of a personified natural world contrasts with the unchristian envy of post-lapsarian human societies:

> . . . las amistades
> con que las plantas fértiles se prestan
> y templan sus contrarias calidades? Y cómo no se impiden ni molestan
> por ver su fruta en extranjeras hojas,
> ni del agravio apelan y protestan,
> como tú, frágil hombre, que te enojas
> si al otro ves tener lo que no es tuyo. (ll. 34–41).

[the friendships with which the fertile plants lend themselves and temper each other's contrary qualities? And how they do not annoy or stand in each other's way when they see their fruit on foreign leaves, nor do they protest and appeal against the offence like you do fragile man, who becomes enraged when you see others have what you do not.]

Symbiotic plant life, tempering extremity and symbolising peaceful co-existence is used as a metaphor to underline the greed for possession characteristic of human society. The ultimate achievement of the garden is an urban civility, the harmonious imposition of order and symmetry on unruly

---

[56] *Ibid.*, fol. 22v.

[57] Lupercio Leonardo de Argensola, *Rimas* (Madrid: Espasa-Calpe, Clásicos Castellanos, 1972), 'Estos tercetos en que se descubre Aranjuez, se escribieron con ocasión de un libro que imprimió el maestro Fray Juan Tolosa, religioso de la orden de san Agustín, al cual puso por título *Aranjuez del alma*', 153–60, here 155, ll. 55–60.

nature: 'Las calles largas de álamos y llanas/ envidia pueden dar a las ciudades' [The long, flat avenues of poplars make cities envious] (ll. 31–2).[58] In both poems about Aranjuez, images of a 'tejido' [weave] of 'yedras' [ivy] which the sun is unable to penetrate appear, as do other Garcilasan topoi of murmuring streams and fertile verdure.[59] Argensola's poem also encloses a series of other topoi that had accumulated around the early modern garden by the late sixteenth century, its reflection of the excellence of the climate, metaphors of paradise and comparisons with famous gardens of myth and antiquity.

In 1589, while in exile in Valencia, Lope composed a *romance* 'Hortelano era Belardo' [Belardo was a gardener] (Belardo was one of the poet's numerous literary disguises),[60] which contained an extensive list of plants, whose medicinal, magical, iconographic and symbolic qualities were applied to different types of women. It advised suggestively, for example, 'lirios y verbena' [lilies and verbena] for widows to green their black mourning 'saya' [skirt].[61] It was published in Lisbon in 1593 as part of the *Ramillete de flores. Cuarta parte de Flor de romances nuevos y canciones* [*Bunch of Flowers. The Fourth Part of the Flower of New Romances and Songs*], just months after Gregorio de los Ríos' *Argricultura de jardines* appeared.[62] Three years later in 1592, Lope composed a 'Descripción del Abadía, jardín del duque de Alba', which appeared in print in the 1604 edition of his *Rimas*. The La Abadía garden in the province of Cáceres created by a Flemish garden designer by 1577, combined statuary, topiary, waterworks and grottoes, rare plants from Flanders and Germany with the myrtles, lemon and orange trees and jasmine typical in the south.[63] Lope's poem is a conventional literary celebration, incarnating the topoi of idealized landscapes in early modern Castile; its aquatic nymphs 'Náyades puras, que de roxo acanto,/ de lirios y retamas amarillas/hazéis a Tormes espacioso manto' [Water nymphs, who make for the river Tormes a spacious cloak of red acanthus, lilies and yellow retama], myrtle hedges dividing beds of floral profusion, 'Entre murtas iguales vertió Flora/ gran parte de la copia de Amaltea' [Amongst myrtles Flora poured out the best part of Amalthea's abundance], and the impenetrable canopy of vegetation shading from the sun 'esta verdura que defiende el passo/ al sol, que a su pessar entrar procura'

[58] Lupercio Leonardo de Argensola, *Rimas*, 154.
[59] Cervantes included a description of Aranjuez's gardens in *Los trabajos de Persiles y Sigismunda*, ed. Carlos Romero Muñoz (Madrid: Cátedra, 2004), 511–12, visited by the tourist group including the protagonists as they pass through Spain.
[60] This chapter owes a massive debt to the seminal article of Felipe Pedraza Jiménez, 'De Garcilaso a Lope: jardines poéticos en tiempos de Felipe II', in Carmen Añón Feliú, dir., *Felipe II: El Rey Íntimo. Jardín y Naturaleza en el siglo XVI* (Madrid: Sociedad Estatal para la Conmemoración de los Centenarios de Felipe II y Carlos V, 1998), 307–30, here 324.
[61] Lope de Vega, *Obras Completas: Poesía*, ed. Antonio Carreño, 6 tomos (Madrid: Biblioteca Castro, 2003), Tomo 6, 843–5, ll. 18 and 20.
[62] On this poem see Miguel Angel Teijero Fuentes, *Lope de Vega, Belardo y su huerta. La mágica pervivencia de una tradición* (Mérida: Editora Regional de Extremadura, 1993).
[63] John H. Harvey, 'Spanish Gardens and Their Historical Background', *Garden History* 3 (1974), 7–14, here 9.

[this greenery which defends against the passage of the sun who despite it tries to peep through].[64] La Abadía was also the inspiration for the descriptions of landscape in his 'pastoral-monster' the *Arcadia* (1598), an allegory of the poet and his master the duke's romantic entaglements and losses in the period 1590–95, that echoed Sannazaro, Virgil's fourth eclogue and Garcilaso.[65] The narrator specifically characterized the imaginative space of the text as an 'ameno sitio', a *locus amoenus*, where shepherds seemed more like 'courtiers' than 'shepherds', more like 'philosophers' than 'rustics'.[66] But despite the implicit nostalgia of its autobiographical elements that look back to the author's affair with Elena Osorio, his love for and the death of his wife Isabel de Urbina, and the similarly scandalous affair of the duke, Antonio Alvarez de Toledo, the representation of love as a positive force that conquers all is displaced by the destructive nature of sexual jealousy, infatuation and obsession, leading inevitably to *desengaño*, the painful knowledge of the passing nature of human love and happiness.[67] The knowledge of where human love and sexual passion lead in the multitude of his plays that concern 'casos de la honra' [honour plots],[68] reach their climax in the *Novelas a Marcia Leonarda*, which have often been likened by critics to *comedias*, partly on the grounds of his own assertion that 'tienen las novelas los mismos preceptos que las comedias' [novels have the same precepts as plays].[69] 'La prudente venganza' typifies this convergence in terms of its highly ambivalent and ambiguous treatment of the theme.[70]

The *Novelas a Marcia Leonarda* are an editorial fiction, originally appearing separately as part of two poetic miscellanies *La Filomena* (1621) and *La Circe* (1624), both dedicated to members of the Pimentel family – the former to Doña Leonor Pimentel, lady-in-waiting to the newly crowned Philip IV's sister, the Infanta María, whose husband the Count of Benavente was *mayordomo mayor* in the queen's household. The latter, *La Circe*, in which three of the four *novelas* appeared (including 'La prudente venganza') was dedicated on its title page to the Count-Duke of Olivares and jointly in the dedication to Olivares' mother, also a member of the Pimentel family, and his daughter Doña María de Guzmán. Lope had been turned down by the new king's father for the post of royal chronicler as recently as 1620. The text has a dual or triple addressee,

[64] Lope de Vega, *Rimas*, ed. Felipe Pedraza Jiménez, 2 tomos (Ciudad Real: Universidad de Castilla-La Mancha, 1993–4), Tomo 2, No. 206, 'Descripción del Abadía, Jardín del Duque de Alba', 203–35, ll. 1–3, 73–4, 342–3. Amalthea was of course the goat/nymph who fed Zeus and whose horn was the cornucopia.
[65] Marsha Collins, 'Lope's *Arcadia*: A Self-Portrait of the Artist as a Young Man', *Renaissance Quarterly* 57 (2004), 882–907, here 883. See also Julián Moreiro Prieto, *Una página en la vida de Lope: Alba de Tormes* (Salamanca: Sociedad Amigos de Alba, 1978).
[66] *Arcadia*, Prologo and sig. A1v.
[67] Collins, 'Lope's *Arcadia*', 889.
[68] This according to Lope was the plot that moved theatre-goers most readily, see Enrique García Santo-Tomás (ed.), *Arte nuevo de hacer comedias* (Madrid: Cátedra, 2006), 149.
[69] Lope de Vega, *Novelas a Marcia Leonarda*, ed. Antonio Carreño (Madrid: Cátedra, 2002), 183.
[70] Originally discussed in Georges Cirot, 'Valeur littéraire des nouvelles de Lope de Vega', *Bulletin Hispanique* 28 (1926), 321–55.

first the noble Olivares family, whom the last story 'Guzmán el bravo' specifically courts by invoking an ancestor and exploring a series of correspondences
between his heroism and strength and the family's illustrious past and
present.[71] Secondly, the innovative framing device that figures 'novelar' [nov-
elizing] as a form of 'cortejar' [courting],[72] points to the muse who had
charged him with writing the short stories, Marcia Leonarda, pseudonym of
the actress Marta de Nevares, whom Lope had met in 1616 and who was to
remain his mistress until her death in 1632, blind and mad. Finally, both of
these supposed addressees figure within the self-fashioning of Lope before a
wider public, his characteristically intimate autobiographical strain subsumed
within a courtly political one, designed to draw in and impress the most
important addressee, his public as an artist 'pretendiendo el vulgar aplauso'
[seeking the vulgar applause],[73] but whose greatest fear was not 'cosa arro-
jadiza' [chuckable things],[74] but to be tedious. His stories according to the
introduction to 'La desdicha por la honra' used:

> ya de cosas altas, ya de humildes, ya de episodios y paréntesis, ya de historias, ya
> de fábulas, ya de reprehensiones y ejemplos, ya de versos y lugares de autores
> pienso valerme, para que ni sea tan grave el estilo que canse a los que no saben,
> ni tan desnudo de algún arte que le remitan al polvo los que entienden.[75]

> [elevated themes at times, humble ones at others, episodes, parentheses, histo-
> ries, fables, reprehensions and examples, verse, commonplaces and authorities,
> so that the style is not so serious as to tire the ignorant nor so bare of artfulness
> that those who know consign it to the dust.]

His prose was directed at a multiple readership both humble and erudite,
intermingling learned and erudite discourse, 'lugares de autores' [common-
places from authorities] with fables, true stories, episode and *exempla*. Their
Baroque excess revels in deviating from classical aesthetic ideals of symmetry
and proportion, offering in place of unity, variety, an emergent poetics of
admiratio brought about by the sheer wealth of what is woven together in a
given story. His decentering congeries are typified in the novellas' most characteristic rhetorical device *amplificatio*.[76] This rhetorical figure is used not to
reinforce, elucidate or expand but more often to undercut, confound and

---

[71] This story is discussed at length by Ali Rizavi, '*Novelas a Marcia Leonarda*' in Alexander Samson and
Jonathan Thacker (eds.), *A Companion to Lope de Vega* (Woodbridge: Tamesis, 2008), 244–55.
[72] Lope de Vega, *Novelas a Marcia Leonarda*, 106.
[73] *Arte nuevo de hacer comedias*, 132.
[74] Miguel de Cervantes, *Ocho comedias y ocho entremeses nuevos, nunca representados* (Madrid: Alonso Martin,
1615), fol. IIIr.
[75] *Novelas a Marcia Leonarda*, 183.
[76] Collins, 'Lope's *Arcadia*', 900. As he had written about the *comedia*, 'que aquesta variedad deleita mucho./
Bueno ejemplo nos da Naturaleza,/ que por tal variedad tiene belleza' [that variety delights a lot. Nature
exemplifies this exactly, it is for such variety that it is beautiful], *Arte nuevo de hacer comedias*, 141.

collapse, drawing attention to the purposelessness of its reductive example or aphorism in driving forward the narrative, as we will see.

In this, he differs significantly from Cervantes. It has been argued that his *Novelas* are an implicit response to Cervantine poetics, underlining his elite credentials through the profusion of learned, didactic exemplification, offering an alternative to the notion of *propiedad* [propriety/appropriateness] at the level of plot[77]: 'habían de escribirlos hombres científicos o por lo menos grandes cortesanos, gente que halla en los desengaños notables sentencias y aforismos' [they ought to be written by learned men or at least great courtiers, people who find in disillusionment notable aphorisms and *sententia*].[78] Again this pose that only great courtiers and philosophers should write novels runs counter to the notion that fiction be judged for the propriety of its imitation of life rather than for its morally salutary effects, a reaction against the humanist condemnations of prose fiction.[79] The term 'ejemplar' found in the titles of many of the collections of short stories produced in this period is notably absent from Lope's presentation of his tales. 'La prudente venganza' ends with a summary of its significance that calls into question the presentation of the narrative: 'Ésta fue la prudente venganza, si alguna puede tener este nombre, no escrita, como he dicho, para ejemplo de los agraviados, sino para escarmiento de los que agravian' [This was the prudent revenge, if any can be described as such, not written, as I have said as an example for the offended, but as a warning to those who offend].[80] The title is signalled as oxymoronic, while the narrative's exemplarity in any moral sense is explicitly eschewed, the consequences are nevertheless admonitory from a pragmatic perspective. Throughout the story, the feelings and motives of its protagonists and victims, Laura and Lisardo, are the subject of a refusal to pass moral judgement, being excused by their love for one another or inexperience, the narrator adding: 'Vuestra merced juzgue si esta dama era cuerda, que yo nunca me he puesto a corregir a quien ama' [Your worship may judge whether this lady was in her right mind, I have never sought to criticise those who love].[81] The refusal to pass sentence ironizes the rhetorical procedure of offering up *sententiae*, even as it undermines the authority of the narrator to do so, with its ironic sideways glance at the author's own autobiographical notoriety for sexual impropriety.

When the avenging husband Marcelo finds the objects, letters, a portrait, and jewels that confirm the adultery, the narrator inserts a warning for those

---

[77] See Marina Brownlee, *The Poetics of Literary Theory: Lope de Vega's* Novelas a Marcia Leonarda *and their Cervantine Context* (Madrid: Porrúa, 1981) and Carmen Rabell, *Lope de Vega: el arte nuevo de hacer 'novelas'* (Woodbridge: Tamesis, 1992) and *Rewriting the Italian Novella in Counter-Reformation Spain* (Woodbridge: Tamesis, 2003).

[78] Lope de Vega, *Novelas a Marcia Leonarda*, 106.

[79] See Barry Ife, *Reading and Fiction in Golden-Age Spain* (Cambridge: Cambridge University Press, 1985).

[80] Lope de Vega, *Novelas a Marcia Leonarda*, 284.

[81] *Ibid.*, 247. He is 'mozo' [young], her letter written 'sin prudencia' [imprudently], *ibid.*, 251–2.

who have lovers against keeping evidence of their illicit relations.[82] Lisardo is discovered by Marcelo in a garden shed of his own walled garden and thrust out into the street through a hidden door. As the revenge of the title unfolds in another aside to his mistress Marcia Leonarda (Marta Nevares), the narrator invokes Christian precept to point to a morality radically different from that on which the familiar dynamics of its plot depends, based instead on imperfection, acceptance and forgiveness, rather than perfect virtue and the bloody avenging of its violation. In order to bear the public shame of infidelity, he suggests husbands exile themselves and offer up their suffering to God, remembering that what has happened to them, could as easily have been done by them:

aunque las leyes por el justo dolor permiten esta licencia a los maridos, no es ejemplo que nadie debe imitar, aunque aquí se escriba para que lo sea a las mujeres que con desordenado apetito aventuran la vida y la honra a tan breve deleite, en grave ofensa de Dios, de sus padres, de sus esposos y de su fama. Y he sido de parecer siempre que no se lava bien la mancha de la honra del agraviado con la sangre del que le ofendió, porque lo que fue no puede dejar de ser y desatino creer que se quita, porque se mate al ofensor, la ofensa del ofendido. Lo que hay en esto es que el agraviado se queda con su agravio y el otro, muerto, satisfaciendo los deseos de la venganza, pero no las calidades de la honra, que para ser perfecta no ha de ser ofendida. ¿Quién duda que está ya la objeción a este argumento dando voces? Pues, aunque tácita, respondo que no se ha de sufrir ni castigar. Pues ¿qué medio se ha de tener? El que un hombre tiene cuando le ha sucedido otro cualquiera género de desdicha: perder la patria, vivir fuera della donde no le conozcan y ofrecer a Dios aquella pena, acordándose que le pudiera haber sucedido lo mismo si en alguno de los agravios que ha hecho a otros le hubieran castigado. Que querer que los que agravió le sufran a él y él no sufrir a nadie, no está puesto en razón; digo sufrir, dejar de matar violentamente, pues por sólo quitarle a él la honra, que es una vanidad del mundo, quiere él quitarles a Dios, si se les pierde el alma.[83]

[although the law for the just pain permits husbands this licence, it is not an example anyone ought to imitate, although here it may be written so that it may be one for women who with disordered appetite risk life and honour for such brief enjoyment, in grave offence of God, their parents, husbands and reputation. I have always believed that the stain on the offended party's honour is not washed away by the blood of the offender, because that which was, can not cease to be and it is a mistake to believe the husband's offence is taken away, because the offending party is killed. What happens here is that the offended party remains injured and the other dead, satisfying the desire for revenge, but not dictates of reputation, which to be perfect can not be touched. Who doubts that the objection to this argument is already being screeched out? Well, although tacit, I reply that it can not be suffered or punished. So, what means are there? Those which a man has when any type of misfortune befalls him: the loss of his

[82] Lope de Vega, *Novelas a Marcia Leonarda*, 280.
[83] *Ibid.*, 283–4.

homeland, to live exiled where they do not know him and offer that pain to God, remembering that the same might have happened to him if one of the injuries he has carried out had been punished. To want those who offend to suffer and to suffer from no-one, is not reasonable; I say suffer, allow to be killed violently, for merely having destroyed his reputation, which is a vanity of this world, he wants to take their punishment away from God, even if it loses him his soul.]

This moment is the crux of Lope's tale, deliberately establishing a dialogue with its non-exemplary ending. The story depends upon a conventional acceptance of reputation even as it destabilizes its lethal significance from the perspective of a tolerant and liberal sexual morality founded in Christian ideals, according to which honour is a worldly vanity, the bloody execution of an adulterer, murder of the worst kind, committed out of pride and self-regard. This juxtaposition uses a discourse of Christian morality to destabilize the honour code.[84] The ambivalence of the narrator's pronouncements about the adulterous passions of the central pair is further ironized by the fact that it is framed by his own seduction. The writing itself is an attempt to gain the favour of his lover, Marcia Leonarda, with whom he has had an adulterous relationship, married during the first two or three years of their relationship and unmarried to him even after her husband's death. Acknowledged within the fictional frame of the text, when he digresses on the origins of the Hymen myth to distract her from the story's unpleasant aspects:

No pienso que le habrá sido a vuestra merced gustoso el episodio, en razón de la poca inclinación que tiene al señor Himeneo de los atenienses; pero por lo menos le desvi del agravio injusto que hicieron estas bodas al ausente Lisardo y la facilidad con que se persuadió la mal vengada Laura.[85]

[I don't think that this episode will have been enjoyable for your worship, because of your little inclination to the Athenian Lord Hymen, the unjust offence that these nuptials did to the absent Lisardo and the ease with which the ill-avenged Laura was persuaded.]

The narrator laments at the outset the aptness of his story at all for the purpose of pleasing her because of its ultimately tragic nature.

This moral complexity is inflected and reflected in his use of outdoor spaces and the garden, playing with symbolic imagery of water and nature, to underline the tragedy and ambivalences of his protagonists' courtship. After two years during which Lisardo and Laura coming and going from mass on feast

---

[84] Recent scholarship has challenged monolithic and particularist assumptions about the honour code in Spain and attempted to situate honour within a broader context of familial relations and European culture concluding that what made Spain different in this regard was the existence of the honour plays, see Scott Taylor, *Honor and Violence in Golden Age Spain* (New Haven & London: Yale University Press, 2008), 5–9 and 231–2.

[85] Lope de Vega, *Novelas a Marcia Leonarda*, 259.

days do nothing more than 'hacer los ojos lenguas' [make their eyes tongues], Lisardo discovers that:

> iban a una huerta Laura y sus padres, donde habían de estar hasta la noche. Tiénelas hermosísimas Sevilla en las riberas de Guadalquivir, río de oro, no en las arenas . . . sino en que por él entran tantas ricas flotas, llenas de plata y oro del Nuevo Mundo.[86]

> [Laura and her parents were going to a garden/orchard/estate, where they were going to spend the time until nightfall. Seville has exquisitely beautiful gardens on the banks of the Guadalquivir, a river of gold, not in its sands . . . but in that it is into this river that rich fleets come from the New World full of silver and gold.]

Although not explicitly described as theirs, it becomes clear later in the story that it is, when Lisardo's servants, disobeying him, go to the house to which the garden belongs, where they are provided with food by the servants and invited by the party to play after claiming to be musicians, so the black slave girls can dance. The public/private nature of the space is perhaps importantly not made excessively explicit. Despite the historicist detail that the riverbanks are not golden, sands feature prominent in the imaginary invoked in describing what Lisardo sees:

> ocupó lo más escondido de la güerta. Llegó con sus padres Laura, y pensando que de solos los árboles era vista, en sólo el faldellín, cubierto de oro, y pretinilla, comenzó a correr por ellos, a la manera que suelen las doncellas el día que el recogimiento de su casa les permite la licencia del campo.[87]

> [He occupied the most hidden part of the garden. Laura arrived with her parents, and believing herself to be seen only by the trees, began to run amongst them dressed in her petticoat, covered in gold, and waist band, as maids do on the day the enclosure of their houses gives way to the liberty of the country.]

At this point the narrator inserts a comparison between Laura and Marcia/Marta: 'si no me engaño, la vi en él un día tan descuidada como Laura, pero no menos hermosa' [If I am not mistaken, I saw you once as carefree as Laura, and no less beautiful].[88] The consistent parallels traced between the story and its narrative frame, titillate the reader(s) to move between them and read ironies in the narrator's reassurances to his addressee that her state, as a widow, insulates her from the dangers faced by Laura and the warning of her example to those who transgress: 'Dios la puso en estado que no tiene que temer cuando tuviera condición para tales peligros' [God placed you {Marta} in a state in which you don't have to fear]. When he alludes to 'tiempo menos

[86] Lope de Vega, *Novelas a Marcia Leonarda*, 237–8.
[87] *Ibid.*, 238.
[88] *Ibid.*

riguroso' [a less severe time],[89] it is studiedly ambiguous as to whether he refers to when Laura's story takes place, his own or the reader's. The narrator again seemingly disavows his own authority by presenting their love as a demonstrably literary discourse, ironically drawn from one of his own poems:

> Lisardo, pues, contemplaba en Laura, y ella se alargó tanto, corriendo por varias sendas, que cerca de donde él estaba la paró un arroyo, que, como dicen los romances, murmuraba o se reía, mayormente aquel principio:
>
>> Riyéndose va un arroyo;
>> sus guijas parecen dientes,
>> porque vio los pies descalzos
>> a la primavera alegre.
>
> Y no he dicho esto a vuestra merced sin causa, porque él debió de reírse de ver los de Laura, hermosa primavera entonces, que, convidada del cristal del agua y del bullicio de la arena, que hacía algunas pequeñas islas, pensando detenerla, competían entrambos, se descalzó y los bañó un rato, pareciendo en el arroyo ramo de azucenas en vidrio.[90]
>
> [Lisardo, then, contemplated Laura, and she ran off so far down various paths, until near to where he was a stream halted her, that, as they say in the *romances*, murmured or laughed, mostly that principal one:
>
>> Laughing flows a stream;
>> its pebbles seem like teeth,
>> because it saw the naked feet
>> of happy spring.
>
> And I have not told your worship this without reason, since he/it must have laughed to see Laura, beautiful spring then, invited by the crystalline water and the bustle of the sand, that formed little islets, thinking to stop her, the two competed with each other, she slipped off her shoes and bathed her feet a while, seeming in the stream lilies in glass.]

The personified stream blurs into and merges with Lisardo, as they compete with each other in their happy laughter, a conceit self-consciously signalled as literary by the narrator pointing to a poem probably by Lope himself. The slight impropriety of the term 'contemplar' [contemplate] and its Neoplatonic resonance is immediately undercut by poetic cliché. While the merging of Lisardo with the water foreshadows his watery grave at the end, the personified water and sand call on Laura to display that most erotic synecdoche, her feet. The moment is brought to a climax with a simile comparing her feet in the water to lilies in a glass vase.[91] This image is doubly suggestive of the

---

[89] Lope de Vega, *Novelas a Marcia Leonarda*, 236.

[90] *Ibid.*, 239.

[91] Curiously the Spanish 'azucena' derives from the Arabic *súsan* which refers to an iris but came to refer to the *lilium candidum* or 'Annunciation' lily. See Harvey, 'Garden Plants of Moorish', 74 and note 19.

virgin Mary, the purity invoked by the lily of the Annunciation and the translucence of glass, so often a poetic trope for virginity and purity. The rhetorical strategy here constructs an image of erotic contemplation out of religious imagery, mixing 'lo divino a lo profano', in a reversal of the *contrafacta* poetry practised by Lope in his *Rimas sacras* (1612). Lisardo's erotic ecstasy is a reiteration of the Annunciation. This passage is evocative of generic models that, with the narrator's ingenuous interventions, are ironized and subverted. Nature is simultaneously an object of spiritual contemplation, erotic suggestion, poetic artificiality and anthropomorphic substitution in this passage. Lope's heterodox use of genre here reminds us of the vertiginous interpenetration of the spiritual and profane. In his poetic celebration of the minor cult figure who later became Madrid's patron saint in 1622, *Isidro* (1599), the protagonist is taunted by jealous fellow labourers for not responding to his wife's suspected adultery by 'herir y matar . . . era infamia callar los que sin honra vivían' [wounding and killing . . . it was infamy to keep quiet those who lived without honour].[92] He is drawn back by the erotic image of Susana in the garden, an image later elaborated on in *Pastores de Belén* (1611), a mixture of prose and poetry retelling from the perspective of the shepherds the story from the Annunciation to the nativity. The erotic evocation of the garden sits uncomfortably in both examples.

A typical example of Lope's use of *amplificatio* occurs when he invokes his own garden to reflect upon the insatiable greed of the courtesan who is bleeding Lisardo's friend Otavio dry, an unnecessary and abstruse allegorical example taken from his own experience as a gardener.

> Hame acontecido reparar en unas yerbas que tengo en un pequeño huerto, que con la furia del sol de los caniculares se desamayan de forma que, tendidas por la tierra, juzgo por imposible que se levanten; y echándoles agua aquella noche, las hallo por la mañana como pudieran estar en abril después de una amorosa lluvia. Este efeto considero en la tibieza y desmayo del amor de las cortesanas, cuando la plata y oro las despierta y alegra tan velozmente, que el galán que de noche fue aborrecido porque no da, a la mañana es querido porque ha dado.[93]

> [I have noted that certain herbs I have in a little garden, which beneath the fury of the dog-day sun wilt in such a way that drooping on the ground I judge it impossible for them to rise again; watering them that night, I find them in the morning as they might be in April after a loving rainfall. In this effect I consider the coldness and failing love of courtesans, when silver and gold awakes them so swiftly that the suitor hated that night because he does not give, is beloved in the morning because he has.]

Here the water signifies wealth and sexual tumescence, with the flowers standing for the ostentatiously, insatiably greedy courtesans. Lisardo's fate is

---

[92] {Lope de Vega, *Obras Escogidas* (Madrid: Aguilar, 1953), pp. 432 and 1218.}
[93] *Ibid.*, 252–3.

similarly tied to the water with which he is compared in his moment of contemplation, when swimming in the river in the hot summer, Marcelo finally completes his revenge two years later by drowning him, his body washing up on the banks. The narrator concludes his story in the river:

> y porque se vea cuán verdadero salió el adagio de que los ofendidos escriben en mármol y en agua los que ofenden, pues Marcelo tenía en el corazón la ofensa, mármol en dureza, dos largos años, y Lisardo tan escrita en el agua, que murió en ella.[94]

> [and so you may see how true that aphorism is that the offended engrave in marble and the offenders in water, since Marcelo held the offence in his heart, stony-hard, two long years, and Lisardo so written in water that he died in it.]

The aphorism is Lope's own and again insubstantial, another improvization on memory, playing on a paradox of permanence and immanence. Lisardo's first exchanges with his beloved take place in an orchard on a riverbank, the same place where he is later drowned by the cuckolded husband while swimming, away from the eyes of potential witnesses. The garden was of course viewed as Edenic and arcadian, pre-lapsarian, a place of philosophical contemplation, but it also always carried within it the seed of its own destruction, the expulsion following the Fall. Flowers symbolized the fleeting nature of beauty and pointed at death. Whilst perhaps the garden does not possess the moral seriousness in Lope that it has within the semiotic architecture of Calderón,[95] it reflects upon the complexity and ambivalence of ornament, rhetoric, poetry, sexual morality and authorship. The climate and geography of Spain produced a very specific set of metaphors and associations for the symbolic and allegorical invocation of the garden, landscapes and their uses for outdoor leisure pursuits. The unboundedness of the *locus amoenus* on the riverbank where Spaniards sought refuge from the pitiless Castilian sun reflected the difference of their unbounded nature. The ambivalence of the garden symbolizes a growing lack of interest in the moral ends of fictional texts and a rejection of artificially imposed notions of aesthetic unity not found in the nature that day by day, Lope the horituculturalist and gardener tended and shaped in his real and imagined gardens.

University College London

---

[94] Lope de Vega, *Obras Escogidas*, 284.
[95] See note 28.

7

Experiencing the past: the archaeology of some Renaissance gardens

BRIAN DIX

Archaeology is concerned with physical remains and material evidence. In relation to historical gardens this can range from earthworks and other upstanding remains to below-ground evidence of previous path layouts and planting arrangements. The proper study of these traces is not only essential for accurate restoration and other reconstruction but at the same time increases understanding of what gardens looked like and how they may have been experienced. The discovery of original methods of surface finishing and other details of appearance, which archaeological techniques expose, makes real the series of contemporary historical maps, views, and written descriptions that generally form the greater basis for interpretation.[1] By showing what actually existed, such information is a vital check upon the accuracy of those sources, as well as indicating the precise form of individual garden elements and their interrelationships.

The regular arrangement of Renaissance formal gardens and the style of those they inspired have left a series of ordered and clearly identifiable sites.[2] Some continue to be used as gardens, where the strength of the original design has influenced subsequent development and remains predominant, but in other places earlier regularity has been subsumed into later, less formal landscaping. Many sites have simply been abandoned, however: given up either because of new ownership or for reasons of economy and changing fashion. The majority are lost or eradicated by being built upon but some survive as earthworks, although now bereft of all planting and much other detail. Of the 5,000 or so gardens which are reckoned to have been created in England during the two centuries to *circa* 1730, for example, perhaps only a

---

[1] Compare, for example, the different approaches using many of the same places and much of the same information demonstrated by Roy Strong, *The Renaissance Garden in England* (London: Thames and Hudson, 1979) and Paula Henderson, *The Tudor House and Garden: Architecture and Landscape in the Sixteenth and Early Seventeenth Centuries* (New Haven and London: Yale University Press, 2005).

[2] See, for instance, John M. Steane, 'The Development of Tudor and Stuart Garden Design in Northamptonshire', *Northamptonshire Past and Present*, 5 (1977), 383–405.

Locus Amoenus, First Edition. Edited by Alexander Samson. © 2012 The Authors.
Journal compilation © 2012 The Society for Renaissance Studies and Blackwell Publishing Ltd.

fifth have left tangible remains.[3] They range in scale from the gardens of royal palaces and other great residences to those of minor country houses and lesser places. Their physical remains may include faint earthworks of previous paths and flowerbeds in addition to the outlines of former canals and ponds, as well as more substantial enclosing terraces and other boundaries.[4]

Renaissance gardens were more than simply linked arrangements of borders and banks, however. The style of individual features and how they were combined and made intervisible expressed the ideas and aspirations of the owner, whose aim was frequently to impress, so that the visitor's experience was carefully manipulated. At the same time, the garden was seen as only one component of the broad estate or setting, which might also include parkland and wider landscape in addition to the main house and other buildings. The way in which this setting was contrived and the association between its different elements could be used to demonstrate the intellectual and aesthetic qualities not just of the place itself, but equally of its owner or 'developer'.[5] As a consequence, modern analysis of the topography and surviving physical traces at an individual site may afford an insight into original intentions, as well as showing the processes by which the desired effect was actually created.

Like any source of information, archaeological evidence has its own shortcomings. Depending upon the nature of an individual investigation and the conditions of survival, it may be a more – or less – reliable guide to what happened in the past. It may prove incomplete or misleading, as for example in specific details of planting, where botanical remains are only partial at best and often confused by the presence of material brought in as fertiliser. The directions provided by contemporary historical gardening manuals and agricultural treatises might therefore provide more useful details about former techniques. Whilst such books helped to shape gardening practice, they were also often written in a way to promote the notion of gardening as an intellectual and recreational pleasure, which could provide the means to contemplation and imagination.[6] These themes were taken up and developed in poetry, which praised estates for the delights of their grounds and the hospitality, or charity, that they might engender, together with highlighting their suitability as places for solitude and contented retirement.[7] Sometimes it is obvious that

[3] Paul Everson and Tom Williamson, 'Gardens and Designed Landscapes', in Paul Everson and Tom Williamson (eds.), *The Archaeology of Landscape. Studies presented to Christopher Taylor* (Manchester: Manchester University Press, 1998), 139–65, particularly 146.

[4] *Cf.* Christopher Taylor, *The Archaeology of Gardens* (Princes Risborough: Shire Publications, 1983).

[5] John Steane, 'Renaissance Gardens and Parks', in Boris Ford (ed.), *The Cambridge Guide to the Arts in Britain. Vol. 3: Renaissance and Reformation* (Cambridge: Cambridge University Press, 1989), 209–21.

[6] *Cf.* Rebecca Bushnell, *Green Desire. Imagining Early Modern English Gardens* (Ithaca and London: Cornell University Press, 2003), *passim* but especially 99–107.

[7] William Alexander McClung, *The Country House in English Renaissance Poetry* (Berkeley, Los Angeles and London: University of California Press, 1977), 115–26.

the garden is being used in a metaphorical sense with a generalized description serving only as a trope, but in other instances details can be tested directly against surviving garden features, with the potential to date them and interpret their previous function.[8]

Other literary genres similarly treated the physical features as generic motifs and often subordinated them to illustrate a particular resonance.[9] Although they provide an important insight into contemporary cultural and intellectual habits, their imagery tends to overlook practical details despite borrowing practices from the garden world.[10] By contrast, travellers' diaries and similar accounts communicate what it was like to move through reality and describe actual situations that might be emulated as well as admired.[11] Yet, as with evidence from bills for seeds and the records of payment for physical works, individual visitor-descriptions vary in their amount of detail and clarity – and ultimately their modern usefulness. Whatever their enthusiasm for a place, they cannot replace pictorial and topographical evidence, which might include glimpses of gardens in the background of portraits as well as specific elevated views and other panoramas drawn in sketches and paintings and sometimes reproduced in engravings.[12]

Despite being subject to the patron's manipulation in addition to the artist's personal interpretation, contemporary illustrations surely bear some likeness to the original and combined with surviving maps and other surveys may give actual shape to an individual garden. With the introduction of scale, measured ground plans started to form the basis of estate maps in the later sixteenth century and began to incorporate woods and other parcels of land in addition to showing specific buildings and their ornamental gardens.[13] But, whilst they may depict the natural setting more accurately than an artist's view, in which topographical constraints might be ignored, the true situation can easily be misunderstood without a sound knowledge of the present form of the landscape and how it has developed.[14] For example, exploration on the ground

[8] See, for example, C. Stephen Briggs and Nesta Lloyd, 'Old Gwernyfed: An Elizabethan Garden in History and Poetry', *Gerddi*, 4 (2006), 7–37.
[9] For example, the garden sundial spoke of the transitoriness of life: *cf.* David R. Coffin, *The English Garden. Meditation and Memorial* (Princeton: Princeton University Press, 1994), 8–26.
[10] *Cf.* A. Segre, 'Untangling the Knot: Garden Design in Francesco Colonna's *Hypnerotomachia Poliphili*', *Word and Image*, 14 (1998), 82–108.
[11] *Cf.* for example, Strong, *Renaissance Garden*, 32–3; John Dixon Hunt, *Garden and Grove. The Italian Renaissance Garden in the English Imagination: 1600–1750* (London: J. M. Dent and Sons, 1986), 103–08.
[12] Roy Strong, *The Artist and the Garden* (New Haven and London: Yale University Press, 2000).
[13] Paul Dean Adshead Harvey, *Maps in Tudor England* (London: Public Record Office and British Library, 1993), 79–93. See further *idem*, 'Estate Surveyors and the Spread of the Scale-Map in England, 1550–80', *Landscape History*, 15 (1993), 37–49.
[14] *Cf.* Françoise Boudon, 'Garden History and Cartography', in Monique Mosser and Georges Teyssot (eds.), *The History of Garden Design. The Western Tradition from the Renaissance to the Present Day* (London: Thames and Hudson, 1991), 125–34. See also *eadem*, 'Illustrations of Gardens in the Sixteenth Century: The Most Excellent Buildings in France', in the same volume, 100–02.

would have avoided the kind of simple mistake that led one recent commentator to describe the watercourses at Vallery in France as flowing in the wrong direction.[15]

A multi-source approach raises serious questions about the conclusions that can be drawn from the single sources that are often relied upon for discussing individual gardens. Ideally, various types of information should be compared and combined wherever possible. Garden archaeology is most effective where documentary and pictorial evidence are also available. Such complementary sources of information and collaboration between the different methods involved in their study are integral not only to our understanding of Renaissance gardens but also to their modern conservation.

The following case studies, one in France and the remainder from England, demonstrate how archaeological knowledge can be combined with other evidence to provide a fuller understanding of the trends and changing attitudes in garden design and technology.[16] At Vallery, in France, the local topography determined the scope of the garden, which was designed to impress the majority of visitors who never got entry into it as well as to delight those who did. Conspicuous splendour is also an abiding image of the even more exclusive garden at Kenilworth Castle, where love poetry was invoked within a theatrical atmosphere of elaborate architecture and sensual planting that probably had all the permanence of a stage-set. Transience of a different kind may have been represented in the gardens at Holdenby, which were designed to excite envy and exploited the natural topography to a fine advantage, creating a prospect over the ancestral land which was transformed into an idyllic countryside made up of productive parkland and woods. Meaning and form were sometimes bound together in a more private and intensely personal way, as at Lyveden where a series of ascents and carefully arranged planting guided the individual sinner towards redemption. Most gardens, however, were designed to be more visible. Kirby Hall, for example, was meant to be seen from the upper windows of the house but was eventually opened up to views from outside when its layout was rapidly updated to be in the latest fashion at the end of the seventeenth century. Its vast grass *Parterre à l'Angloise* contained cut-out shapes but lacked flowerbeds, unlike the almost contemporary Privy Garden that was built for King William III at Hampton Court Palace. Its modern reconstruction well

---

[15] William Howard Adams, *The French Garden 1500–1800* (London: Scolar Press, 1979), 28 with Fig. 22 – probably based upon Marie Luise Gothein (ed. Walter P. Wright and trans. Mrs Archer-Hind), *A History of Garden Art* (London and Toronto: J. M. Dent and Sons / New York: E. P. Dutton and Co., 1928), Vol. 1, 404.

[16] The selection of sites is unashamedly personal, being places where I have acquired an intimate knowledge of their physical characteristics either by carrying out intensive fieldwork or through teaching and research interests.

illustrates the value of combining diverse sources of information and is an exemplar for how interdisciplinary studies should be carried out.

VALLERY

Archaeological investigation at Vallery in present-day Burgundy shows how the surroundings of a medieval castle were transformed into an impressive Renaissance setting. A new residence for Jacques d'Albon, Maréchal de Saint-André and favourite of King Henri II (1547–59), was created by Pierre Lescot, who as well as adding garden pavilions may also have designed their location.[17] Modern archaeological studies were carried out between 1995–8 for the regional office of the French Ministry of Culture as a preliminary to the partial restoration of the gardens, which previously extended along the valley bottom

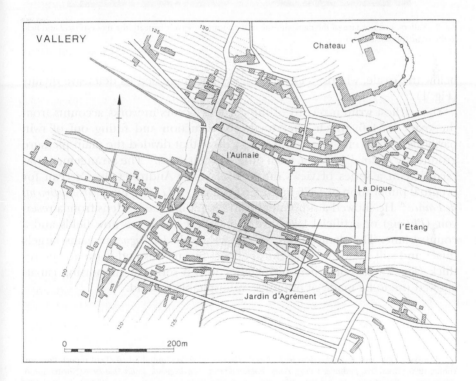

Fig. 1   Chateau and gardens at Vallery in Burgundy, France (after Brian Dix, *Jardins de Vallery, Yonne. Recherches Archéologiques de 1997*)

---

[17] Brian Dix, 'Vallery Revealed', *European Gardens*, 3 (1996), 28–31; Jean Guillaume, 'Pierre Lescot, 1515–1578', in Michel Racine (ed.), *Créateurs de Jardins et de Paysage en France de la Renaissance au XXIe siècle; I: de la Renaissance au début du XIXe siècle* (Arles: Actes Sud, 2001), 17–18. For the castle and later house, see also René Planchenault, 'Les Châteaux de Vallery', *Bulletin Monumental*, 121 (1963), 237–59.

Fig. 2   Vallery. Exterior face of the dam with site of the former reservoir beneath the modern road and field
to the right (photo: author)

below the castle, where wet ground had once increased its defensive quality
(Fig. 1).[18]
    The earliest written record of the gardens occurs in works accounts from
the years 1554–6, which refer to the construction and fitting out of twin
pavilions at each end of a connecting gallery that divided the main pleasure
ground, or *Jardin d'Agrément*, from other garden areas.[19] The arrangement was
recorded in a series of views drawn by Jacques Androuet du Cerceau for
eventual publication in 1576 in the first volume of *Les Plus Excellents Bastiments
de France*.[20] He showed a substantial dam separating the gardens from a reservoir (*l'Étang*) or artificial lake upstream, where there are now fields and a
country lane. The dam, known locally as simply *La Digue*, remains largely
intact and still stands to a height of almost five metres and is twenty metres
thick (Fig. 2). Its construction, together with a series of supporting canals
allowed use to be made of otherwise inhospitable ground.

    [18] Jean-Yves Prampart, *Recherches dans les Jardins du Château de Vallery* (unpublished client report, Pont-sur-
Yonne, 1995); Brian Dix, *Jardins de Vallery, Yonne. Rapport d'Évaluation-diagnostic, Juillet-Août 1996* (Northampton:
Northamptonshire Archaeology, 1997); Brian Dix, *Jardins de Vallery, Yonne. Recherches Archéologiques de 1997*
(Northampton: Northamptonshire County Council, 1998).
    [19] Catherine Grodecki, *Documents du Minutier Central des Notaires de Paris. Histoire de L'art au XVIᵉᵐᵉ siècle
(1540–1600); I: Architecture-Vitrerie-Menuiserie-Tapisserie-Jardins* (Paris: Archives Nationales, 1985), 144–7: Nos.
169, 171, 172, 174.
    [20] J-A. du Cerceau, *Les Plus Excellents Bastiments de France*, 2 vols. (Paris, 1576–9). *Cf.* single volume reprint, ed.
David Thomson (Paris: Sand, 1988), 107–17. Original drawings are preserved in the Department of Prints and
Drawings, British Museum, London; the most relevant are Nos. 1972 U. 825–U. 827.

Analyses of pollen, plant and snail remains from the original ground surface and other layers show that the area was previously open but damp and marshy, and frequently under water.[21] Drier conditions followed after damming-up the valley and the creation of canals to carry water through the main garden and beyond, where remedial works were more extensive. They comprised a long central watercourse flanked by narrower channels with the ground in between under-drained and filled by a regular arrangement of double rows of trees that du Cerceau noted as being alders, which thrive in damp sites. A similar style of planting then continued for a distance downstream beside the inner banks of two streams, which diverged along the base of the valley after forming at the other side of a roadway across the end of the alder-ground, or *l'Aulnaie* (Fig. 1).[22]

The dam crossed the base of the valley at a right angle, with the result that the approaching visitor using it as a causeway would have looked up towards the new chateau and the walls of the older castle, with the greenery of woods and vineyards on the hillslope at the rear framing a pleasant backdrop. The scene would be mirrored on the surface of the lake or reservoir, which du Cerceau depicted as a straight-sided feature extending across the entire face of the dam.[23] A later plan provides a more complete picture and shows that it held back a large body of water fed by the local river and another stream.[24] The regularity of its outline beside the dam presupposes artificial deepening, as still characterized by a steep scarp along one edge where the valley slope has been cut away. Analysis of archaeobotanical samples from a series of test pits dug into the base of the former reservoir indicates that it held deep moving water.[25]

Examination of the structure of the dam and its retaining walls revealed that its construction was coeval with the creation of the garden in the mid-sixteenth century. It had been formed by dumping material at either side of a clay core, with the mass held in place by strong outer walls.[26] The wall facing the lake was built with a slight batter to withstand pressure and the choice of bright, off-white sandstone will have been visually striking, especially when gleaming in sunlight reflected by the water. The effect with the castle and new house on the slope to one side therefore would have been spectacular.

The wall was built upon a timber spreader-plate above a series of wooden piles, which had been driven into the underlying marsh to provide a stable footing. The opposite wall, beside the garden, may have been similarly supported to prevent sinking, but its base could not be reached due to the height

---

[21] Dix, *Rapport*, 12–13 (Trench 3) and 15 (Trenches 5 and 10).

[22] du Cerceau (ed. Thomson), *Les Plus Excellents Bastiments*, 109. See also Dix, *Recherches*, 19–23.

[23] *Loc. cit.*

[24] Henry Sengre, *Atlas des Terres de Bourgogne par Berry* (1682), preserved in Musée Condé, Chantilly, archives: armoire 81, 1597.

[25] Dix, *Recherches*, 3–8.

[26] *Ibid.*, 8–11 and Pl. 11.

Fig. 3   Vallery. Top of counterfort behind rear wall of the dam; scale rod in 0.5-m. divisions (photo: author)

of the modern water table. It was strengthened by a series of massive coun-
terforts, which held it fast in the thickness of the dam (Fig. 3).[27]

The top of the wall below the parapet bordering the garden was used as a
pavement.[28] Its surface was mortared to provide a smooth walkway, although
the outlines of stones remained visible and some were left protruding, giving
a 'rustic feel'. Only fragmentary evidence survived to show how the

[27] *Ibid.*, Pls. 13 and 15.
[28] *Ibid.*, 12–13 and Pls. 14, 17–18.

Fig. 4 Vallery. Modern view of the *Jardin d'Agrément* looking from the top of the dam (photo: author)

contemporary carriageway had been surfaced, but it seems likely that it was made up of sand and gravel hoggin.

Access into the *Jardin d'Agrément* was by means of a centrally placed twin staircase, although the present structure is a rebuilding using the earlier foundations.[29] Like its predecessor, therefore, it leads to the end of an axial canal that extends along most of the length of the garden (Fig. 4). According to du Cerceau the ground at either side was divided into a series of ornamental plots with trees planted at the corners (Fig. 5).[30] Each compartment was laid out with geometric patterns that were symmetrical in themselves although no two were identical. There appears to have been sixteen rectangles in all but the published view shows only twelve, presumably due to engraver's error.[31]

The walls of the garden enclosure originally formed a rectangle 120 metres long and 110 metres wide but the north-east corner has since been modified to provide a new entrance at modern street level. Until then, the only points of access at ground level appear to have been located beside the corner pavilions at the opposite end of the garden, where a pair of ornamental alcoves presumably contained gates. Despite the historical mention of a separate doorway connecting the gallery between the pavilions with the alder ground beyond,[32] no traces remain since the corridor has long been demolished and the dividing wall between the two gardens has been rebuilt. The

[29] *Ibid.*, 13–14.
[30] British Museum, Department of Prints and Drawings, 1972 U. 827.
[31] Du Cerceau (ed. Thomson), *Les Plus Excellents Bastiments*, 114–15.
[32] Grodecki, *Documents*, 144–5 No. 169.

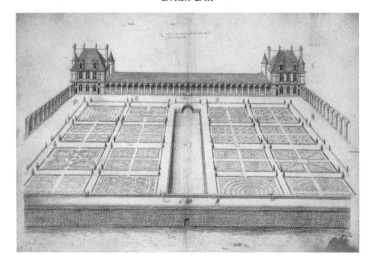

Fig. 5   Vallery. Drawing by J-A. du Cerceau overlooking the causeway and dam to the *Jardin d'Agrément* at the rear (London, British Museum, Department of Prints and Drawings, 1972 U.827; reproduced by permission. © Trustees of the British Museum)

Fig. 6   Vallery. Remains of the northern garden pavilion seen from the rear in *l'Aulnaie*, for a view of the opposite side see Fig. 4 above centre right (photo: author)

individual pavilions are likewise much altered. The northern one is the most complete, following its conversion for later residential use, but it has lost its upper floors and one corner has been demolished (Fig. 6). Its southern counterpart is more fragmentary, with only the lower part of one corner still standing. Both originally looked splendid, however – each two storeys high and containing attic windows with turrets at the rear.[33]

The sense of grandeur continued around the sides of the garden, which were decorated with blind arcading, and the open arches of the gallery or loggia connecting the pavilions were mirrored opposite by a series of deep alcoves set into the retaining wall at the rear of the dam.[34] It seems, however, that these recesses proved to be a source of perceived, if not real structural weakness and they soon appear to have been filled in and the wall was re-faced as the need to ensure stability overtook the earlier aesthetic.[35]

Whilst the central layout of the *Jardin d'Agrément* occupies a raised platform above the surrounding walks in du Cerceau's drawing (Fig. 5), the discovery of original steps and associated ground levels leaves no doubt that the actual situation was different.[36] By contrast, the archaeological evidence indicates that the area formed a sunken garden surrounded by a broad, low terrace approximately two feet high (0.65 m.), as was shown correctly in the published view.[37] In later years it was filled with soil and gradually built up to the same level as the top of the terrace, eventually necessitating the introduction of steps down to the canal and resulting in today's largely flat appearance (*cf.* Fig. 4).

The stone-lined canal in the middle of the garden was fed water from the reservoir through an underground conduit beneath the dam and a sluice controlled the outflow at the other end.[38] Its form is that of a long, thin rectangle with semicircular apsidal ends flanked by a pair of ramps, which may have been intended for use by waterfowl. The top of the surrounding walls slopes gently towards the far end, thereby creating an illusion of greater length when viewed from the carriageway above the dam. The floor of the pool comprises a continuous pavement of neatly squared white sandstone blocks and with a similar lining around the sides would ensure bright water, which could be used to good effect for displaying fish and other aquatic creatures. The structure was made watertight through the use of hydraulic mortar, in contrast to the canals in *l'Aulnaie*, which were built using porous mortar and had puddled clay bottoms.[39] They were also linked to a series of field drains, further indicating their more utilitarian purpose.

Whilst the differences of construction between the main canals in the two gardens emphasize their different roles, it is also clear that the ornamental pool in the *Jardin d'Agrément* could not have been used to drain the surrounding garden, and excess groundwater was presumably directed into soakaways.

[33] As shown in the bird's-eye view by du Cerceau (ed. Thomson), *Les Plus Excellents Bastiments*, 110–11.

[34] Dix, *Rapport*, 19–20 (Trenches 21 and 23). See also Dix, *Recherches*, Pls. 23–4.

[35] Dix, *Recherches*, 15. Instability presumably caused the top of the wall to split away from the counterfort shown in Fig. 3 above.

[36] Dix, *Rapport*, 10.

[37] du Cerceau (ed. Thomson), *Les Plus Excellents Bastiments*, 114–15.

[38] Dix, *Recherches*, 18–19 and Pls. 29–30.

[39] *Ibid.*, 19–22.

Although snail evidence indicates that soil conditions had improved, with dry ground species now predominant, there was still a measure of dampness and the general habitat seems to have been rather open and largely devoid of vegetation.[40] A continuing element of ground moisture is further suggested by the apparent dearth of associated seeds and other plant remains, which might be expected to have survived, and it is significant that the decorative designs were deliberately picked out using inert materials such as fine yellowish brown sand, orange gravel, and broken white sandstone.[41]

The paths surrounding the patterns were made up of dense compacted chalk and although equipped with shallow side drains would soon become dirty and slippery when wet.[42] It is possible therefore that they were not intended generally to be walked upon, but rather to be viewed from the surrounding terrace and the upper windows of the pavilions, or even to be seen more distantly from the viewpoint of the causeway and its pavement. Thus, whilst the gardens could be looked down upon from the new house and its carriage-approach, they might have been kept largely as a showpiece with exclusive admission. Indeed, the scale and openness of the *Jardin d'Agrément* does not lend itself to intimacy, but its robust mix of strong architecture, geometrical elaboration, and land reclamation through clever water engineering fits well with the authority of Vallery's martial owner.

KENILWORTH

A different kind of stage effect was created at Kenilworth Castle in the heart of England in July 1575 to provide the setting for nineteen days of lavish entertainment organised by Robert Dudley, Earl of Leicester, for a visit by Queen Elizabeth I.[43] The entire landscape served as theatre, with its different elements linked as a series of deliberately framed views in a continuous narrative of events and tableaux. The deer park and mere, already vast pleasure grounds, were used in scenes of pageantry and spectacle, reached via a new turreted gatehouse that was reminiscent of an earlier age. Inside the castle walls, a recently built lodging was refurbished for the queen's use and an elaborate garden was laid out below the twelfth-century great tower or keep, which was partly remodelled to accommodate a picture and viewing gallery.[44]

In contrast to the very public spaces of other parts of the castle, the garden provided a secure and convenient private place that could appeal to the senses through a mixture of sights, scents, and sounds. A contemporary description

[40] Dix, *Rapport*, 13 (Trench 3).
[41] *Ibid.*, 18 (Trenches 6 and 22).
[42] *Ibid.*, 17–18 (Trenches 6, 7 and 17).
[43] Elisabeth Woodhouse, 'Kenilworth, the Earl of Leicester's Pleasure Ground, following Robert Laneham's Letter', *Garden History*, 27 (1999), 127–44.
[44] Richard K. Morris, *Kenilworth Castle* (London: English Heritage, 2006), 11–13, 25–9.

by Robert Langham conveys the image of a *locus amoenus*, or place of joy and delight, where beauty could be enjoyed and lovers might meet.[45] He described a series of pretty conceits, which alluded to the queen as well as to Dudley, and the layout that contained them, comprising a high bank or terrace along one side of the garden with a timber aviary directly opposite and arbours at each end. The area in between was divided into quarters by grass and sand walks, and filled with flowers, fragrant herbs and fruit trees. Such luxuriant planting emphasized the sensual quality of the garden, which was clearly intended both to enchant and seduce the onlooker. In the middle of all there stood a tall, sculptured marble fountain with side-panels decorated with amatory scenes from Ovid's *Metamorphoses.*[46]

Apart from the altered remains of the terrace at the base of the castle keep, there were no obvious visible remains of the Elizabethan garden when English Heritage began to investigate the feasibility of reconstruction in 2004.[47] Archaeological evaluation at that time, however, discovered the foundations of the central fountain, which has proved a vital key to understanding the original geometry.[48] Upon complete excavation, it became clear that its octagonal form matched that in Langham's description and its dimensions were also consistent with measurements he had recorded (Fig. 7).[49] A central scar showed where the main fountain-sculpture had risen from the middle of the basin and small pieces of Carrara marble, discarded during later dismantling, further confirmed the accuracy of the historical account.[50]

Used in conjunction with the historical account of building dimensions, the archaeological evidence has provided a firm basis for recreating the arrangement of the garden, although much finishing detail remains necessarily speculative (Fig. 8).[51] The lack of firm foundations for the arbours, obelisks and some of the other features which Langham described suggests that they were only of light construction, and most likely made out of wood and painted to look like stone. This may certainly be expected for the tall porphyry obelisks that were mentioned in the centre of each quarter: such a quantity of material

[45] Roger J. P. Kuin (ed.), *Robert Langham: A Letter* (Leiden: E. J. Brill, 1983). For a new edition of the text see Jayne Elisabeth Archer, Elizabeth Clarke and Elizabeth Goldring (eds.), *John Nichols's The Progress and Public Processions of Queen Elizabeth I: A New Edition of the Early Modern Sources* (Oxford: Oxford University Press, forthcoming).

[46] Elisabeth Woodhouse, 'Propaganda in Paradise: The Symbolic Garden Created by the Earl of Leicester at Kenilworth, Warwickshire', *Garden History*, 36 (2008), 94–113, in particular 107–09.

[47] Graham Brown, *The Elizabethan Garden at Kenilworth Castle* (Swindon: English Heritage Archaeological Investigation Report Series AI/3/2005, 2005), 2–4.

[48] Brian Dix and Joe Prentice, *Archaeological Evaluation in the Elizabethan Garden, Kenilworth Castle, Warwickshire, September 2004* (Northampton: Northamptonshire County Council, 2004), 3.10 (Trench B). See further Brian Dix, Brian Kerr and Joe Prentice, 'Archaeology', in Anna Keay and John Watkins (eds.), *'Worthy to be Called Paradise': Re-Creating the Elizabethan Garden at Kenilworth Castle* (London: English Heritage, forthcoming).

[49] Brian Dix and Joe Prentice, *Summary of the 2005 Season of Excavation within the Elizabethan Garden at Kenilworth Castle* (Northampton: Northamptonshire County Council, 2006), 2.2.3–6.

[50] Brian Dix and Joe Prentice, *Assessment Report on the Excavations within the former Elizabethan Garden at Kenilworth Castle, Warwickshire* (Northampton: Northamptonshire County Council, 2007), 12.2.16.

[51] See, for instance, the critique by Roy Strong, 'Gloriana's Garden', *Country Life*, 5 August 2009, 46–50.

Brian Dix

Fig. 7   Kenilworth Castle. Excavated Elizabethan fountain remains; scale rod in 0.5-m. divisions (photo: author)

Fig. 8   Kenilworth Castle. The reconstructed Elizabethan Garden (photo: author)

would have been almost impossible to obtain in sixteenth-century England, especially since only thin veneers appear to have been used in Roman Britain.[52]

It is significant that only thirty years later the sole items of any quality and value listed in the garden were the marble fountain and 'the Queenes seat of freestone'.[53] This would fit with the other elements having been of flimsy construction – and they might already have long disappeared from the garden, especially if they were erected to create an atmosphere just for the duration of the queen's visit. In that instance, it may have been intended that they should be admired as much for the extravagance of their ephemerality as for their ingenuity.

'MANIE ASCENDINGS AND DESCENDINGS'

John Norden's words, used in describing the garden terraces at Holdenby in Northamptonshire,[54] would have applied just as fittingly to other places where variety was experienced through movement and the chance of unexpected discovery. The organization of split-levels was most easily achieved on a sloping site, where the garden space could be ordered into terraced descents. Indeed, the inequalities of an individual site might be viewed as an advantage rather than something to be avoided. Although few English places had a steep hillside location to match that of many Italian villas, their more gentle slopes were nevertheless transformed to equally dramatic and fine advantage.

At Holdenby a sequence of garden construction can be identified in Elizabethan surveys made seven to eight years apart.[55] The property was the family home of Christopher Hatton, the queen's trusted favourite and Lord Chancellor from 1587 until his death four years later.[56] In addition to building the largest private house in England at the time, he provided a setting of elaborate formal gardens alongside a large deer park that was laid out over common fields covering almost one-third of the parish.[57] The two maps, dated 1580 and 1587 respectively, show the creation of the park and development of the gardens around the new house, which occupied a commanding site uphill from the modest manor house that it replaced.[58]

[52] Andrew Pearson, *The Work of Giants. Stone and Quarrying in Roman Britain* (Stroud: Tempus Publishing, 2006), 81.

[53] British Library, London, *Cotton Tiberius* Eviii, fol. 212v.

[54] Written by 1591 and revised *c.* 1610, but not published until a century later: John Norden, *Speculi Britanniae Pars Altera; or, a Delineation of Northamptonshire being a Brief History and Chorographical Description of that County in the Year 1610* (London, 1720), 50–51.

[55] Northamptonshire Record Office, *Finch Hatton Collection (FH)* 272, fol. 59 and 62.

[56] Eric St John Brooks, *Sir Christopher Hatton* (London: Jonathan Cape, 1946), in particular Chaps. 1–2 and 16.

[57] Maurice Beresford, *History on the Ground* (1957; rev. edn. Stroud: Sutton Publishing, 1998), 213–14.

[58] *Ibid.*, Pls. 15–16; Royal Commission on Historical Monuments England, *An Inventory of the Historical Monuments in the County of Northampton. Vol. III: Archaeological Sites in North-West Northamptonshire* (London: Her

The latest mansion was built around two courtyards and had tall symmetrical facades with central towers in the long sides and turreted corner pavilions, which will have formed a striking silhouette against the sky.[59] Its large windows with their lavish glazing, particularly along the south-facing garden side where the façade was over 100 yards long (approximately 105 m.), would have been a similarly impressive sight, whether seen from the slopes below or viewed across the deer park and out of the countryside beyond. Its potential to sparkle in daylight and glisten in the evening sun, and then shine by the brightness of lights at night would have added to the sense of awe and splendour.

The visitor approached the house from the east along a strong axial drive leading straight to an entrance at the end of a large rectangular enclosure known as 'The Greene', which Lord Treasurer Burghley described as 'a large, long, straight fairway' (Fig. 9).[60] A large pond next to a freshly planted spinney and a long stables building hid the nearby village from view. At the end a gatehouse provided access into the Base Court and it was only after entering this forecourt that the towering front of the house was fully revealed. The archways that pierced the walls at either side still survive and are dated 1583. One led out towards the village, where a new inn was built to provide additional accommodation for visitors; the other opened into the gardens (Fig. 10).

A series of plantations separated the house from the common fields around the north and west sides, in part replacing an earlier arrangement of nine square flowerbeds but allowing greater privacy, particularly where the outlying ground dropped away and the woodland would therefore screen off the view from any workers. Tall, close-boarded fences of pointed planks divided off other parts of the private area, but several circular and snail-mounts constructed in the corners permitted views out.[61]

In addition to being pleasant areas, the woods could also be used for profit, as Norden noted.[62] Likewise, various fishponds appear to have been well stocked and the adjacent 600-acre park (approximately 240 hectares) contained a large rabbit warren and a herd of fallow deer in addition to other woodland. The creation of a cruciform arrangement of rides through one area known as 'Colepitt Ashes' shows how the existing functional aspects of a hunting preserve were already starting to fuse with the aesthetic and economic values of a landscape park.[63]

Majesty's Stationery Office, 1981), Pls. 16–18; Mark Girouard, *Town and Country* (New Haven and London: Yale University Press, 1992), Figs. 186–7, all reproducing details of the original maps in Northamptonshire Record Office, *FH* 272 (see note 55).

[59] Girouard, *Town and Country*, 197–210 and especially Figs. 182 and 184. See also John Heward and Robert Taylor, *The Country Houses of Northamptonshire* (Swindon: Royal Commission on Historical Monuments of England, 1996), 235–8.

[60] Quoted in Brooks, *Hatton*, 158.

[61] See, for instance, Royal Commission on Historical Monuments England, *Sites in North-West Northamptonshire*, Pl. 18.

[62] See note 54.

[63] Depicted in the 1587 map. See note 58.

Fig. 9　Holdenby. Aerial view showing 'The Greene' at top right with the remains of the Base Court, house site, and terraces overlooking the church and lower gardens towards centre right and former park below (photo: author)

The formal gardens separating the parkland from the house were divided into several areas (Fig. 9). Thousands of tonnes of earth were used to create a level, roughly square platform that extended along the entire length of the south front of the house between the end pavilions. It still projects up to five metres high above the sloping ground where flights of terraces drop down at either side.[64] The flat area between appears to have been raised for walks around the edges but otherwise was divided into four identical compartments, which in 1587 were depicted with knots. The outlines of some of the plots can still be traced, together with the remains of a low circular mound that they previously surrounded. The two Elizabethan surveys show this central feature containing a series of radiating lines or spokes, with a gap in the southern arc that suggests that it was an immense flat sundial.[65] The presence of such a feature in so prominent a position may have been a deliberate reference to transience, particularly since a double-sided portrait painting alluding to the same theme may have been placed near the entrance to the house.[66]

The series of terraces at either side of the 'dial garden' remain prominent earthworks (Fig. 10). In the 1580 survey, both groups were described as 'ye

[64] Royal Commission on Historical Monuments England, *Sites in North-West Northamptonshire*, 106–09 and Fig. 83.

[65] *Cf.* Pete Smith, 'The Sundial Garden and House-Plan Mount: Two Gardens at Wollaton Hall, Nottinghamshire, by Robert (*c.* 1535–1614) and John (– 1634) Smythson', *Garden History*, 31 (2003), 1–28, in particular 6–7.

[66] Tarnya Cooper, 'Double-Sided Painting with a Portrait of Sir Christopher Hatton, *c.* 1581', in Susan Doran (ed.), *Elizabeth. The Exhibition at the National Maritime Museum* (London: Chatto and Windus with The National Maritime Museum, 2003), 137–9.

Fig. 10   Holdenby. Gateways of 1583 with remains of 'ye Rosiary' terraces in the foreground (photo: author)

Rosiary', indicating that they may have been set apart for the cultivation of roses or, possibly at the same time, an abstruse reference to the mysteries of the Rosary. Hatton is known to have had an ambivalent attitude towards Catholics and employed Hugh Hall, a Catholic priest, as the gardener at Holdenby – if not its actual designer – prior to the latter's arrest in 1583 for involvement in Somerville's plot to murder the queen.[67] The original paired arrangement of six terraces had been modified by 1587 through the insertion

---

[67] Brooks, *Hatton*, 216, 257–8.

of a large rectangular fishpond into the base of the western group and the addition of a bowling alley below the other series, where a separate raised walk provided access to a new banqueting house built at the far end.[68] Within each flight of terraces the separate levels appear to have been connected by gentle slopes enabling an easy, winding descent.

The medieval church of Holdenby, containing a series of recently added family memorials and earlier dynastic tombs,[69] lay at the foot of the western series of terraces and occupied the corner of a lower garden compartment that provided access into the newly created park. Before that, the 1580 survey had identified the area as 'the orchard', showing it with trees and a single pond as well as containing the site of the old manor house. By the time of the later survey, the pond had been enlarged and two smaller ones constructed to the side. A separate block of five larger ponds was also created in the hollow at the centre of the garden, where they still survive. A series of broad terraces today rise up the slope to the west and include an area that may have been a knot garden in 1587.[70] The prospect mount mapped at that time on top of the opposite slope in the facing corner has been refashioned on several occasions but still affords panoramic views. The earthwork of a zigzag path leads up to it from the central ponds, but as with other features in this area does not appear in the two historical maps and thus may post-date them.[71]

King James I bought Holdenby in 1608 as a country seat for Prince Charles but after the English Civil War the property was seized by Parliament and subsequently sold. Following its purchase in 1650 by Captain Adam Baynes, the house was demolished except for a small part that was kept as a residence, and much of the surrounding garden also appears to have been abandoned and its woodland cut down. The property returned to the Crown at the Restoration and thereafter passed through numerous hands by grant or purchase, culminating in the rebuilding of the present house and gardens towards the end of the nineteenth century.[72] Since they hardly impinge upon the earlier gardens, the greater part of the late sixteenth-century layout of terraces, sloping walks and ponds survives as tangible testimony to elaborateness and scale, despite the accompanying luxury of architecture and other art having largely disappeared.

The development of specific routes and different plantings through a succession of individual garden spaces enabled a variety of narratives and imagery to be presented. Whilst places like Holdenby were meant to be highly visible, others were designed to be more private, yet no less appealing to the observer who was educated enough to understand the associations and allusions being offered.

[68] See note 61.
[69] Brooks, *Hatton*, 165.
[70] Royal Commission on Historical Monuments England, *Sites in North-West Northamptonshire*, 108.
[71] *Loc. cit.*
[72] Girouard, *Town and Country*, 210; Heward and Taylor, *Country Houses*, 235–6.

Fig. 11   Lyveden. Aerial view looking over the valley slope before recent tree clearance, showing the manor house at top and lodge in bottom right with former gardens and orchards in between (photo: author)

Each of the gardens so far discussed provided a framework for the processes of social and cultural exchange, as well as a means of projecting family and personal image. In contrast to them, the gardens that the Catholic recusant Sir Thomas Tresham created from 1594 onwards at his Northamptonshire manor of Lyveden formed a symbolic scheme that served as a religious witness.[73] Despite being left unfinished when he died in 1605, enough remains upstanding to be used, in conjunction with surviving details of some of his original directions to workmen, to demonstrate the intended experience.

The gardens occupied a long strip of ground, rising for almost a half-mile (approximately 530 m.) up the hillslope that forms the valley side above the manor house (Fig. 11).[74] They terminated in a lodge or banqueting house that was designed in the form of a Greek cross and ornamented with emblems and inscriptions proclaiming devotion to Christ's Passion and the Blessed Virgin Mary.[75] It overlooked a bowling green and quincunxes of nut and fruit trees to one side, but stood at the centre of a separate raised garden that was deliberately offset from the main axis behind the brow of the hill.[76] The gaze of the visitor approaching from the manor house was thus directed upwards,

[73] Andrew Eburne, 'The Passion of Sir Thomas Tresham: New Light on the Gardens and Lodge at Lyveden', *Garden History*, 36 (2008), 114–34.

[74] A. E. Brown and Christopher C. Taylor, 'The Gardens at Lyveden, Northamptonshire', *Archaeological Journal*, 129 (1972), 154–60.

[75] John Alfred Gotch, *A Complete Account Illustrated by Measured Drawings of the Buildings Erected in Northamptonshire by Sir Thomas Tresham Between the Years 1575 and 1605* (Northampton: Taylor and Son, 1883), 31–44 and accompanying plates.

[76] *Cf.* Eburne, 'New Light', Fig. 1.

Fig. 12 Lyveden. Terrace and stepped mounts between the two orchards (photo: author)

although the destination and other features which lay ahead were not immediately visible but only revealed during the ascent.

The sense of discovery began at once with a series of broad terraces climbing the hill from beside the house and leading towards a high embankment
along the edge of a large orchard that rose up the rest of the slope. Its far end
was closed off by an elaborate stepped bank with a double truncated-pyramid
mount at each end, which marked the boundary of a square moat around a
second orchard above the crest of the hill (Fig. 12). The lower orchard
appears to have been planted with several hundred fruit trees, consisting of
varieties of apples, pears and plums arranged in regular rows with walks
running in between.[77] In addition to forming an exquisite collection, the
abundance of trees could have been capable of being interpreted in several
different ways – from recalling the Garden of Eden and implications of the
Fall, to a concept of the Virgin with Paradise and association with the Garden
of Gethsemane.[78]

Within the moated orchard, an arrangement of ten concentric rings or
flowerbeds, no longer visible but identifiable as cropmarks in an aerial pho-
tograph taken by the Luftwaffe in 1940,[79] resembles the manuscript, pavement
and turf labyrinths of medieval Christian thought.[80] Like them, it may have
been intended as a devotional aid to evoke a notion of pilgrimage to Jerusalem
or as a reference to Christ's entry into the city on Palm (or Willow) Sunday. It
may be significant that palaeobotanical evidence for willow trees has been
recovered from silts within the moat canals, whilst the roses and raspberries
that Tresham recommended to be planted in the circles were specifically

[77] *Ibid.*, Table 1.
[78] *Ibid.*, 121.
[79] *Ibid.*, Fig. 3.
[80] *Cf.* Edward Trollope, 'Notices of Ancient and Medieval Labyrinths', *Archaeological Journal*, 15 (1858),
216–35; Hermann Kern, *Through the Labyrinth. Designs and Meanings over 5,000 Years* (Munich, London and New
York: Prestel, 2000), Chaps. 7–9.

Fig. 13   Lyveden. View towards the lodge from the top of the adjacent spiral mount within the moated orchard
(photo: author)

associated with Christ's Passion.[81] It seems likely that the mounts surrounding
the orchard were similarly intended to evoke other locations associated with
the Passion and the spiral ascents of the two largest overlooking the lodge
from the top side of the moat may have been particularly suited to specific
devotions (Fig. 13).

The symbolism of the different garden elements such as the orchards and
mounts culminated in the lodge itself with its eclectic mix of Catholic

[81] Eburne, 'New Light', 125–6.

emblems, inscriptions, and numerology.[82] The careful placing of words in the exterior inscriptions ensured that the names *IESVS* and *MARIA* were repeatedly linked at either side of the bay on the end wall of each wing. A triumphalist note was expressed by juxtaposing emblems of the Crucifixion and Resurrection in a lower frieze over the bay front, thereby proclaiming the salvation of the world that results from Christ's Passion and the Virgin's intercessions – and surely holding the key to the nature of Tresham's devotion.[83]

Following Sir Thomas's death in September 1605 the property passed to his son, Francis, but was forfeited in only a few months owing to his involvement in the Gunpowder Plot. Construction of the gardens came to an abrupt halt and was not resumed on any significant scale thereafter.[84] Modern dewatering and dredging of part of the canal system around the moated orchard has revealed the moment when groundwork ceased. At one end of the last section of the canal, which would have completed the square around the garden, a ramp was exposed. It was clearly used as a haul-way for the excavated spoil to be taken out and dumped to create the nearby snail mount, which is still in the partially formed state that it was left in when abandoned (Fig. 14).

'DIGING OF BORDERS'[85]

Studies of short-lived gardens like Holdenby and Lyveden provide important information about contemporary historical trends in design and the close-dating of their remains can help to identify and interpret similar types of earthwork that are not so well documented. However, other archaeological methods involving non-intrusive geophysical survey techniques as well as actual excavation will often reveal unsuspected and sometimes complex substructures, and thereby caution against too simplistic identification.[86]

It is in the nature of gardens to be transient places. While they constantly alter as the plants they contain flourish and die, they also develop in response to changing fashion. The careful examination of what remains below ground can indicate the stages of evolution at an individual site as well as demonstrate specific details of original design and fabric.[87]

Kirby Hall, near Corby in Northamptonshire, is an important Elizabethan prodigy house that was abandoned during the eighteenth century and there-

---

[82] Gyles Isham, 'Sir Thomas Tresham and His Buildings', *Reports and Papers of the Northamptonshire Antiquarian Society*, 65.2 (1966), 28–31; Mark Girouard, *Lyveden New Bield, Northamptonshire* (London: The National Trust, 1990), 20–22.

[83] *Cf.* Gotch, *Buildings*, Pls. LNB 3–4, 12.

[84] Eburne, 'New Light', 130–31.

[85] Northamptonshire Record Office, *FH* 2146 referring to Kirby Hall: *The Acounte of the Great Garden from December ye 5ᵗʰ 1685 to November ye 5ᵗʰ 1686.*

[86] Brian Dix, ' "Of Cabbages – and Kings": Garden Archaeology in Action', in Geoff Egan and Ronn L. Michael (eds.), *Old and New Worlds. Historical/Post Medieval Archaeology Papers from the Societies' Joint Conferences at Williamsburg and London 1997 to Mark Thirty Years of Work and Achievement* (Oxford: Oxbow Books, 1999), 368–77.

[87] *Ibid.*, 370–72.

Fig. 14   Lyveden. Abandoned cutting of the final arm of the canal around the moated orchard with unfinished
mount in the background (photo: author)

fore remains largely untouched by later alteration.[88] Archaeological excavation has shown that a grander scheme of gardens replaced the initial simple
layout when King James I began visiting in the early seventeenth century.[89]
Their creation involved extensive earthmoving to form a level, rectangular
platform overlooked by a long gallery in the west side of the house, with tall

[88] Heward and Taylor, *Country Houses*, 245–56.
[89] Brian Dix, Iain Soden and Tora Hylton, 'Kirby Hall and its Gardens: Excavations in 1987–1994', *Archaeological Journal*, 152 (1995), 291–380.

Fig. 15 Kirby Hall. Aerial view showing previous reconstruction of the Great Garden beside the house and remains of the canalised stream below (photo: author)

terraces around another two sides and a free-standing wall along the other edge. The main, shorter axis was aligned on a crosswalk that extended from the house towards a pedimented arch in the middle of the terrace opposite, where it framed steps leading to the top.[90] The discovery of discarded fragments of stone balustrading[91] indicates that a miniature arcade ran along the

[90] *Ibid.*, 321–3.
[91] *Ibid.*, Figs. 52–4.

Fig. 16   Kirby Hall. Reconstruction of ornamental parterres in the northern half of the Great Garden prior to the reintroduction of associated statues and urns (photo: author)

top of the brick walls that formerly retained the inner edge of the terrace beside a soil border; otherwise, broad paths divided the garden-floor into an arrangement of quarter-plots (Fig. 15).

Towards the end of the seventeenth century the axis of the garden was turned through ninety degrees to create a longer view.[92] The walls surrounding the Jacobean garden were pulled down and the terrace opposite the house was converted into a grass-covered bank. At the same time, the existing arch was moved to its present position in the middle of the north side of the garden to form a new focus at that end.[93] Instead of being looked upon from the house, the intention now was that the layout should be viewed from the top of the valley slope to the south, where the gardens had been newly extended.[94] They culminated there in a wilderness planted with 'almost the whole variety of our English trees'[95] from which avenues led the eye to distant views, looking beyond the owner's estate and thereby appropriating the wider landscape.[96]

The extension of the gardens appears to have been accompanied by canalization of the local brook, which was directed along a series of straight lengths linked by right-angled turns. A stone dam and sluice built on the downstream side of the main part of the streamcourse where it crossed the alignment of

[92] *Ibid.*, 325–8. See also Teresa Sladen, 'The Garden at Kirby Hall 1570–1700', *Journal of Garden History*, 4 (1984), 139–56.

[93] British Library, London, *Add. MSS* 29574 331. See Edward Maunde Thompson (ed.), *Correspondence of the Family Hatton*, Camden Society n. s., 23.2 (1878), 206.

[94] Sladen, 'Garden at Kirby Hall', 152–4 and Fig. 10.

[95] John Morton, *The Natural History of Northamptonshire with Some Account of the Antiquities* (London, 1712), 493.

[96] British Library, London, *Add. MSS* 29575 43: '. . . I am inclinable to think if yr Loppe cut a riding straight forwards from thence thro ye woods you might from ye top of ye Wilderness see to Gretton if not into Rutlandshire.'

gardens would have enabled the channel to be filled with water, thereby creating a reflective ribbon at the foot of the garden.[97] The previous arrangement of plats beside the house was retained but given a makeover, whereby the surface of each was raised prior to the introduction of stone- or 'gravel'-filled shapes in grass (Fig. 16). A series of clinched iron nails survived where they had been used to fasten together a framework of wooden boards which formed the outline of the latest design.[98] The employment of such fretting, combined with laying turf taken from local meadows, would facilitate swift creation of the new effect, as might be demanded in between seasons. The surrounding paths were renewed at the same time and replenished with loose limestone chippings, which were laid sufficiently thick that a visitor's feet would sink slightly into the surface and produce a crunching sound during walking. The display in pots and urns of new plant varieties and other rare specimens from the owner's collection would have heightened the sense of delight, as well as the feeling of specialness from having access into the garden.[99]

The kudos of privilege was felt nowhere more keenly than in the exclusiveness of royal gardens, as for instance in the Privy Garden at Hampton Court Palace, where the accession of William III and Mary II to the English throne in 1688 heralded a period of great change.[100] Sir Christopher Wren was soon commissioned to build a new palace to be the centrepiece of a vast Baroque landscape. The Privy Garden lay directly in front of the new king's apartments and was initially enlarged to match their width. Work fell into abeyance after the death of Queen Mary in 1694 and it was only in July 1700 that William decided finally to extend the garden to the River Thames, clearing from the site the Water Gallery and other buildings that stood in the way. It took nearly another year of deliberation to adopt the final design, for which construction was almost complete when the king died on 8 March 1702.[101]

In 1991, the Historic Royal Palaces Agency embarked upon a major project to restore the garden of 1701, which had lost both its original form and vistas through later replanting.[102] It was widely accepted that it needed to be brought back into harmony with the palace, where the adja-

[97] Dix *et al.*, 'Kirby Hall and its Gardens', 341–2.

[98] *Ibid.*, 330–31.

[99] Sladen, 'Garden at Kirby Hall', 152. Unpublished lists of *Plants for the Gardens of Kirby Hall, Northamptonshire, 1658–1704* were compiled from contemporary bills and family documents by the late Dr John H. Harvey and show the extensive range of flowers that may have been grown for display. See further Brian Dix, 'The Reconstruction of the Great Garden at Kirby Hall, Northamptonshire', forthcoming.

[100] Simon Thurley, *Hampton Court. A Social and Architectural History* (New Haven and London: Yale University Press, 2003), 229–32 with Chap. 10.

[101] *Ibid.*, 233–7.

[102] Simon Thurley (ed.), *The King's Privy Garden at Hampton Court Palace 1689–1995* (London: Apollo Magazine, 1995). See also Mavis Batey and Jan Woudstra, *The Story of the Privy Garden at Hampton Court* (London: Barn Elms Publishing, 1995).

cent apartments had been returned to their original condition following the repair of recent fire damage. Archaeology was an integral part of the scheme.[103]

Geophysical prospection was carried out initially to reveal the original arrangement of steps and planting along the terraces that flanked both sides of the garden. Small-scale trial excavation at the anticipated locations of former steps and statue bases confirmed that their remains survived. Further excavation of narrow circular trenches around the bases of selected trees in the parterre, as a preliminary to transplanting them, revealed the edges of paths and showed that soil-filled trenches had been dug into the natural gravel to form planting beds. Other sample excavations along the terraces located former tree holes and showed that many of their positions coincided with slight hollows and changes of surface vegetation.[104] At the same time, researches into the rich archive of contemporary historical documents detailed the garden's original construction and studies of concurrent planting design led to a convincing scheme for replacement based on the surviving receipts for shrubs and flowers.[105]

Encouraged by such results, the decision was taken to clear the later trees and surface vegetation in order to recover the previous garden design. Mechanical excavators were used to remove the recently cultivated and root-disturbed soil and the underlying surface was carefully cleaned by hand, enabling later features to be recorded before attention turned to redis-covering the layout of borders, or *plates-bandes*, from King William's garden.[106] The original flowerbeds comprised trenches up to three feet deep (0.95 m.), which had been immediately backfilled so that their sides remained as sharp as when they had been freshly dug (Fig. 17). They were filled with deliberately improved soil, which had a high clay content to retain water. Soil microfabric analysis and related chemical and botanical studies also identified inclusions of finely broken bricks and mortar that were intended to make the soil more calcareous, and showed evidence for the use of domestic waste as manure. Finally, a top layer of sandy soil had been added to protect the roots of the new plants from being scorched.[107]

Archaeological excavation also determined the relative levels between the different parts of the garden, using the evidence of surviving features such as statue plinths, drain funnels, and the original rim of the fountain basin.[108] The exact positions of topiary along the terraces could be reconstructed from the

[103] Brian Dix and Stephen Parry, 'The Excavation of the Privy Garden', in Thurley (ed.), *The King's Privy Garden*, 79–118.

[104] Brian Dix, *Archaeological Evaluation of the Privy Garden, Hampton Court Palace, 1992: A Summary Report* (Northampton: Northamptonshire Archaeology Unit Contracts Section, 1992).

[105] David Jacques, 'The History of the Privy Garden' and Jan Woudstra, 'The Planting of the Privy Garden', in Thurley (ed.), *The King's Privy Garden*, 23–42 and 43–77 respectively.

[106] Dix and Parry, 'Excavation', 109–10 and Fig. 145.

[107] *Ibid.*, Appendix II.

[108] *Ibid.*, 102.

Fig. 17 Hampton Court Palace. Original trenches of the *plates-bandes* in the Privy Garden emptied by modern re-excavation (photo: author)

Fig. 18 Hampton Court Palace. Brick foundations of steps located along one of the terraces in the Privy Garden (photo: author)

Fig. 19   Hampton Court Palace. The reconstructed Privy Garden (photo: author)

rediscovered tree holes,[109] while the brick footings for flights of steps provided an important clue to the former terrace profiles and their gradients (Fig. 18).[110] Other foundations uncovered along the top of the west terrace established the width of the bower or tunnel arbour that had originally stood there, and indicated the size of the portico that was attached to it.[111]

The geometry of setting out the garden was analysed by comparing the excavated path dimensions and details of other major features with informa-

[109] *Ibid.*, 97–9; Woudstra, 'Planting', 69–70.
[110] Dix and Parry, 'Excavation', 97–9.
[111] *Ibid.*, 90–91.

Fig. 20   Hampton Court Palace. Replanting the Privy Garden (photo: author)

tion scaled off historical surveys. Such studies indicated that an eight-foot module had been used, which was therefore adopted to remodel the different finishing elements of topiary, sand alleys, and cutwork.[112] In consequence the garden has been accurately reconstructed to its original form, reusing the historical features to reproduce the previous layout of four plots surrounding a central fountain basin, which lay on an axial path between the palace and the river (Fig. 19). Each quarter contains perimeter and internal *plates-bandes*,

[112] *Ibid.*, 92.

which as in the original garden are planted along their centre-lines with clipped evergreens: yew cones or pyramids in the middle of the plots and alternate yews and round-headed hollies around the outer borders. Woody shrubs planted in between include roses, sweet briars, honeysuckles, savins and lavenders. Along the dwarf box edging at either side, seasonal bulbs and flowers prevent the different materials of gravel, sand and earth from mixing together (Fig. 20).[113]

Such full-size reconstruction allows the effects of historic planting schemes to be rediscovered and in conjunction with actual physical remains can demonstrate how individual places may have been experienced, providing an important insight into feeling as well as style. In addition, the restoration of a garden within its original space enables us to perceive inner landscapes and views to the outside world, which may be both metaphysical and real. Through such understanding we become aware not only of designers and their patrons but of others who worked in or used and visited such gardens, and we can more readily enter into their time and the spirit of their involvement.

Independent scholar

---

[113] *Cf.* Batey and Woudstra, *Story*, 24–32.

Index

Index compiled by Terry Halliday